About the Author

L inda Marie Brown is a retired physics teacher and working organist. Her undergraduate degrees are BA in medieval history, BS in science, MS in science, with a strong minor in music. The study of medieval history has always been her passion. *Musings of a Medieval Abbess*, Book I of The Cumbrian Chronicles, is her first novel of historical fiction. She is presently writing a sequel, *Eawynn's Daughter/The Gospel of Isolde*. Ms. Brown grew up on a farm in New York State and presently lives in a very rural area with two dogs, a horse and an undetermined number of cats.

D1521024

Musings of a Medieval Abbess

Author: Linda Marie Brown

Publisher: Courtableau Press

Book Jacket Design: Pluto

© 2024

Paperback ISBN: 9798303624955

Musings of a Medieval Abbess is dedicated to all the courageous women of the medieval period who made a difference despite overwhelming odds of government and the Church.

FOREWORD

A journal of Isentrude, Abbess of Lambley, was recently recovered from the back of a cabinet in the bell tower of the church of the Blessed Mary Magdalene, which is located on the grounds where the abbeys of Lambley and Lanercost once stood. Isentrude began to journal the important events at Lambley Abbey when she became abbess in 1448. The writing for this journal began on her birthday, March 23, 1454.

Lambley and Lanercost were Augustinian communities that were close to each other on a parcel of land that was donated by the landowner Robert de Vaux in 1169. Before 1157 this property had been under Scottish rule. Lanercost was a monastery comprised of Augustinian monks and a few priests. Lambley, a convent of nuns, also contained an orphanage and a simple hospital. The abbey was destroyed twice, burned in 1296 by the Scottish Army during the Scottish War for Independence, then later ransacked and desecrated by David II of Scotland in 1346. The convent, as well as other buildings, were rebuilt. The abbeys were located in what are called the borderlands between Scotland

and England in an area just south of the wall built by the Romans. Both communities continued in ever-diminishing capacity in the fifteenth century until they were finally dissolved during the policy of "rough wooing" under King Henry VIII. Parts of the monastery remain; however, the convent was completely destroyed. The church of Mary Magdalene is still operational under the present Church of England.

Borderland skirmishes happened often in this area, usually over the theft of cattle and sheep. The convent at Lambley was cloistered until 1401, when the nuns became an integral part of the surrounding community as a healing and teaching order.

PROLOGUE

Isentrude of Lambley was born in 1404 during the reign of Henry IV to Elizabeth de Vrie and Henry Clifford of Appleby. Isentrude and her brother Daibhidh, ten years her senior, were issue from her mother's first marriage. Their father, Henry Clifford, was killed in the battle of Yeavering in 1415 against the Scots. Two years later, her mother remarried a Dacre of the local landed gentry, and the family continued to reside in her ancestral home. This second marriage produced three more daughters and an infant son. Isentrude, born with a shortened twisted left leg, was destined for the Church because of her deformity and was dedicated to Lambley Abbey at age 14 (1418), during the reign of Henry V.

As a child, Isentrude learned to read and write French and Latin and play the lute. Tutors directed the child's education to subjects she would need to know as an Augustinian nun. Little interest was shown in this daughter with a deformity, and while Isentrude was provided with an education, she received little maternal warmth. Horsemanship and knowledge of the countryside were the gifts of her maternal grandfather, William de Vrie, who came to live with the family in 1411 after the death of his wife. He took a special interest in the introverted girl. Prior to this, Isentrude's only companions had been tutors. At Lambley Abbey, she was trained to take care of household matters, medical practices, and midwifery. The Augustinians were and are a healing and teaching order. She was appointed abbess in 1448 and retired from that position in 1456.

ISENTRUDE OF LAMBLEY

THE YEAR OF OUR LORD

1454

MARCH

23 March 1454

Cake

It is mid-afternoon. Hearing from a whisper in the wind that there is to be a birthday celebration for me at the evening meal, and not being sure if this is supposed to be a surprise, I walk to the kitchen to observe if anything out of the ordinary is taking place. Having been born with a twisted, shortened left leg, I have used a cane most of my life, both to take the pressure off my leg and for stability. It is difficult to creep quietly along, but I have years of practice in such stealth, and I hobble silently down the stairs to the kitchen door, avoiding the places where the steps creak. Peeking through the door I see Guda, who is in charge of a great many things, but mainly in charge of the kitchen, cutting what appears to be a very large cake into squares. She looks up at me, grinning, and motions me to come in. Holding one forefinger to her lips to indicate silence and turning her head to see if others are watching, as quick as can be, she puts a piece of the cake on a plate, grabs a small wooden spoon, places them both in my hands, and scoots me back out the door.

I do not normally eat anything too sweet during the day as I tend to experience sudden weakness a few hours later. It is not usually an issue, as there is rarely anything sweet coming from the kitchen unless there is a special occasion, such as a birthday or holiday. I must conclude that my birthday celebration is not a secret after all. Feeling like a child that has just gotten away with some misdeed, I walk outside to a bench, sit down, and vow to take just one bite. Just one bite, and I will leave the rest for later in the evening. I will even feign surprise at the evening meal.

How can I begin to describe heaven in my mouth. The cake is my favorite, made with flour, eggs, honey, and shredded carrots. I can taste the dried fruits and berries as well as the walnuts. It is topped with a layer of creamed goat cheese mixed with honey. I take another bite. And another. Before I can comprehend, the cake has disappeared. I even scrape up the bits left on the plate. Putting the plate down on the bench beside me, I proceed to lick the creamy topping off each finger.

With not a little guilt, I return the plate and spoon to the kitchen, quietly putting them on a side table. If anyone notices me, they do not look up. I make my retreat to my study to await the evening meal. I do not even care what is served, as long as there is cake for dessert.

APRIL

2 April 1454

Sheep

I rise from sleep as a pale, pink color appears in the eastern sky, just before Prime. The faint bleating of ewes and lambs is beginning. It is usually a full-blown racket by the time we finish our devotions and make our way to the dining area to break our fast. Things are much quieter this morning, a sign that lambing is almost finished. During the summer, our two shepherds work together with the shepherds of Lanercost Abbey to tend our small flock of sheep with their much larger flock in the summer pastures. When the flock is back at our barns in the winter months, the shepherds in charge of the lambing work ceaselessly to care for the ewes, especially if there is a difficult birth. I was a bit upset when

I lately learned from Sister Cwenhild that the sheep returning from summer pasture last fall were two less in number than when they had left. She was surprised that I did not know. I should have been informed immediately by the shepherds when the flock returned. Perhaps the shepherds in charge do not realize that we keep records of the number of sheep in our flock.

Only three lambs were lost during the birthing process this spring. At present, the task of shearing the sheep of their long woolen coats is ongoing. I stop in the barn this morning for a few moments to watch this process, while on my way to speak with Cwenhild. The barnyard and stables are her domain. Shearing sheep is a not a simple task, but the barn laborers work together in such a coordinated fashion that makes shearing look easy. Cwenhild is in a stall with an older boy, two lambs, and a ewe. Wearing an apron that extends past her knees, she is bending over one of the lambs, her wimple, veil and scapular hung neatly on a peg on the wall. As I approach, she hears my footsteps and stands up with annoyance. Sunlight slanting through a crack in the barn wall lights up her thick braid of white-blond hair. With her height and slender, muscular build, she is the very image of a Norse goddess. Glancing over her shoulder at me, her ice blue eyes finally show recognition, and she smiles. As she holds one of the lambs, she explains, "This lamb is an orphan, and the lamb over there has been rejected by its mother. The ewe gave birth to a stillborn lamb last night. We are trying to make the ewe accept these lambs." The boy restrains the ewe while Cwenhild rubs the placenta of the dead lamb on the two live lambs in hopes that they will be accepted by the ewe. She gently brings one of the tiny, trembling creatures to the ewe, who snorts and backs away. She repeats the action, but on the other side. The ewe sniffs the lamb again, then allows it to suckle, noisily. The process is performed again with the second lamb, who takes hold immediately with little resistance from the ewe. Cwenhild stands back as the boy completely releases his hold on the ewe. We watch for a few moments as the lambs greedily continue to suckle, and the ewe begins to munch contentedly on some hay. Cwenhild turns away from the ewes and faces me. "We have been feeding the orphaned lambs goat's milk in a ceramic bowl, which is very messy and often does not give them enough nourishment. I have seen my grandfather use this method to attach orphaned lambs to a ewe," she says, wiping her hands on an apron. It is obvious that Cwenhild is very busy, so I ask her to speak with me when she can manage it and continue my way through the barnyards to the convent.

From all appearances, the remaining lambs, kids, chicks, ducklings, and goslings are prospering.

I make my way through the convent to peek into all the other areas. The large room for carding and dyeing wool is empty this morning. However, in the library, where research is conducted and copying is done, several sisters and novices are working under the direction of Sister Yvonne. Sister Eawynn also works there when she is present. Yvonne nods at me as she looks up from the music manuscript that Sister Joan is working on. I continue, looking into the nursery for orphans who are infants, as well as the special quarters for the older orphans. In the learning room, Sister Mathilde is busy telling a story to the children, who sit around her in a semicircle, listening with rapt attention. She does not look up, although I know she has seen me. My last stop is the spacious room for sewing, weaving and knitting, under the direction of Sister Rosamund. She is busy looking over the work of several novices, attended also by Sister Margarethe, who is Mistress of Novices. Yvonne's special assistant, Alfred, is busy embroidering a large tapestry. All three glance in my direction and nod their heads. This is a familiar routine every morning. When I arrived at Lambley to become an oblate of the Order of Saint Augustine at the age of fourteen, due to my mother's shame at my misshapen left leg which rendered me unfit for marriage, I had had no idea whatsoever what kinds of knowledge I would need for this vocation.

9 April 1454

Eawynn

We are eating our evening meal when the thundering sound of horses coming from the west causes us to look up with concern. As I stand and glance through the open window, I can see the riders. My heart races with anxiety until I spot the reddish mop of hair spilling out from underneath a cowl. "Eawynn is back," I state in my best matter-of- fact voice. She is riding without her veil and wimple again. She is returning from Carlisle with Abbot Alexander Walton of Lanercost Abbey and several of the brothers. Rosamund and Yvonne, who made their vows at the same time as I did, look up, smile slightly, then resume eating. Cwenhild also looks up, grins widely, and then looks at me, mischief on her face. Eawynn is one of her favorites. A few other heads glance knowingly in my direction. We have secrets here at Lambley Abbey. No one asks personal questions. We come from many different backgrounds and circumstances. Some willingly, some not. Some with a real devotion. Some with hardly any belief at all. We have learned to respect our differences and mind our own business.

Eawynn has been gone for at least a fortnight with some of the brothers from Lanercost to negotiate for the sale of Lambley Abbey's wool once the shearing is completed. I have missed her greatly, both as my scribe and my dearest friend. I always miss and fear for her when she leaves, as she also assists the brothers at Lanercost with their calculations and records. Lambley Abbey is very close to the border, and while skirmishes are less frequent, raiding parties do happen, especially after a hard winter when food has become scarce. Eawynn is the smartest person I know and the most honest, but she does not speak, which is why Abbot Alexander Walton seeks to make deft use of her muteness by requesting her help from time to time. Her record-keeping is impeccable. The abbot disregards her use of hand signs but accepts her written communications. Most of the brothers are literate, but few are as talented as she is. Eawynn watches everything and misses nothing. She also has access to Lanercost's records of all transactions. It was from her that I learned of Lanercost's increase in adult sheep last fall, which then prompted me to have our own flock recounted. It is the reason I requested a meeting with Cwenhild.

Eawynn is responsible for the records at Lambley. She works with Sister Yvonne in the library. Greek mythology and the writings of the ancients are part of the curriculum that our novices must complete. The library at Lambley Abbey is extensive, as is the library at Lanercost Abbey, perhaps even more so than the library at the archbishop's palace in York. Before becoming abbess, I worked in the library as well. Those who work there must be able to read Greek and Latin. It is our work to translate from ancient texts to the common vernacular. Besides translating, copies of these writings are made by hand for the universities at Oxford and Cambridge. The writings of Aristotle, Plato, Plutarch, and Hippocrates are in great demand. Eawynn excels at translation and often oversees the process of making copies. I recently learned that a method of using a mechanical press is now in use in Germany. We are most eager to know this process.

12 April 1454

Inquiry

After speaking with Cwenhild about the decrease in our flock of sheep, I send for the two shepherds who tend the flock during the summer months. They are a middle-aged man and his young son who have worked for Lambley for the past two years. Until now, I had not questioned their abilities or their honesty. The flocks of both abbeys are pastured together in the summer. The shepherds from Lanercost and Lambley Abbeys work together to keep them safe and move them from pasture to pasture. The shepherds arrive just as I am about to send for Eawynn. I ask them to wait because I want Eawynn to hear their explanation. As Eawynn arrives, the older shepherd shifts his feet nervously and speaks without making eye contact with either of us. He explains that the two ewes disappeared one night when there was a chorus of wolves, causing the flocks to mill about nervously. He claims that they searched for the sheep but had no success in finding them. By the shiftiness of his eyes, I suspect he is not being truthful. It is my intention to send Eawynn and Cwenhild, who was raised on a farm and is very knowledgeable about sheep, to take a closer look at Lanercost's flocks. The moon will be almost full tomorrow night. As the flocks are in pens for shearing, it should not be difficult to find ewes with different markings. Our sheep have a notch on the right ear, while Lanercost Abbey's sheep have a notch on the left ear.

Actually, the more I consider this path of action, the more I am convinced we should go tomorrow during the daylight hours. With enough help, we should be able to go through the sheep pens quickly. If we are questioned by the abbot, I will reassure him that we are simply checking to see that a mistake has not been made when separating the two flocks upon their return from the summer pastures last fall. This needs to be done before the flocks set out for summer pastures again.

13 April 1454

Inquiry

This morning Eawynn, Cwenhild, and I set out early, walking quickly to Lanercost Abbey. Two older stable boys, Derian and Lunden, accompany us. I stop for a mosment at the abbey to speak with Abbot Walton, informing him of our intentions, while the others continue on to the sheep pens. Surprise crosses his face, but also anger. "How could this have happened without my knowledge?" he asks. His surprise seems genuine.

"It may have simply been a mistake," I reply, knowing full well that it was not. He makes no attempt to stop us, so I proceed to the sheep pens where shearing is taking place. After telling the man who appears to be in charge of our intentions, we proceed to go through each pen, sheep by sheep. Sheep do not offer to stand still so their ears can be examined, especially if they have a young lamb to protect. Cwenhild and the boys force each sheep and its lamb into a narrow chute where they cannot escape. Eawynn and I stand on either side and check the ewe's ears. After being examined, we open the latch and release the ewe and her lamb into an adjacent empty pasture. Soon after we start, several workers in Lanercost's barnyard, who were shearing the animals, join to assist us, which makes the work progress much faster. We find our two missing ewes in separate sheep pens after we have gone through about one third of the flock. They are big, healthy ewes, just freshly shorn of their wool. They both have newly cut notches in their left ears as well as older, well-healed notches in their right ears. They have also just given birth to lambs, that are still suckling. I do not believe this so-called mistake was an accident. Cwenhild asks one of the workers who is helping us to separate our ewes and their lambs from the flocks and return them to our flock, along with the amount of wool they would have produced. He apologizes profusely, claiming not to have noticed that two new ewes had mysteriously joined the Lanercost's flocks. It does not matter whether I believe him or not. I do believe our own shepherds did have knowledge of this theft and must have received some reward for transferring the ewes. They will need to be replaced by men I can trust.

We walk back to the barnyard at Lambley Abby, a sorry sight indeed. Only Cwenhild seems unscathed by our morning adventure. She had already donned her apron and mucking boots and left her veil behind. I should have followed her example, as I have mud over my shoes and halfway up my habit. I am carrying my headdress. The boys are in much worse shape, as they needed to capture and wrestle each sheep into the chute, along with its lamb. They are covered in mud, even their heads and faces. They look so comical; I turn away so I do not burst out laughing. Cwenhild informs me that she will wash them off with their clothes on at the well. Sister Rosamund's assistant, Alfred, is standing in front of the abbey as we walk past toward the barn and completely loses control at the sight of us. He is laughing so hard that he loses his balance and sits down abruptly on the ground. We simply continue to walk, although I am glad it was Alfred and not me who started the laughter. By this time the boys, Cwenhild, and Eawynn have joined in.

14 April 1454

Breakfast and Orphans

It snowed again last night, an early spring snow with big wet flakes, the kind that piles up quickly on the ground. Hopefully, it will have melted by tomorrow when Eawynn and I are scheduled to make our visits with several families in the surrounding community. Breakfast is gruel with goat milk and a scant handful of dried berries. I am heartily tired of plain gruel, and our store of berries is low. A great many herbs and dried berries were used up during the bouts of illnesses this past winter. The supply of eggs is also low, as some of the hens are broody and others have gone into the spring molt, a little early it seems. As I leave the dining area, I mention to Guda, who rules the kitchen and gardens with an iron hand, that we should have some roast fowl for supper. I am not serious, but she nods in agreement.

Later this morning, as I am rounding the corner of the convent by the herb gardens while on my walk through the grounds, I see the children under the care of Lambley Abbey, as well as some of our workers' children, playing in the snow, supervised by two of our novices, Bernia and Kendra. I draw back, so as not to affect the manner of their play by my presence, and watch. There seem to be three separate groups of four to five children playing, and two older girls of about twelve, who are sitting quietly, deep in conversation. The littlest ones are having a tremendous time building snow figures and flopping in the snow to make body imprints, and there is a group playing hide and seek that is being bossed about by a rather large girl, one of the kitchen worker's daughters. It occurs to me that she might be old enough to be helpful in the kitchen.

It is an experience to see how they manage their play and their friendships, as well as their feuding and animosities. However, our newest arrival, Odelyn, does not join in, but sits quietly on a bench and watches. She is not invited by any of the others but does not seem to be discouraged or discontented. I find her active observation interesting. As I stand there, hidden from view, Kendra approaches Odelyn to encourage her to join the others, but she pleasantly declines. I guess this is the way we learn. Sometimes watching is the best and smartest way to assess a situation. It would be wise to watch this child. A child this smart may well be an asset in the future

I am not completely surprised when three very tasty, roasted chickens appear on the table for the evening meal, along with a variety of cheeses and a platter of freshly cooked fish. Guda is a marvel! She has also prepared freshly baked rolls and boiled grains mixed with honey, dried apples, and herbs. There is enough chicken for everyone to have a taste.

Later this morning, as I am rounding the corner of the convent by the herb gardens while on my walk through the grounds, I see the children under the care of Lambley Abbey, as well as some of our workers' children, playing in the snow, supervised by two of our novices, Bernia and Kendra. I draw back, so as not to affect the manner of their play by my presence, and watch. There seem to be three separate groups of four to five children playing, and two older girls of about twelve, who are sitting quietly, deep in conversation. The littlest ones are having a tremendous time building snow figures and flopping in the snow to make body imprints, and there is a group playing hide and seek that is being bossed about by a rather large girl, one of the kitchen worker's daughters. It occurs to me that she might be old enough to be helpful in the kitchen.

It is an experience to see how they manage their play and their friendships, as well as their feuding and animosities. However, our newest arrival, Odelyn, does not join in, but sits quietly on a bench and watches. She is not invited by any of the others but does not seem to be discouraged or discontented. I find her active observation interesting. As I stand there, hidden from view, Kendra approaches Odelyn to encourage her to join the others, but she pleasantly declines. I guess this is the way we learn. Sometimes watching is the best and smartest way to assess a situation. It would be wise to watch this child. A child this smart may well be an asset in the future

I am not completely surprised when three very tasty, roasted chickens appear on the table for the evening meal, along with a variety of cheeses and a platter of freshly cooked fish. Guda is a marvel! She has also prepared freshly baked rolls and boiled grains mixed with honey, dried apples, and herbs. There is enough chicken for everyone to have a taste.

15 April 1454

Visits

As I look out the window, I see Brother Edward from Lanercost Abbey riding up to the courtyard this morning, leading a pack mule, just as Eawynn leaves to walk to the stable and fetch our horses. I visited the kitchen earlier to see what could be spared. Guda did her best to scrape together some cheeses, wrapped portions of smoked hams, and grains. We have been riding out to visit families in the outlying areas at least once monthly, sometimes more often, but do not visit during the harsh winter months. This is our first visit since last December. The area that we cover follows the River Irthing up to the Roman fort, which is situated on the Roman wall, then on toward Gilsland and the waterfalls. There are five families in several small communities that we have visited for years, poor people who have great need, especially at this time of year. We began this calling soon after Eawynn professed her initial vows. A few of the other sisters such as Mathilde, Margarethe, and Cwenhild, also feel called to visit the poor in other parts of the area surrounding our abbeys. Most have a brother or two from Lanercost as an escort for safety.

Brother Edward has been our escort on these visits for several years, but it is only recently that we learned from him that he is Sister Yvonne's younger brother. As we ride on a path along the River Irthing that goes past the ancient Roman Fort, he is regaling us with tales of his childhood. My mare spooks at a movement from a fish jumping in the river, and I realize that I have not been attending to much except Brother Edward's stories. Getting the mare back under control, I ask about Yvonne. I have always been curious about her vocation, even though it is not my concern. Eawynn begins to chuckle. "Yvonne has about as much calling to the religious life as we have," she says. "I work with her day in and day out, and her only interest is in historical research." Brother Edward nods his head in agreement. He adds, "Yvonne was never interested in marriage or children. She has sought the vocation of historian in the only way she could find, by becoming a religious of a teaching order."

We ease our horses to a trot as Eawynn adds, "You should see how put upon Yvonne is when she must teach the novices. She does not even particularly like children. She leaves that work to me."

21

We stop at the fort built into the side of the Roman wall and dismount to take a break in the shade of a wall of the fort, where we share some bread and cheese. A slight breeze ruffles the horses' manes as they search for any new growth of grass. Snow still remains in areas which are permanently shaded. Eventually we remount and ride on toward the hamlet of Gilsland. Edward tells us that he is the only one in his family to have a true religious calling. He and Yvonne have other, younger siblings who have grown up and married, with plenty of offspring to ensure the family name. When I press him for his surname, he replies that he is a Dacre. Imagine my surprise, as my stepfather is also a Dacre. Giving my stepfather's name, I ask if they might be related. Edward shakes his head, adding that he does not recognize the name, and laughingly replies that Dacre is a common name in the North. Still, I wonder.

Our visits hold no surprises. We leave as much as we are able, dividing the supplies among the five homes we visit. One of the families has lost two grandparents since our last visit. Feeling sad, because I know how much my grandfather meant to me, I express my deepest sympathy. Eawynn, who sincerely despises her family, also goes through the motions, then walks outside to pet a dog. She is not very good at pretending.

16 April 1454

A Summons

A summons arrives this morning from Archbishop William Booth of York. Abbot Alexander Walton from Lanercost has also been summoned along with William Percy, the Bishop of Carlisle. Archbishop Booth recently replaced John Kemp, who was transferred to Canterbury. The abbot and I will join with the bishop and accompany his group as they pass through. It is possible that we are being gathered because of trouble brewing under the reign of King Henry VI of Lancaster. Apparently, the trouble comes from York. The abbeys and the city of Carlisle are under the Archbishop of York and Richard, Duke of York. Henry VI has had increasing bouts of instability in recent years, and it is common knowledge that Richard, Duke of York, also has a claim to the throne. Richard is the chief deputy to the king and acts on the king's behalf during these periods of mental collapse. Although Richard vows that he has no wish to become king, there are those who do not believe him, just as there are those who would gladly support him. I believe we will be asked where our loyalties lie.

It is a long journey, at least five days. Urgency demands that we travel lightly. I had learned to ride as a child from my grandfather, whom I affectionately called Bampy. I still have the saddle that my grandfather had made especially for me to accommodate my twisted left leg; however, it was constructed for a pony. I have since commissioned a saddler in Carlisle to fashion two more saddles, one for the larger bay horse that I occasionally ride, as well as a saddle that fits my sturdy highland mare, who is short, but rather wide, a very comfortable mount for a long journey. All my horses have been taught to mount from both sides as I must mount from the right side instead of the left. Eawynn and I ride astride with split skirts, and my left stirrup is fashioned so that there is no discomfort for my twisted left leg. I will only take one trusted confidant, Eawynn, who will scribe for me. She is very observant and gifted at judging all the nuances of a situation.

17 April 1454

Saint Mary of Magdala

Today, as spring bursts to life all around us during the week of our Lord's passion, reflecting on His death as well as the eternal renewal of life, the thought strikes me that the only ones who stayed with Jesus during his crucifixion and death were women: Mary, Jesus' mother, Mary Magdalene, and Mary, the wife of Clopas. Following their example, as the women who daily took care of Jesus and his followers throughout his ministry, (how else would they have been fed and sheltered), we must daily renew our determination to feed the hungry, care for the sick and dying, comfort the broken-hearted, and love and care for all of God's creation. May the message of the risen Lord, the message of love, triumph over the hatred, apathy, and cruelty in our world.

Our chapel, which serves both Lanercost and Lambley Abbeys, is the church of the Blessed Mary Magdalene. She has always been a great comfort to me. I have often felt her presence by my side, giving comfort when I feel overwhelmed or overburdened. I try to make time daily to sit alone in her chapel, especially when I have a difficult decision to make, or need guidance to deal with some new problem. The Church teaches that Mary Magdalene was a harlot who repented her ways, but I have read the Gospels thoroughly several times and have found no evidence of this. Why would the Church encourage this belief? What would be the benefit to the early church fathers, or indeed all Church fathers since, to portray Mary Magdalene as a harlot who repented? (This question would make a fine research project for Eawynn or Yvonne.) It seems that she was a truer disciple than the rest of the twelve.

18 April 1454

A Journey

Our journey to York begins this morning. We are up very early and ready to travel. The Bishop of Carlisle and his small retinue arrived late yesterday afternoon and spent the night at Lanercost. Shortly after breaking our fast, we ride to join them. The kitchen has already packed supplies for us on a mule that we will take turns leading. The group is traveling at a fast trot, which the horses can sustain for miles. So far there has been little regard for the two of us struggling with our mule. As we lag further and further behind, I see the abbot beckon to his small group of brothers to take turns leading our pack mule. One of them rides back to us, taking the mule's lead while smiling at us in sympathy. Gratefully, we accept the help, because it is obvious that we are slowing them down. It is also a relief not to have to drag that stubborn animal and keep my seat on my mare at the same time.

Riding behind Eawynn, I notice that a few locks of her hair have escaped her veil. She refuses to cut her hair short, as is customary. In the sunlight, there are now some gray hairs mixed in with the copper ones. It seems like only yesterday when I was a sixteen-year-old novice preparing to take my initial vows, and she was an uncontrollable, stubborn, red-haired, eleven-year-old girl that had been brought by her father to the abbey for the purpose of making her marriageable. Her family did not inform the abbess that Eawynn did not speak. At the time, when she did not even attempt to speak, everyone in the abbey assumed that she was mute. I know now that acting as though she was mute was a ruse that Eawynn thought might give her some control over her situation. She had no intention of ever returning home to marry the older widower to whom she had been promised. At first Sister Elseyth Dacre, who was in charge of the education of the children at Lambley, assumed that Eawynn was just being stubborn when she refused to answer questions. Eawynn was quite able to follow simple directions but refused to respond vocally to any dialogue. My first inkling of her aptitude came two days later, during the morning hours the children spend with several novices, myself included, in our school room learning to read and write. Yvonne, who was also a novice, asked Eawynn a direct question. I watched as Eawynn did not respond to the question but wrote an answer with her chalk on her small slate instead. This went unnoticed by Yvonne, who had turned her attention to another student. Eawynn then tried to regain her attention by repeatedly tapping on her slate. Frustrated by the lack of response, Eawynn stopped tapping on the slate and hurled it to the floor. I intervened by picking up her slate from the floor, the neat script of her response to the question a glaring indication of the gap between her actual intelligence and everyone's perception of her, as if her inability to speak had rendered her stupid as well. Although it was obvious that Eawynn was angry and very unhappy at her circumstances, and remembering my own when I arrived at Lambley, I made every effort to befriend her and help in any way I could. I asked Sister Elseyth if I might be given the job of supervising the stubborn child. Somehow her inability to speak was never questioned by Abbess Isabeau Sysson or Sister Elseyth Dacre. There must have been some communication with her parents during her first years at Lambley. I can only conclude that the subject of her inability to speak never came up. I did not learn the truth until a few years later.

21 April 1454
Easter

We are in route to York during Holy Week, the most important time of the year for the Catholic Church. When I inquire of Abbot Walton why the Archbishop of York saw fit to have not only the leaders of two abbeys, but also the Bishop of Carlisle, separated from their flocks during the most holy time of year, he shrugs, replying that Archbishop Booth had probably not even considered the ramifications of his decision. Today, we celebrate a short mass for Easter led by Bishop Percy. Then, we pack up and continue on our way.

Knowing that I would not be there for the Easter celebration, I left Sister Yvonne in charge, along with Guda in the kitchen. My instructions were to celebrate Holy Week and Easter as we always have, and to send good thoughts to us, and prayers to Our Lady for safe travels. I know that Eawynn and I are missing the Easter feast of roast goose and lamb, along with an amazing dessert of cake filled with dried fruit and walnuts and topped with a creamy, rich cheese, dripping with honey. These thoughts make me hurl mental curses at the archbishop in my mind, for all the good it will do. To make things worse, my buttocks are sore from our hurried journey, and it is beginning to rain. Eawynn does not complain, but I know her thoughts run parallel to mine.

30 April 1454

Time Away

Five miserable days of travel for a brief meeting where we have been kept waiting for hours by Archbishop Booth. Abbot Walton, Bishop Percy, and I are seated in a dark, damp room that has no windows. We have been here for the entire morning and well into the afternoon. Other than a small meal to break our fast in the morning, no notice has been given to us until now, as someone arrives to escort us to the archbishop's chambers. Bishop Percy is already in a rage, pacing the floor and muttering all manner of unspeakable things. In contrast to the bishop's behavior, Abbot Alexander Walton is sitting quietly and does not complain. I am faint with hunger. We have been allowed no contact with the rest of our party during this time. I think the archbishop is playing both sides of the coin to be safe. He must swear fealty to the king, but also protect his interests with the Duke of York, who is his immediate superior. I think he wants us to be very clear about who is making the decisions and pulling the strings. We are to be his puppets. I do not like being put in this position. It is difficult and often a conflict of interest when the head of the country is by divine right also the head of the Church in that country, only answerable to the Pope and perhaps the Holy Roman Emperor. At least England's conflict with France is resolved for the time being. I mention to Abbot Walton that I think we are playing a dangerous game, and he agrees that we must be cautious. When the archbishop asks whether I favor the Duke of York or the king, I reassure him that I will stay loyal to the crown, no matter whose head it is on.

While returning home, we are accompanied by some of the Duke of York's own men, who are riding north to rumors of a skirmish on the border west of Carlisle. At forty and six, Eawynn still attracts the attention of men, although she seems totally unaware of it. More than a few heads turn in her direction, as we are the only women in the group. Nevertheless, we stay close to the abbot and the brothers to avoid unwanted attention. The soldiers seem glad to be heading out. I sense that they thrive on danger and adventure and have missed it since the cessation of hostilities with France. What is it that drives us to seek conflict?

The trip home is worse than miserable, as it has rained the entire way. Even our well-oiled coats cannot adequately keep us from getting drenched. We ride for hours each day in cold, driving rain. By each nightfall, my fingers and toes are numb. It is a miracle that we stay on our mounts. It is impossible to get a fire going in the evenings to warm us as the wood is damp. Our rations are cold. We arrive home looking and feeling like frozen, drowned rats. Even our boots have water in them. I pray we do not get sick.

MAY

2 May 1454

Sickness

Finally feeling well enough to get out of bed and sit for a while, every movement continues to bring discomfort, weakness, and a yearning to lie down again. It seems the Mayday festivities have concluded. I have lost track of time. This morning, Sister Margarethe looks in on me and says that I have been incoherent for five days with fever and chills. Even now, I would be happy to meet God immediately if I truly thought that would be my final destination. I do have some doubts about that. Evidently, Eawynn recovered faster. She also looks in on me and signs that she has been up for two days, helping tend to the others who are sick.

My mind spins in circles as I try to figure out how we contracted this illness. Believing at first that we became ill from the terrible weather as we journeyed back from York, now I am not so sure, as the illness is passing to those who were not with us. Hopefully, we can keep this sickness from spreading into the surrounding area as one of our older sisters has already passed on. Her body has been washed, wrapped with linens, and carried to one of the colder cells until such time as there are enough people who can be spared to bury her. Cwenhild visits later in the morning with news that the illness has also affected the community of brothers at Lanercost. The latest reports are that two of the older brothers have died. The others are either too sick or too weak to assist with their burials, so the dead have been placed in a cellar. By afternoon, so many sisters have dropped by, perhaps to ascertain that I will live, that I feign sleep to avoid speaking to anyone else. Except for Sister Yvonne, who does not leave, but sits in a chair next to my bed for a few moments before speaking. "I know you are awake, Isentrude," she says. "You are not breathing the way one breathes while sleeping. I want to discuss the events leading up to this plague when you are well enough, every detail." My eyes open briefly, and I nod, then she departs. Thankfully, someone had the sense to send everyone away who does not reside at the abbey for the duration of this illness.

8 May 1454

Recovery

Several of us have now recovered enough to help others who have developed symptoms, mostly those who cared for us at the start. The younger ones seem better able to handle this illness. I instruct everyone that we must drink lots of herbal tea, and hard bread dipped in tea seems to settle the stomach. The physician from Brampton village tries to attend us and suggests leeches to rid the body of impurities. I send him away. I refuse the leeches, as I have noticed that they always seem to further weaken those already ill. I have faith that most of us will recover. It seems a few of us are well enough to care for the others at any given time, as well as feed the livestock. It will pass, God willing.

10 May 1448

An Adventure and a Rescue

The flocks left this morning for summer pastures. The shepherds have checked the meadows and maintain that there is ample grass. They have joined with Lanercost's flocks for the summer. Eawynn and I ride out this afternoon to check on their progress as the shepherds move the flocks through the valleys to the hills where they will remain until fall. It is an excuse to get away for a few hours. I notice blackberry blossoms in several spots along the way and make a mental note of their location. I will check them again in a few weeks.

We stop by a stream to let the horses drink and Eawynn allows her horse to walk into the stream as the water is not deep. Before she can stop her gelding, he begins to paw at the water, goes down on his knees, and rolls in the water. Luckily, Eawynn manages to free her feet from the stirrups in time and rolls off, falling into the water. The horse spooks and takes off, back toward the abbey. The stream is very cold from snow melt, and Eawynn is shaking as she manages to scramble out of the stream, laughing. She is not hurt, but has lost a shoe in the stream, and her socks and clothes are soaked. I dismount from my mare and make her strip down out of her wet clothes, which we bundle up and tie to the front of my saddle. I remount and she mounts behind me with only my cloak to cover her.

It is not long before I realize that my little mare cannot take both of us back the entire way, so I get off and walk beside her, holding on to a stirrup to steady myself. We are about halfway back to the abbey when we are met by a stable boy riding a draft horse and leading Eawynn's gelding. I thank him and ask to borrow his jacket and socks. He smiles with confusion on his face but complies with my odd request. Eawynn is thoroughly chilled by this time. We send the boy back with instructions to tell Cwenhild that we are well and are on our way back. As soon as he leaves, I give Eawynn a leg up to mount the gelding, and I mount my mare again. It is necessary for her to ride the gelding because, unlike my mare, he has not been trained to be mounted from the right side. It is almost dark by the time we reach the abbey, where we ride to the back of the convent, I leave Eawynn by a side door with the wet bundle of clothes before returning both horses to the stables. When I make it back to our rooms, with Cwenhild by my side, Eawynn, wrapped in blankets, is sipping hot tea by the fire with Sister Mathilde, who has been waiting to speak with me. Mathilde is kind enough to sense our fatigue and sends a novice to fetch some hot soup and bread for us. Cwenhild will not leave until she has heard the entire story, smiling broadly as I retell of Eawynn's magnificent dismount into the stream. Convinced that we are not hurt, she takes her leave. We go to bed after finishing our meal in hopes that we do not come down with an illness, so soon after the last plague.

12 May 1454

Sleep

I have always thought that getting up at all hours of the night to pray is one of the most absurd practices ever conceived. The idea most certainly was not thought up by a woman. At my age, I need to sleep. Waking Eawynn up for the prayers during the night is always a challenge. When I wake at midnight for Matins, it is a full hour before I can get back to sleep and two hours after that we must be up for Lauds. I have literally dragged Eawynn from her bed and walked her down the corridor to the chapel, during which time she never opened her eyes. It is like we are all sleepwalking, except for the few who actually enjoy this kind of torture. I am certain the good Lord would rather we all got a full night's sleep, and instead spent three times as long at our worship in the early morning at Prime, before we break our fast. I will get resistance to this idea from some of our more traditional sisters, but we will all be healthier for not having our sleep disturbed twice during the night! I am most certain Our Lady would agree; any sensible woman would.

I am pondering these thoughts as I eat my porridge this morning. It rained last night, but the clouds are gone. I can see sparkles of light where the rising sun reflects off raindrops on the needles of a pine tree that is in my line of vision. I am so mesmerized that I do not notice when Eawynn stands behind me, with her hands on my shoulders to see what I am staring at. Very soon after that, a small group of sisters join her. One very large drop sparkles blue, while a tiny drop just above it sparkles gold. As I continued to watch, I can see more and more flickering drops, more beautiful than fireflies on a summer's eve. Today, I will work out a suitable worship plan for Prime, and tonight we will all sleep until daybreak.

15 May 1454
Concerning the Archbishop

All my life I have tried to make sense of the many traditions of the Church, but I do not disclose my true thoughts or misgivings to the rest of my sisters. Sickness is not retribution from God. Sickness is not the result of wickedness. Good people often experience bad fortune. There seems to be no reason why this is so. If sickness is God's retribution on evil people, why are the hypocrites in the Church spared? Only Eawynn knows my true feelings, although I have always felt that Sisters Rosamund and Yvonne, who were novices with me, are suspicious. Rosamund is very devout, but also seems not to judge others. After speaking with Yvonne's brother, I am not sure Yvonne is even interested, except in an academic way. My beliefs are safe with Eawynn, as she has similar misgivings.

Apparently, the cities of York and Carlisle have not been afflicted with the illness. The illness must have come from the soldiers of the Duke of York who shared their meals with us. When the Archbishop of York learned of the outbreak of sickness here at Lambley and Lanercost Abbeys, he claimed that this must be a manifestation of God's vengeance for some offense. This is probably just a way to justify his lack of aid in our time of need. He does not support us at all. It is easy and convenient to say that people who experience misfortune are being punished for their wickedness. I do not know and cannot even imagine what our abbeys could have done to deserve this plague. Apparently, this archbishop agrees with the views of the vengeful God of the Old

Testament. The God of the Hebrews often indiscriminately punished everyone, in fact, whole nations. Even as a child I had difficulty understanding the actions of that God. The vengeful God of the Hebrews cannot be the same as the God of love as taught by Our Savior, Jesus Christ. The God of the Old Testament thrived on worship, revenge, and obedience, much like some of the leaders of the Church. Obviously, the Church emphasizes the Old Testament over the teachings of Christ. Indulgences are sold to those who can afford them to excuse them from their sins. Little is done to help the widow with children or the elderly. I have heard of saints in Spain being boiled after their deaths so their bones could be sold as relics to bring in more money for the churches. Every church wants a piece of the true cross to display. I often wonder, not aloud of course, how many crosses all these "true pieces" of the cross would make. Following the God of the Old Testament gives those in authority the divine right to force their followers to obey. It allows the Church to control the lives of the people. I could go on and on about this hypocrisy. Even so, I feel a change is coming, especially from some of the religious orders who have chosen to follow a life of poverty and the teachings of Christ.

I do not often pray to God, or even to Jesus, as I feel no real connection to them. I rely on the intercession of the Blessed Virgin Mary. My prayers are to her and to Mary Magdalene for guidance. They are my safety. As a novice, I spoke more freely about my thoughts than I do now. As abbess, I must be careful how I play my part. There are only a very few that I trust with my innermost thoughts. A loving God would never visit a plague like this on those who worship Him, although, in truth, a little vengeance on our archbishop seems like justice. I must now pray to Our Lady and Mary Magdalene to intercede for me for my wicked thoughts! But intercede to whom?

18 May 1454

Inspection

This morning, immediately after Lauds, I feel the need for a solitary walk around our abbey compound. I retrieve my cane and skip breaking my fast with the rest, resolving to find something to ease my hunger from the kitchen later. Our younger adults and children are always hungry, so there is usually a supply of rolls left out for pillaging during the morning hours.

New plants are emerging in the herb gardens behind the kitchen. This morning, I find tiny shoots of chamomile and spearmint. Garlic, parsley, and thyme have also been planted, but they have not sprouted yet. The rosemary bushes are beginning to show new leaves. The areas where the herbs were planted are marked for each herb, but occasionally, volunteer plants from last year appear all over. Most can be identified easily by their second growth of leaves. A few kittens are chasing each other in the gardens but disappear when I approach.

Someone has already thrown mash and cracked corn on the ground for the chickens in the barnyard. Two hens have small flocks of chicks that they viciously guard. I carefully circle around those. Straying near the sheep pens, I notice that the shearing is almost finished. Great piles of wool are stacked inside wooden crates. Some wool will be taken up to the convent where it will be washed, dried, and carded. During the winter months the wool is dyed and spun into yarn for the weaving of cloth. The yarn is also used for knitting garments, either for the abbey or for sale in Carlisle. All of this is Sister Rosamund's domain. Wool that is not used by the convent is sent in wooden crates to be sold as raw wool in Carlisle. From there it is shipped to many cities in Europe.

There are two new arrivals at the barn, puppies that a local man, also a shepherd, has promised us in return for something, though I forget what. The puppies are from one of his special guard dog's litters. Unlike our regular sheep dogs, who are trained to herd the flock, these are to be trained to guard them. They are wrestling with each other as I approach but stop immediately and run to greet me. I cannot resist picking them up, petting and cuddling them. I am scolded and told rather adamantly by a worker not to try and make friends with them, as they are not pets, but must be raised with the lambs. Entering the mews, I greet my little mare with a scratch under her chin as she noses around my arms, looking for a treat. I have not ridden her since my illness, and I miss riding. Hopefully, I will be well enough to ride again soon. A surprise awaits inside the stables. A new foal of one of our draft mares is hiding behind his mother. He is a big handsome boy, chestnut with a flaxen mane and tail, and white stockings on his front feet. I am not sure if we will keep him to work the fields or sell him at the spring fair. I had not heard of his birth, so it must be very recent.

I end my walk near the lake. The ducks and geese gather close to the water to escape if I come too close. A few of these also have ducklings. It amazes me how well they swim immediately after hatching. There is an island in the middle of the lake where they can escape predators. We have many predators: foxes, badgers, and raccoons, not to mention the hawks and falcons that can swoop down and pick the ducklings off. Every year, quite a few are lost. I turn to go back to the convent just as the sun is peeking over the trees, turning the clouds into vibrant ribbons of pink. Despite my deformity, I walk through the convent grounds as often as I can. I am grateful to Alaric, who has been the groundskeeper since before I came to Lambley, for carving a cane to fit my height shortly after I arrived as a novice. He replaced the cane with a new one every few years. The cane I have now was fashioned by his grandson, Timothy, who is a carpenter. Having a cane gives me the ability to oversee the abbey much better than I could have done without one. Walking also lifts my spirits, clears my head, and gives me the motivation to continue the work of our abbey. Morning is my favorite time of day.

21 May 1454

The Grandfather

Sitting in the gardens drinking my tea this morning, I am very much aware of old Alaric, who is cleaning away the debris from around the roses that are blooming along the walkway. He lives in a small hamlet about fifteen minutes west of here by horseback. When I first came to Lambley many years ago, he was not referred to as old Alaric. He had a family then. His wife died several years ago, and all his children except his eldest son have moved away. His son's family lives with him, although his two grandchildren, Donal and Timothy, are almost grown. They have all worked for the abbey in some way over the years. Alaric spends his time puttering around the flower beds and vegetable gardens. I often see him sitting or playing with the children when they come outside. They gather around him as he tells them stories. He plays hide and seek with them, often rushing out at them, making terrible faces and noises that leave the little ones squealing with delight. He does not need to work anymore, but I think he continues to come here each day because he misses being around the children. He is always somewhere nearby during their morning breaks. As I watch, a side door opens and five of our youngest come running and yelling onto the grounds. Although my time for silent contemplation is over, I stay for a few more moments to watch Alaric put his tools away and walk over to take a seat on one of the benches that are placed around the yard. He is immediately surrounded by the young ones. They call him Bampy and clamor to sit on his knee, each in turn, while he bounces them up and down, pretending to give them horseback rides. He is very gentle with the youngest children but makes the older children yell and laugh as he acts like a bucking horse. He takes great care to give attention to each child individually, even the shy, tiny, three-year-old the sisters call Margy. He sings silly rhymes to them, which makes them laugh with delight. The rhymes bring back memories that I had forgotten.

My maternal grandfather came to live with my family when I was seven. His manor was only an hour away by horseback or coach, and we visited three or four times each year until my grandmother died. I have few memories of her except that she was a stern woman who had no time for children. When we visited, my grandfather, Bampy, always took me to the stables to see his horses. He would lift me onto his shoulders, and we would wander through the estate as he pointed out anything that he thought might interest me.

He often sang as we strolled along, stopping to point out a fawn nestled in the bushes beside a wooded area, or a group of wood ducks by the pond. I loved visiting him. I was even more thrilled when he decided to stay with us, leaving the care of the estate to his youngest daughter and her new husband. He trained a small mountain pony to be mounted from either side, and had a saddler construct a saddle for me to ride astride with a special stirrup that angled outwards for my twisted left leg. Every day we spent an hour together while I learned how to mount the pony, as well as walk, trot, canter, and even jump small logs. When he felt that I rode well enough, he would saddle my pony, mount his grey gelding, and we would ride around the estate. He often sang songs in Gaelic, and I learned to sing with him. I missed him terribly when I left for Lambley in 1418. He died two years later.

25 May 1454

Trouble in the Kitchen

We are facing an uncomfortable situation in the kitchen at Lambley Abbey. Guda has overseen the kitchen for as long as I can remember. All the novices must work in the kitchen under Guda at some point during their training. Wonderfully efficient, she is stern, but fair with her charges, and a wellspring of knowledge about preparing and preserving food and herbs. Besides the novice helpers, a few village women also work in the kitchen with her. Her knowledge is immense, but I am sure all that wisdom has not been passed on. Guda is very stubborn, and she does not read or write. More concerning, she guards her recipes by refusing to have them recorded, so her vast knowledge has never been written down. Unfortunately, we have witnessed several mistakes of judgment from Guda these past few months, although she has tried to pass the blame to others.

Last week, two of the older novices, Eugenia and Alyce Marie, who are presently working in the kitchens, sought me out. They came to express their distress at being accused of making a mess of the bread that was baked this morning. It is their job to make the bread every day, and they have been doing this for a few months. They know the recipe well, but Guda demanded that they change the ingredients they usually use, and the bread did not rise. There will not be any rolls for pillaging today. A surplus is always made to feed hungry children, who often stop by the kitchens for a snack in the morning. Guda insisted that she had not told them something different, but others who heard the conversation backed up the young women. Guda dismissed the novices, stating that she would no longer allow them in her kitchen, that they must go work elsewhere. They explained to me that they did not want to be blamed when they had done nothing wrong. Refusing to punish the girls, I spoke with Guda with my decision. (It is strange and uncomfortable to reprimand someone whom you have previously worked under.) Eugenia and Alyce Marie were transferred to work with the children under Sister Mathilde. In turn, the two novices working under Sister Mathilde were transferred to the kitchen. Guda would not accept any blame, though she must abide by my decision. She left my study very unhappy.

Yesterday, I heard that she had also taken a barn boy to task for not washing the eggs before he delivered them to the kitchen. Of course, it was not his job to wash the eggs, but simply to deliver them. As a result, there was an argument between Guda and the boy's father, who also works in the barns. The matter was brought to me. Once again it resulted in an argument between Guda and me. At the time, I was quite busy with other matters and lost my temper. She left my office, her face red with frustration and tears. Many of Guda's mistakes have been trivial, but the increasing frequency has been worrying, and they upset the peace of this place.

Today it came to my attention from another kitchen worker that a few of the kitchen staff have been watching Guda carefully for some time. One of them, who has worked with her for years, is very concerned about her change in behavior. It seems this worker has identified at least part of the problem. Guda is losing her sight. Finally knowing what to look for, I can see the gray film that is beginning to cover her eyes. Could her hearing and mental faculties be worsening as well? She was in her thirties when I entered the convent at fourteen and is now well advanced in age. There are several things that need to be accomplished to make this transition smooth, as it is extremely important that her knowledge not be lost. I can task someone with writing down as much as Guda can remember. I feel strongly that her accomplishments be acknowledged and recognized, both to save her pride and reward her for a lifetime of service. At the same time, she will need to be removed from her present position, perhaps by finding something else for her to do. I have no wish to hurt this wonderful woman, who has devoted her life to the health and happiness of those who live at Lambley. Reasoning with her might be difficult, and it will take all my skills as a diplomat, which have sometimes been a bit lacking.

30 May 1454

The Problem of Aging

The situation with Guda has me grappling with the issues of aging and the challenges these bring to those who are experiencing them, as well as those who must work with or care for them. As someone who has experienced debilitating bouts of excruciating pain in my leg all my life, I have great sympathy for those who are suffering, as well as for their caretakers.

As we age, we increasingly experience bodily aches and pains: twisted fingers, crippled knees and feet, fading eyesight, and loss of hearing. It had been annoying for me to keep asking people around me to repeat themselves, to stop mumbling, until I realized the problem was my diminished hearing! Gradually, over time, these changes affect our abilities to function as we are accustomed to. We may even lose our ability to walk or speak. Worst of all, our mental faculties can diminish. The elderly and infirm often refuse to acknowledge their diminished capacity. Coming face-to-face with the frailty of growing old is a humbling experience, a path I have personally already set my feet upon. We sometimes become like querulous children, difficult to deal with. I am hopeful that Guda will accept the changes in her life with grace. If she does, I will probably ask Eawynn to record Guda's wealth of knowledge about managing the kitchen. Yvonne may be our historian, but Eawynn has more tact. Blessed Lady, pray that it may be so.

JUNE

5 June 1454

The Despair of a Child

E arly this morning, a child is dropped off at the convent by her mother. A girl child. She is seven, appearing on our doorstep as a small, solemn figure in an old dress that is a few sizes too large. She seems alert but does not speak one word as her mother explains the situation to Sister Mathilde and me. The mother is educated and apparently from a good family of lesser nobility. She explains that her husband passed away five years ago. She and the girl, Lynet, have been staying with the mother's family, who are not supportive, and the child, of course, has not had a father. The mother has decided to remarry, and her future husband does not want this girl child. It seems the mother is not much attached to her either. As the mother leaves, without even hugging her daughter, Lynet begins to cry, silently. I give her into the care of Alyce Marie, but not before I attempt to hug her and tell her we will take care of her. Her little body, all angles, with bones like sharpened twigs, stiffens immediately, but she eventually relaxes as I continue to hold on. Then, she grips me fiercely and begins to sob, her small body shaking. We will take care of Lynet. We will love her and give her all the comfort she has never had before. We will watch her grow and bloom. She will lighten our days, as the young ones in our care always do. We will truly see her.

These situations, which occur all too often, always bring back memories of my own short childhood. My father and elder brother Daibhidh left when I was ten, called up for service to the king to fight the Scots in the Battle of Yeaverling. My father died in that battle, whilst my brother remained in the king's service for several years. I was already at Lambley when Daibhidh returned. Daibhidh had made my childhood a misery. When I was four, he began taking me on walks. The first time he did this I was so happy that he had even taken notice of me, and I went with him gladly, skipping by his side and holding his hand. He laid me down on the ground on his coat at the edge of the forest where we could not be seen. The pain I experienced was excruciating as he forced himself inside my tiny body. I tried to cry out, but he held his hand over my mouth. I remember watching the sky, with small white clouds drifting slowly by. When he was finished, he stood up and towered over me menacingly. He told me that I was an evil child, that my twisted leg was proof that I was evil, and that I would go to hell if I ever told anyone of the experience. Despite this, I told my mother immediately. She did not believe me. She never checked to see if I had been misused. She sent me to bed without supper and told me never to make up lies about Daibhidh again. I tried to avoid him, but he often caught me unawares. I learned to go away, to be somewhere else during each ordeal. The torment continued until my grandfather came to live with us. I never mentioned the situation to my mother again. I had learned my lesson. I had also learned to hate my brother, and that my mother was not to be trusted. Even now, trust does not come easily for me.

My mother doted on my other sisters. She was embarrassed by me because of my obvious deformity. It is assumed that a deformity can be passed on to one's children, which made me unfit for marriage. She kept me from the public eye as much as possible, embarrassed that my appearance might reflect upon her bloodlines. I never knew the comforts of a warm mother who was physically demonstrative. I only received affection from my tutors and my Bampy, my maternal grandfather. It was his loving attention, his warm affection, and his sense of humor that gave me the strength to survive. I have deep feelings for the pain this child is suffering. As Our Lady loves all her children, we will love this little one as well. We will love her.

7 June 1454

Honey and Berries

The wild blackberries and strawberries are ripening. They grow near tree lines and stonewall fences. They must be picked every other day until their season is past. This year Sister Margarethe and her novices are gathering them. Guda and her helpers will assist with drying or processing the berries into tinctures. Some will be mixed with honey from the beehives. Some will be made into preserves and stored in jars sealed with beeswax.

I accompany Sister Mathilde on a walk this morning to watch Alaric remove the first honeycomb of the season from one of the skeps, woven bee boxes, accompanied by Donel, his grandson. We stand quite some distance away as Alaric explains that bees can be dangerous if they become upset. The hive had separated two weeks ago when a young queen bee left with many of the workers, and they were presently swarming in a nearby tree. Donal had rushed in early that morning to tell us not to go anywhere near that meadow until his grandfather had the swarm under control and settled into a new skep. The transfer was successful, giving the abbey a new source of honey. Alaric has established several skeps in various spots on the abbey's grounds. Apparently, Alaric knows how to talk to bees.

This morning, we watch as he and Donal use smoke to calm the remaining bees in the original skep so the honeycomb can be extracted safely. Over the years our annual supply of honey and beeswax has grown. Lately, I have noticed that much of the job of keeping the bees has been passed to Donal, except when gathering the honeycomb. Alaric still assists with that. Timothy, who is Alaric's other grandson, often accompanies them as well, particularly if it looks like the work might be dangerous. Timothy has been apprenticed to a local carpenter and has made himself very useful in repairing barns, sheds, and doing other odd jobs on the abbey grounds. It appears that Donal will take over as chief groundskeeper.

17 June 1449

Summer

G uda has asked for assistance in processing the honey that has been retrieved from Alaric's bee boxes. The honey must be extracted from the honeycomb. It is a process that takes several hours for the separation to be complete.

Margarethe comes to assist accompanied by a couple of new novices. I send to the library for Eawynn, as this is one of her favorite tasks. Cwenhild also joins, saying she would not miss this for anything. We sit around a table, each with our own piece of honeycomb and a finely woven mesh covered with cheese cloth that are placed in the bowl. We place the honeycomb in the bowl and crush it with a wooden pestle, cutting apart the beeswax with knives when necessary. It is important that we do not touch the honey or beeswax with our hands, as this can cause it to spoil. When most of the honey has drained into another bowl, the beeswax from each bowl is tied up in the cheese cloth and twisted to remove any remaining honey. The honey is poured then stored into containers that are sealed with melted beeswax. The containers cannot be moved until the beeswax has become solid again. All our utensils are left spread out on a table in the sunlight, and we watch as bees discover the bits of honey and wax that are left. Miraculously, the bees clean everything for us.

After sealing the jars, the beeswax that remains is used to make candles. Wooden furniture is preserved by rubbing it with beeswax. Separating honey from the beeswax is sticky work. As hard as we try not to, a little honey always gets on our fingers. We are tempted to lick our fingers, although Guda says that makes the honey spoil, so we refrain. When we are finished, Guda brings out some fresh rolls for us to dip into a small bowl of honey. Only those who participated are allowed this treat. Our conversation at the table is light-hearted, a very enjoyable task. My favorite part of this process is the plate of honeybuns that is served with our porridge for breakfast the next morning.

JULY

3 July 1454

Eawynn

The first two years that Eawynn was with us, like everyone else, I did not question that she was mute. At the beginning, she was a stubborn, belligerent child who refused to follow the rules. She would not get up in the mornings. She refused to do anything at lessons except stare blankly at the wall or out a window. She would not play with the other children. As I was one of the novices working with the children, Sister Elsyth agreed to make Eawynn my responsibility. Slowly, ever so slowly, a change came over this unhappy child. She began to respond to my questions with hand signals. At first, communication between us was very frustrating, but gradually improved as I learned her signals. Whenever she was not in the learning room, she began to follow me around, taking an interest in my tasks and helping me with them. She became my shadow. She increasingly took more care with her appearance and attempted to communicate with the other children. Although they were uncooperative at first, even mocking or laughing at her, there were a few that responded positively, with interest. They became her friends. They learned her signing. The method of silent communication spread throughout children in the learning room, and onward to any adult that Eawynn had repeated contact with. The abbess even remarked that the change in this formerly miserable child was remarkable. What is remarkable is how quickly she must have invented these signs as she needed them. I still marvel at a mind that is capable of such creativity.

Riding horses, especially my little mare, has always been one of my greatest pleasures. I often rode out around the abbey grounds, which are extensive, when I had an hour to myself in the afternoons. Eawynn had been begging with silent hand signs to be allowed to accompany me for a few weeks, and I had refused. At the time I was nineteen and preparing myself to take my initial vows as a nun. She had just turned thirteen. I finally relented and allowed her to accompany me on a sturdy bay pony that I knew was well-trained. Imagine my surprise to find out that she was already an accomplished rider. She was so well-behaved on that first ride that I allowed her to accompany me whenever I could, which was quite often. On the day that I discovered that she could speak, I was riding a little ahead of her on a path through a forested area when a boar suddenly rushed at me from the side. A nearby rustling in the undergrowth caused me to turn and look just as Eawynn screamed for me to run. Kicking my mare into a full gallop, I realized that Eawynn was still behind me on the trail, as was the boar. Skidding to a stop, I turned, only to see that she had taken off in the opposite direction. The boar had also disappeared. Carefully, I back tracked to the mews only to find that Eawynn had already dismounted, thrown her bridle to a stable boy, and fled to her room. By the time I finally I caught up to her, she had flung herself down on her bed and was sobbing. Demanding an explanation, because she was obviously not mute, as we had all been led to believe, I stood by her bedside and waited. At first, she offered no response and continued to weep, possibly hoping that I might consider the incident a one-time event. I continued to stand over her, glowering at her, waiting. Such sobs of despair! When she finally quieted down, she pleaded with me not to tell others. I had difficulty believing that this child could have fooled us all for so long, but I left her after vowing that I would not reveal her secret yet, not until we had a long discussion and some understanding between us.

7 July 1454,
Home Visits

The pink brilliance of dawn is just visible in the eastern sky when Brother Edward arrives on horseback, leading a packhorse loaded with supplies, to ride out with Eawynn and me toward Gilsland and the Roman wall. This month our stock of foods and herbs is much greater than our last visit, due to our summer harvests of berries and greens. I have decided that teaching these households to grow their own herbs and forage for wild berries and edible greens, as well as the knowledge of their usage for illnesses is long overdue. I will try to remedy this with short explanations at each cottage we visit. We mount our horses using the mounting block by the barn and take turns leading the packhorse that Guda has loaded with our supplies, as we ride on the path beside the River Irthing that leads to the Roman wall and fort. The last time we ventured this way was a few months ago. The house at our first stop is deserted, appearing to have been abandoned. There are no animals, and no planting has taken place in the little garden plot. Though we dismount and walk around, calling out greetings, there is no one here. Concerned, we hurriedly remount, with Edward giving Eawynn a leg up on her tall gelding, and we ride to the next home. Thankfully, the family is still in residence and appears to be healthy. When I ask about the deserted homestead, which is only two miles away, the husband replies that the family moved because they had been threatened. He does not want to say more, but I press him for information. Apparently, someone from Thirlwall Castle has been threatening to evict families in this area, as the land has been claimed by the powerful Thirlwall family. Surprised, I have been under the impression that the land around Gilsland was part of the de Vaux estate, so I will need to look into this. Perhaps Yvonne can find the historical records. Although we ask for information from the next three families, they say they have heard nothing, so the reason given for this family abandoning their home may not even be true. I may have to visit Thirlwall Castle to inquire about this matter. It might be best if I involve the abbot as well.

We journey a little past Gilsland to the waterfalls, where we dismount and have a meal of bread and cheese. The waterfalls are a little quieter today than they were in early spring, when the snowmelt causes the water to roar in great torrents down the falls, although it has not been a dry summer. I suggest a short nap, which we manage, leaning against a tree, or on one of the large boulders on the side of the falls. I am accustomed to taking a short nap after the midday meal. Eating always makes me drowsy. There is a gentle breeze, accompanied by a few ravens that scold us from the top of an elm tree. Nearby, the sound of bees going from flower-to-flower lulls me to sleep. I wake with a start as my mare nuzzles my shoulder. Alarmed at first, I quickly realize that we have not been asleep long. Edward is already stirring and gently wakes Eawynn. We mount and begin the ride back to the abbeys, stopping at the abandoned cottage once more for another look, then continuing on. Providing instructions about herbal remedies and edible wild greens slipped my mind during our visits. This will need to be accomplished at another time.

11 July 1454

Secrets

This morning's schedule leaves me with no time to myself! Summer is a busy season. I have just finished washing my hands at the outside well, after digging up beets and carrots from the garden, when Eawynn comes out from the kitchen carrying a cool drink for us both. She convinces me to sit in the shade for a few minutes to rest before the midday meal. She makes sure I do not overexert myself.

I had planned to ride out and survey the surrounding countryside in the afternoon, as I still do from time to time. I ask Eawynn to accompany me. At my age it is best not to ride alone. She is an excellent horsewoman now, probably better than I am. As soon as we are out of hearing range and certain that we are not being observed, we laugh and carry on the way we did when we were young. We speak of many things, some being information that we have already shared over the years. I find that the need to give voice to and relive difficult situations lessens as the years go by, but never disappears completely.

She speaks of her first time on horseback, how the smell of horses and tack is one of her earliest memories. I tell her about my wonderful grandfather, and the abuse that I had suffered from my brother. She confides that she had become an uncontrollable child in hopes that her parents would send her away. She knew what they had planned for her future, marriage to a wealthy older man in the south of England, and she wanted no part of it. She had met him once and he had touched her in such a way that she thought she might be sick. She protested, as she disliked him immensely, but her parents were adamant about the match. Her parents knew that she could speak. She had no idea why the sisters had not inquired about her condition when it became apparent that she was mute at Lambley. She had expected to be found out at any time. The convent seemed to be an acceptable alternative, even though it was only supposed to be temporary. It is a miracle that her ability to speak has not been discovered by anyone else. It is a ruse we have kept up for years. In the beginning the idea was hers alone. I agreed to keep her secret at first for her sake, although now it suits me to have a mute as my scribe. People often ignore a mute person, assuming their mental capacity is diminished as well. This works very well, as Eawynn is extremely unobtrusive, yet very observant.

20 July 1454

Root Cellars and Harvests

Guda is supervising the cleaning of the root cellars and the harvesting of vegetables from the gardens. Although the cellars are cleaned each year, we still find dead skeletons of small creatures, spiders and the occasional snake. I have watched many slither away over the years, avoiding us just as we avoid them. Our lamps do not illuminate all the corners, so I am careful where I place my hands. The drying of herbs is ongoing as many are stored for the winter. Herbs are essential to our health in times of sickness, and several, such as rosemary and thyme are essential to Guda for cooking.

The farm laborers are also cutting and storing hay for the winter. Stopping momentarily as I walk past the hay barn, I stand and breathe in the smell of newly dried hay! It is the very scent of summer! Cwenhild often asks for a rotation of novices and anyone else who is not busy to aid in bringing water to those cutting the hay, as the work is hot and strenuous.

Having surpassed my own expectations at the organizational skills necessary to be successful as an abbess, I would not have been as successful without Eawynn's ideas and encouragement. Even at a young age, I realized that a position of some authority would afford me both a measure of protection and control over my life. I also knew what work would be needed to learn these various skills. As a child, it was necessary to learn to read and write in Greek so that I could make correct copies of both the Greek authors and the translations of their works into common English. I helped with the orphan school, first as a novice helper and later as head novice in charge of the education of our orphans and some of the children from the surrounding area that were sent to us specifically for that purpose. I enjoyed my time spent in the kitchen although I would never claim to know how to cook. Under Guda, I learned to follow the simple directions for food preparation and preservation.

Being outside has always been my favorite, either working in the gardens with vegetables and herbs, or learning the care of our many types of animals. Due to Eawynn's foresight, the hen houses and duck roosts have been enlarged to accommodate a larger number of fowl, and the stables have been rebuilt with more and better stalls, as many of the sisters and workers often need a horse for travel. There are three large work mares that are used for cultivating the fields and pulling heavy wagons, along with two shaggy cows and several goats that produce milk for our cheeses. Our most important source of income comes from the wool of our flock of sheep. I have very little to do with their care but must keep accurate accounts of their numbers and the amount of wool we sell. Not all nuns know how to keep accounts, but I insisted on learning that as well, although I turned the job over to Eawynn, who enjoys working with sums much more than I do. She has made every effort to assist me in whatever way she can, even bringing me tea and bread when I am overtired or have forgotten to eat. Together we have a thorough working knowledge of the administrative skills necessary to make Lambley flourish.

Although neither of us ever felt a calling to live a religious life, the path had been forced on us by circumstances. It would be a lonely and somber life without Eawynn. She entertains all the convent, and me in particular, with her antics, pantomimed stories, and impersonations of those she does not particularly like. My life would be a dull day-to-day ritual without her. With her, it is everything I could have ever dreamed of, so if I give thanks to God, it is for her.

27 July 1454
The Weather

I do not think I have ever seen a July with this much rain. The last month it has rained three or four days each week. The rain has made the harvesting of vegetables difficult, the result being that many of them could rot. For the last three days Guda has been adamant that the vegetables must be picked daily, sometimes in the rain. Tables, covered with cloth, are set up to allow the vegetables to dry sufficiently before storing them in the cellars. Working barefoot with our shifts tied up between our legs, we make our way down the rows of cabbages, parsnips, carrots, onions, and kale. Baskets of muddy vegetables are then rinsed with water from the well and set out to dry on tables set up in an empty room, or hung, tied on strings. Upon finishing our labor in the rain each day, we receive some good-natured grins from the brothers at Lanercost, who are also working in their gardens, as we make our way to the banks of the river to clean the mud off our legs. In some cases, as with Alyce Maria and Eugenia, after slipping in the muddy field, some need to rinse every part. On the third day, always the one to lighten the mood at the end of the day's labor, Eawynn pushes Cwenhild into the mud, and chaos ensues. The mandatory rinsing before we are allowed back in the convent is embarrassing, as Lanercost Abbey lies between Lambley and the river.

AUGUST

10 August 1454

On Music

One of the skills that I learned from a tutor, an unusual young man who had come to stay with us, was a rudimentary knowledge of harp and lute. He was a relation of my father, although I was never told what the connection was. He only stayed for a few years. He was slight of build with what my mother called a "sensitive nature." I never did find out why my parents employed him, although he was knowledgeable about reading and writing as well. I regard it as strange that his name was Angus, as I tend to think of anyone named Angus as a big, burly Scotsman. Angus was quite the opposite. In the summer he would sit in the garden and sing, accompanying himself on the harp. I loved to sit close by, in secret, and listen. He introduced me to the works of Hildegard of Bingen and Guillaume de Machaut, as well as the contemporary music of Guillaume Dufay, but what I loved most was learning the popular troubadour songs from the English courts. My voice is acceptable and the singing we do at chapel is inspiring, but I do miss the secular songs. When time allows, I continue to practice both instruments at the convent. Of music and horses, music is a close second.

12 August 1454

On Death and God

I have spent much time contemplating what we are taught by the Church about the afterlife. I confess that as I grow older, I increasingly doubt the truth of it. Our libraries at Lambley and Lanercost are extensive. The writings of the ancient Greeks have led me to question many of the teachings of the Church. I would probably be burned at the stake as a heretic if this was known, so my journals and my views are not shared with others, except for Eawynn. When we witness how men treat each other in the most abominable ways, what does it say about God, that man is made in His image and likeness? Perhaps it is God who is man-made.

Despite my doubts about the Church, I have never questioned the teachings of Christ, found in the four

Gospels. If the members of Church hierarchy, including the pope, followed His teachings, it would be a much different world.

15 August 1454

Cats

Cwenhild surprises me with a visit this morning, telling me that a litter of small kittens has been left by the road leading into the orchards. They are quite wild, but fortunately, Cwenhild, Eawynn and I catch them with some milk from the goats. They are being kept in an empty stall in the stable at present. There are two with grey stripes and white paws, one that is black, white, and orange with a black spot on its nose, and a tiny, fluffy black one that I may keep for myself.

While I feel anger toward those who abandon helpless creatures and expect others to take up the responsibility for these creatures' care, I am nonetheless grateful for the abandonment of these kittens this morning, as we have recently lost several of our older cats. We did have two litters of kittens born in the stables earlier this spring but lost all of them to an eye sickness that runs through a litter like a plague, despite our efforts. Fortunately, these five seem to be healthy. We need to tame them, as I wish to have at least two of them housed in the pantry with the grains. Guda has seen evidence of mice in there again. Unfortunately for Lanercost, the abbot and several of the brothers have an unreasonable dislike for cats. As a result, their sacks of grains, both for their livestock and for their personal use, are filled with rodent dirt and grain hulls. I have repeatedly told him that cats can solve this problem. He is old-fashioned and thinks that their very independent nature and inability to be trained like a dog makes them untrustworthy. Despite the opinions of our abbot, I can only see the good in these creatures, and I do tend to enjoy their independence. Perhaps I should also tell him that the harmless brown snakes we find in the barnyard are also excellent for controlling the rodents, although telling him that snakes are also good is probably not a good idea. After the serpent in the garden convinced Eve to eat the apple, I cannot see Abbot Walton allowing the presence of snakes!

17 August 1454

What to Do?

Everything goes just fine, until it does not! Last month we received a young oblate. She comes to the abbey from a wealthy family that is situated some distance from here, very far indeed. She is a headstrong, clever girl who does not want to be here and is causing no end of trouble with the sisters. As she has several older sisters, apparently her father thought there would be an issue with finding her a husband. Although the donations to take her in were ample, I am not sure it is worth the disturbance of the peacefulness of the abbey that her stubborn refusal to follow guidelines is causing. I cannot send her back. Her family would refuse to take her. I cannot turn her out. Where would she go? She is only eleven. What to do?

19 August 1454

The Promise of Cats

We have finally finished cleaning out the storage cellars for the root crops. Despite the rains, and because of Guda's insistence of harvesting in the rain, there is an average harvest from the gardens of turnips, parsnips, onions, and cabbage. Ah, cabbage, by spring we are all so tired of cabbage and gruel! I should not complain.

The kittens are thriving. We are so blessed to have some mousers among us again, although they are probably too young to be of much help this year. We are training two of them to stay near the grain storage area. Our winter supplies of oats and barley were badly damaged about ten years ago when we had an infestation of mice and rats. It is a winter I will never forget. The abbot at Lanercost had convinced our mild-mannered abbess that cats should not be allowed inside the convent or treated as pets. Cat became outside animals. Our stable manager still insisted on keeping a few cats in the grain room at the barn, especially at night. I think he locked them in there and let them out in the morning. Unfortunately, the rodents got into our supplies in early winter and ruined several sacks of grain. Barley and oats that are full of grain husks and rodent droppings are not fit for human consumption. By March we had used up the last of our barley and had to use some of the oat supply kept at the barn for the horses. We used it sparingly, so the health of our livestock would not be negatively affected. Our meals were much diminished in size, especially when the hens went into spring molt and stopped laying while our cows gave birth to calves that required most of their milk. It was a difficult spring. We did not discuss the necessity of having cats in the storage rooms with the abbot but have made sure that we have cats to guard the grain supplies since that winter. I will endeavor to change his mind at some future time if we ever have a surplus of kittens.

One of our new kittens has been designated a kitchen cat. The fourth will be our prowling house cat. I insist they be fed their goat milk in the places we want them to patrol. I sincerely hope this works out. One little tabby seems to know all the feeding places already. Training cats. Is it even possible?

On another note, the child whose name is Mildred, but whom we are calling Maud, is slowly adjusting. She is very headstrong, like the great Empress Maud, daughter of King Henry I. She is under Sister Mathilde's care. She seems to like being outside to work in the herb and vegetable gardens. She is also quite adept at writing, and drawing, in fact, her drawing is quite remarkable for one so young. I tried to interest her in singing, and then I did not. She has no ear for melodies and throws others off. We will keep working to find a vocation for her, perhaps working in the library. At least I occasionally see her smiling.

21 August 1454

God's Hands

Today I wake up with the resolve to do better. I never look forward to the harvest season. So much work! So little time for reflection. Everyone is engaged as we need provisions for the winter not only for ourselves, but for the poor of the local community as well. The landowners take so much and give so little back. Even the Church requires its pound of flesh from the poor. I have always heard that with faith, God will provide, but that does not happen by itself. God provides through us, through our foresight, our care, our understanding, and our love. We are the hands of God, through our acceptance and tolerance of each other's differences.

Wherever there is division, look to see who benefits. We must stand united against the tyranny of the powerful, and sometimes that means those in power in God's most holy offices. The Church may be Christ's most holy bride on earth, but greed and the hunger for power are invasive everywhere. Where there is turmoil, the poor suffer the most. We are called to love unconditionally.

26 August 1454
Elderberries

Novices Kendra and Bernia are processing our dried elderberry flowers into syrup under Guda's watchful eyes. The berries themselves are not quite ripe. They usually ripen in the third week of September, and they must be harvested before the birds eat them. Elderberries have been used by healers at least since the time of the Greeks, as both Hippocrates and Dioscorides recommended the use of the berries and the bark as treatments for illness and snakebite. The abbot had previously inquired about our use of elderberries, as several of the bishops have declared from the pulpit that elderberries should not be used, that any effects of the berries are associated with witchcraft and the devil. They claimed that Judas hung himself on an elderberry tree. I question that, because our elderberries grow on bushes. Maybe the elderberries are different in Jerusalem? Abbot Walton has since seen and accepted that elderberries have strong medicinal properties. The brothers now process them just as we do. Thank goodness there are ample bushes in the vicinity. They grow everywhere.

When the berries are ripe, we will make a tincture with them in spirits with some honey from our hives. The solution is allowed to sit for several months and is then strained through cloth. I find it to be a marvelous remedy for the illnesses that colder weather brings. It is also excellent when poured over bannocks or scones for afternoon tea. We always make the tincture for the following year. Last year, Eawynn took it upon herself to experiment with making elderberry wine, for medicinal purposes, of course. The results were quite remarkable. Care must be taken that one does not imbibe too much as it is also rather delicious. I say this from personal experience as Eawynn and I drank quite a bit with a few of the other sisters and it loosened our tongues. I cannot remember what was said, but we really need to be more careful. I believe that Eawynn may have also spoken out loud. I pray that everyone else was as inebriated as we were. Most of our sisters did not come here from personal choice, and many are just as suspicious of some of the questionable traditions that the Church teaches as we are, but there are a few like Sister Rosamund, and possibly Sister Yvonne, who are conservative, devout, and very sincere. I do not think they would endanger us intentionally, but we are still careful to keep our opinions to ourselves.

I also know that some of the older, wise women in the villages who are well-versed in herbal lore are often regarded with suspicion. Perhaps this is where the association with "witches" comes from. There are recent rumors that women have been burned at the stake in Scotland for being witches. The rumors come from the area just south of Edinburgh. I fear that this may develop into a hysteria where vulnerable women, or women who are seen to be a threat to the local authorities, are accused for anything that goes wrong in a community. It is easy to accuse a woman. Most have no defense. Often, the women who are accused have something someone else wants. It is a difficult and scary time for women. These occurrences are driven by greed or jealousy. I do not believe in witches. I do think older women who are midwives and healers, who know about herbal remedies, and have influence in a community are often resented by priests of the Church. Accusing them of witchcraft removes that influence.

SEPTEMBER

3 September 1454
Cats Can Fetch

As I make my rounds this morning, I witness a curious event. I stop in the kitchen to grab a bread roll from the basket where the midday meal is being prepared. One of the rescued kittens has been relegated as the official Kitchen-and-Pantry mouser. It has several small balls of yarn to bat around to keep it occupied, as it is not yet fully grown and has become a favorite of some of the kitchen staff. I watch as Bernia surreptitiously tosses a small yarn ball across the floor. I am amazed to see the kitten retrieve the yarn and return it to her. This action is repeated several times until the kitten tires of it and flops in a corner by the hearth to rest. I had no idea cats can play "fetch." It is nice to learn something new.

5 September 1454

Rain

It continues to rain, more than usual for late summer. The amount of rain we have received the last two months has made harvesting crops and hay difficult. Fortunately, we have had a few dry days, and Guda's quick thinking has saved most of the root crops. It is raining as I sit here watching the skies open in the gardens next to my window. Streams of water are cutting rivulets between the bushes and rushing down the hill. Eawynn saves the day by showing up with two scones flavored with dried berries, a small pot of honey and hot tea.

9 September 1454

The Fate of Girls

Oh, the senseless tragedy! I am weeping this morning. Yesterday, the body of a young, very young, girl was discovered in a nearby hamlet. She died in a failed attempt to abort a pregnancy that resulted in her death. Through some inquiry, it was revealed that she had repeatedly had sexual intercourse with one of her older stepbrothers. Pregnancy was inevitable. When questioned, the stepbrother admitted that he had been having relations with her for some time, but that it was consensual and that she had seduced him. She was just twelve years old and had likely flowered only a few months earlier. There are few consequences if any for the young man. This is a common tale.

The irony of it all is that she cannot be buried in sacred ground, as the Church has deemed this a suicide and has also condemned her as a murderess. Such an injustice! I cannot believe God to be so unforgiving, although there is nothing to forgive. She was a desperate child. If she did consent, it was for something she needed. Boys are considered to be more valuable to a family than girls. They were a poor family with few resources.

The fate of a poor girl child is of no consequence. This child was malnourished. She never had a chance. She and her child, if it had survived, would have placed a greater stress on the family's resources. Boys can always find some kind of labor to contribute to the family's well-being. Young girls are often given away in marriage, usually to a widower with children. Once this child had been used sexually by her brother, even marriage was not an option.

It is a sad truth that poor women have little value. They can be ill-used, then blamed, and thrown away. They are possessions, worth less than the family cow. There will be no justice until the courts and the Church hold men accountable. Unfortunately, the courts and the hierarchy of the Church are made up of men. We do what we can to aid girls who are in this position in our community, but it is often not enough. There are too many poor families with unwanted female children.

12 September 1454

A Visit and a Puzzle

Yesterday, I walked out to the orchards and gathered some ripe apples for the children, as well as two for myself and Eawynn. The harvesting of apples and pears will begin any day. Some will be sliced and dried. The rest will be stored in boxes in the cellars, where the temperature is quite cold. They last a long time that way, even if they eventually look like shriveled old men. They are still sweet, sweeter still when they are dried, it seems.

It has stopped raining, so today seems the perfect day to check on the families by the Roman ruins and Gilsland, and also to check with the de Vaux family about the ownership of that abandoned cottage. Although we have been out twice since May with Brother Edward, our time was restricted to morning travel and the de Vaux estate at Triermain Castle is quite a bit further on. We decide to take as long as needed today and visit the families on our way to Trierman Castle. Yesterday, I walked to Lanercost Abbey to ask Brother Edward if he would accompany us, but he was absent on a mission for the abbot. Eawynn and I know the area quite well, having spent many of our younger years on errands for the abbess, being only too glad to ride out for just about any reason.

Immediately after Prime, we take our leave with a packhorse and supplies. Visiting a few cottages on the way to Gilsland, we then turned northwest and continued to the castle, arriving around noon. A man meets us at the door with news that the Earl is not in residence. We ask him about the land around the Roman fort and he is nice enough to pass on the information that we need. The land on which the abandoned cottage is located is indeed part of the de Vaux estate. Although the land is located between the Triermain Castle of de Vaux and Thirlwall Castle, the land does not belong to the Thirlwall family.

Returning from Triermain Castle, we ride up to Gilsland to visit a family there. While on route from the hamlet of Gilsland to the gorge, Eawynn notices that a traveler has appeared on horseback some distance behind us. It is difficult to see him clearly at that distance. As we ride on, the distance between the traveler and us remains constant. Reaching the waterfalls, we dismount to eat a meal packed by Guda consisting of cheese, bread, and a delicious piece of apple cobbler from last night's supper. What a pleasant surprise! We rest out of sight of the road for about one quarter of an hour. Returning to road toward home after our brief rest and assuming the traveler has passed by us and continued on his way, we are surprised to find that he is following us again, in the opposite direction, although not close enough to make out his features. This continues until we reach the Roman fort on the wall, at which point he disappears from our sight. Incidentally, I realize later that the spot where he left the road was at the abandoned cottage. Assuming that the cottage is still abandoned, we have not visited it for some time. The whole episode gives me a feeling of unease. Next time we will be sure to have an escort.

18 September 1454

Brigitta

There are many reasons why women come to us at the convent. Many have no choice, although such is not the case for a young girl who showed up last night. She was dressed in rags as a boy, her hair cut short, her face filthy, perhaps to keep from being recognized. Her story is a curious one, although more common than we might imagine. She says she is fourteen-years-old. She is one of the older children in her family and was married early last summer to a local tradesman, a butcher. Apparently, the butcher had recently lost a wife and babe in childbirth. According to our little refugee, she became his third wife. His first two wives had died, leaving behind three small children. There had been some rumors of neglect and abuse. Even so, the girl's parents insisted on the wedding. She ran away after a week and would not disclose what had happened during that time. She would not, and still will not, tell us where she is from, or her name. She is the same age that I was when I entered the convent. Her strength and resilience are palpable. I have named her Brigitta, and she has accepted the name.

She was a long time wandering before she stumbled up our walkway. I have not told the abbot about her. I am sure he would try to find her husband and return her to him, as marriage is a sacred institution. Neither have I encouraged her to become a novice, as that might also involve the bishop learning about her background. He is a stern man, and he will do what he thinks is right, that this child should do her duty in her marriage.

As the girl is too old to go to morning lessons with the other children, Eawynn has taken her on as a special project. She is teaching her the system of speaking with her hands, a system Eawynn developed fully while a novice at Lacock Abbey. Brigitta has made a good start at reading and writing under Yvonne's instruction, and we will attempt to teach her a trade. That is the best we can hope for at present. I fear for her future but pray that she will flourish here with us. She practices everything with enthusiasm and has a lovely young singing voice. I always praise God when He sends us someone who can sing! God willing, Brigitta will also benefit.

20 September 1454

The Harvest

The harvesting of apples and pears begins today, and the quantity of fruit looks to be adequate this year. The picking of fruit involves climbing ladders and is done by farm laborers. We help by picking up the apples and pears that have fallen to the ground. These are brought to Guda. Some are ground up, mashed, and filtered into a cider that turns alcoholic or sometimes into vinegar. Many are cut into slices and dried the same way the berries are dried, often in the still house. Unprecedented rain has caused unbelievable growth of grass and scrub bushes, so much so that I feel this is what it must be like to live in a jungle. There are vines everywhere. We plan to provision our false root cellars well this year. It was Eawynn's idea a few years ago to install hidden spaces for our root crops that only a few sisters and the kitchen staff know about. Even Abbot Alexander Walton has not been informed of these areas.

The hidden spaces are behind the regular dirt walls, dug out with doors in front of which we have placed large, movable shelves. We had a very small harvest three years ago and the bishop at Carlisle took most of our stores. It was a difficult winter. Although we helped as much as we were able, many of the local villagers in the surrounding areas starved. After the pillaging by the bishop, we were very limited ourselves. I cannot feel guilty about deceiving the bishop and his men when they come to audit our winter stores. They take and squander. They do not do without, as we must in a lean year. They profess to care for the common people, but they express their care only through prayers for their immortal souls. Prayers do not feed the starving. Hypocrites! If they truly followed the teachings of Christ, they would also care for the bodily health of their human flock.

OCTOBER

24 October 1454

Guests Outstay Their Welcome

For three days we have endured daily visits from Bishop Percy and a few of his entourage, and they have plans to remain for two more before journeying on. At least they are in residence at Lanercost, rather than with us. This visit has been a little more pleasant than the last one, as the priest who was making life very unpleasant for some of the younger oblates and novices did not accompany the bishop this time. In other respects, the visit, or more appropriately, the "inspection," has been as usual. Two of the bishop's men spent the better part of one day inventorying our stores of crops and negotiating what they deemed should be sent on to the bishop's residence. I accompanied them the entire day that they made their rounds, only allowing them out of my sight to relieve themselves in the privy. I worried that a worker might inadvertently mention the hidden storerooms, as a few of our kitchen helpers are simple. I value them for their kind, cheerful hearts, but they need supervision. Thankfully, the hidden storerooms have not been discovered. Our stores of grains and root crops are slightly below average this year, and we will need to be frugal to make it through the winter with enough for ourselves and those of the surrounding countryside who might need assistance before spring. The tremendous rains this summer are also making the harvesting of wheat and barley difficult.

Timothy and several laborers are presently strengthening and finishing the livestock shed. We lost too many lambs in the late winter storms two years ago. I will try to have a plan to avoid that should winters continue to prove difficult in the future. God willing, we will make it through in good health.

27 October 1454

A Surprise

The bishop departed yesterday morning from Lanercost. They stopped at Lambley mid-morning to give a final report of their visit. As usual, Bishop Percy expressed his gratitude for our dedication to the Church and to the surrounding community. At the same time, he hinted that more revenue was needed from the abbeys. He spoke briefly about the political situation, imploring us to pray fervently for a solution to avert the coming war between the Yorkists and the Lancasters. I do not think our prayers will be answered on that issue. The king is unstable and Richard, Duke of York, is the only one who can keep the peace at this time. War is inevitable.

As is the yearly custom when the bishop is in attendance, two of our novices, Eugenia and Alyce Marie, made their initial vows as nuns. As is tradition, the rest of the sisters also renewed their vows at this time. The ceremony was brief and without celebration. This morning, Guda and the kitchen staff surprised us with delicious griddle cakes, made with diced apples and walnuts and topped with butter and honey. It is a very pleasant change from the porridge we are usually served. There is also a hint that our evening meal will be special. I believe there are three wild geese waiting to be plucked in the pantry. I am glad we can celebrate without guests as the atmosphere is much less subdued. At morning chapel, we pray for the safe travels and arrival of the bishop back to his palace in Carlisle. We also give thanks that his visit was satisfactory and short. I silently add a prayer that we will not see him again until next October.

NOVEMBER

3 November 1454

The Joys of Being an Abbess

Managing a convent offers no end to complications. There are so many reasons why women come here. Some come willingly, others have no choice. We presently have fifteen fully professed sisters. Of these, some are widows who have chosen to dedicate their lives to God, although I suspect that a few of the wealthier sisters are here because they can live in relative ease without men telling them what to do. Some have brought their wealth with them and in this way have "purchased" an easy life. Their tasks may include some spinning, weaving and embroidery, but little hard labor. Oftentimes, when a family has too many daughters, one or more are sent to the convent as young girls with a sum of money that is much less than might be spent on a dowry. These become oblates and then novices. They are educated and taught skills. They may choose not to profess; in which case they eventually find work here or elsewhere. The abbey is always in need of cooks, gardeners, teachers, and healers.

Last year, two young widows, Beatrice Percy and Avice Mowbrey, were placed here by their husband's families to get them out of the way for inheritance. Neither had children yet, so it was easy for the husband's family to simply send them away with a small donation to the convent. Although they are adults, they are still novices. They do not want to be here and have done everything in their power to disturb the peace of our convent. They have refused to follow the rules. They will not help with the daily chores. They refuse to rise from their bed in time for morning prayers. Worst of all, they attempt to create an atmosphere of discord with the other novices, most of whom are much younger. I was also not given a choice by my family when they considered that I should have a life devoted to God, but I made my peace with it. The sisters and staff of the convent have become my family. With Eawynn as my dearest friend, I am blessed indeed.

Although I sympathize with these young women, there is no alternative for them now except to be cast out into the street or returned to their family or their deceased husband's family. I have explained their situation to them. Apparently, they do not believe me, as their belligerent behavior has continued. I have spoken to the entire community about the discord and disharmony that has been felt in our convent lately, and today I will ask that we now observe periods of silence and quiet meditation during the day, times which are meant to help bring us closer to God, but they serve to help keep the peace as well. I will also ask the nuns who oversee these novices to watch this situation carefully and identify any others who might be sowing discontent. If this does not work, I will need to take more drastic measures to restore our harmony. Lambley is a small community.

Sometimes the daughter of a prominent family is sent here because she is in the family way. We have had many such instances over the years. The girls who come to us in the family way are usually grateful for our care and understanding. Their families are obligated to donate enough money for us to raise the child or find a family to adopt it. Most girls are sent home after the baby is delivered, although a few have chosen to stay on, often against the family's wishes.

Occasionally a young girl professes a desire to join a convent on her own. I must confess, this does not happen very often.

4 November 1454

Matilde

I stop at the open door of the sunny room that was recently set up to be used for the children's lessons. When Sister Matilde asked to use this room, instead of the larger but darker hall that had previously been their classroom, I questioned her judgment. There are large windows here that let in the morning sun, but also are low enough that the children can look out at the lawn leading down to the wooded area beyond. All manner of creatures can be observed from this view, a rabbit quietly nibbling on grass while being stalked by one of our cats, foxes looking for a snack of mice, a doe with a fawn. The bare-leafed trees are a stage for the ever-changing dance of brightly colored birds as they chitter and scold each other and the squirrels. I questioned Mathilde that the view would cause no end of distractions. She smiled and asked me if I did not trust her to keep the children on task. She also added that the pleasant atmosphere of a sunlit room would cause the children to be more cheerful, especially since she had promised that if they worked diligently, she would allow them a few more minutes of their morning playtime outside. I could tell how pleased she was with the new arrangement, as the room also had a door that opened straight out onto the grounds.

As I peek into the room, the children are indeed totally immersed in their educational studies despite the panorama of activity outside. Just as I am about to leave, I spy a doe step slowly from the woods onto the grounds beside the building, followed tentatively by her two fawns, born last spring. Mathilde notices at the same time. Gathering the children around her, she quietly holds her finger to her lips, indicating that silence is needed. She slowly herds them to the windows to watch. Although it is apparent that the children are in awe of the spectacle, they move slowly and silently to the windows so as not to scare the doe away. Even their movements are controlled. It is obvious that they have been drilled how to react. I now understand the reason for the change of classrooms. How extraordinary it is to use this method to teach the wonder of creation.

Mathilde is one of our finest teachers and has made herself indispensable in the practice of caring for our orphans. Her mother brought her to Lambley when I was in my twenty-third year. She was sixteen at the time and pregnant. She could have chosen to go home when her child was delivered. Her parents are landowners of a small estate just north of York. They had made it clear that they would welcome her back. After giving birth, she chose to stay on, refusing to abandon her little son. As a novice she would be able to watch him grow up, even though she would not be allowed to have him recognize her as his mother. His name was Philip, and he was given to the brothers at Lanercost at the age of five. As a novice, Mathilde spent every free moment interacting with the convent's children. It was only natural that she became a teacher after making her vows, eventually taking charge of the education of the novices and our children at Lambley. Over the years she has trained several novices in childcare as well. We are grateful for her presence, innovation, and dedication.

7 November 1454

Results

The atmosphere at Lambley is much improved. I am thankful to have some peace restored, even though I personally dislike having mandated periods of silence. The families of Beatrice and Avice have been contacted to inform them of their daughter's behavior and the possible consequences. We wait to see if either family will allow their daughter to return home. Meanwhile, the young women are under a mandate of silence unless spoken to by a professed sister. Eawynn thinks they should be kept in their rooms until we have heard from their families. I think this is harsh, but it might be necessary if they continue their rebellion.

It is difficult for young girls and women adjust to convent life, even if they have chosen this path voluntarily. They miss their parents, siblings, and friends. They even miss their possessions, as those are given up upon entering the monastery. Three years ago, Judith Devereaux joined our community as an oblate. She was thirteen. She convinced her family and herself that she must join because she felt she had received a calling to serve God. I believe she was sincere, and since she was the third daughter, the family did not object. She was shy and did not make friends with the other girls but spent most of the time kneeling in the chapel in prayer when she was not involved in convent duties. She ate little at meals and it soon became apparent that she was losing weight. Eawynn was informed by one of the novices that the girl cried herself to sleep at night.

I leave issues with the oblates and novices up to Eawynn and Sister Mathilde. They decided to intervene before the girl made herself ill. Sister Mathilde asked Judith to accompany her and assist her throughout the day, giving her tasks that would compel her to work with others, to assist with the children. The process was lengthy, but Judith eventually began to assimilate into the community as an important contributing member. She is now a novice and has developed a real talent for singing and working with the abbey's children, where I believe she has found her path.

10 November 1454

An Anchoress

When the Bishop of Carlisle had visited earlier, he hinted that more revenue was needed from the abbeys to support the larger establishments of the Church.

He also said that he had been instructed by the archbishop to encourage convents and monasteries to establish an anchoress or anchorite, and so we have been "encouraged" to establish an anchoress here at Lambley. An anchoress would attract pilgrims, as she or he would be considered a living saint. I have tasked Eawynn with researching any historical records that we have on the subject. This is more a practice of the Benedictines.

Eawynn has finally reported her research to me. An anchorite or anchoress is a man or woman "chooses" to be walled up for life in a monastery or convent with only a screen through which to communicate to the outside world. It is through this screen that they observe Masses and daily offices, receive meals and communicate with others. There have been hundreds of cases of men or women all over Europe and England who have followed this path. While it is true that some have willfully chosen this path, and that their presence does indeed increase the revenue of the parish or abbey they are associated with, there have been many for whom this vocation was not voluntary or was made for reasons other than dedication to God. Katherine of Ledbury, a notable example, was a Welsh heiress who became an anchoress at the Church of Saint Michael's after the death of her husband and father. It is well known that she spent some time in hiding and became an anchoress to escape an unwanted marriage. Julian of Norwich and Hildegard of Bingen are perhaps the anchoresses that we know the most about, as they wrote and published many works on religion. It is to be noted that Hildegard did not consent to the life of an anchoress and left it immediately after her companion, the Blessed Jutta, died. All of Hildegard's writing and music date from after she established her own abbey at Rupertsberg.

The Bishop of Carlisle felt that the perfect place for an anchoress would be one of the small rooms near the sacristy at the local church of the Blessed Mary Magdalene that is used by both Lambley and Lanercost Abbeys. I will agree to this only if the vocation is requested by someone who truly has a calling for this kind of life. From what I have discovered during Eawynn's research into the subject, that is most often not the case.

17 November 1454

Rejection

We have had letters back from the family and from the husband's family of Beatrice Percy. Her husband's family expressed regret that they could not accept her return to their estate. In short, they claimed that she had been a disruptive daughter-in-law before their son's untimely death. The fact that Beatrice had remained childless meant that they no longer had a responsibility towards her upkeep. They had already spent what remained of her dowry to have her installed as a novice at Lambley. Her own family also felt they could no longer help her as they had already given a large dowry to her future husband's family to have her wed, and they had no more funds to support her.

This afternoon, I send a novice for her and ask that she be brought to my study in the presence of Sisters Margarethe and Eawynn, where she is given the letters to read for herself. I expect tears. She reacts instead with outrage and accusations against us. She has been with us for almost a year. I tell her that we will refund a part of the money given to place her here. After that, she can go wherever she chooses. It might be possible for her to find an occupation in a household, perhaps as a maid or nanny for children. We will do everything we can to aid her in her search for a position elsewhere. We will not offer her work as a laborer because, in the year she has been at Lambley, she has never made any attempt to learn any of the skills necessary for convent life. She will be given a month to decide. In the meantime, she is to cease all activities within the convent and keep to herself, in particular, the disruptive actions she has encouraged among the other novices. Regardless of whether she succeeds in finding a position, after one month she will be required to leave. The convent is no longer an option for her, either as a novice or as a laborer. As reality finally sets in, she sits in stunned silence. I feel sorry for her. It is difficult to watch someone who refuses to change, even for her own self-preservation.

Of Avice Mowbrey, we have only received a reply from her deceased husband's family stating that they are no longer responsible for her. In truth, Avice is not an instigator, but a follower. Sister Margarethe has vouched for her, reporting that Avice has ceased being disruptive and, indeed, seems to avoid Beatrice's company. We await communication from Avice's family.

DECEMBER

5 December 1454

Strength and Attachment

B eing out in nature, in the meadows and forests around the convent, always renews my spirit and gives me strength. Winter is a time for solitude and contemplation. I take daily walks, weather permitting, often with Eawynn. Our time together outside allows us to discuss and share our concerns. This morning, we focus on the problem of establishing an anchoress at Lambley. I am outraged at this suggestion, but we must be circumspect about how we react. We must appear to obey the mandate of our archbishop.

As we walk, we discuss how to approach the establishment of an anchoress, or rather, how to avoid doing so in such a way that it would seem we are being compliant with the archbishop's request. The wind is rising, making our return to the convent problematic. We hold on to each other as we push forward. It is at this time that I observe how the great gusts affect the bare trees very little but cause those that retain their leaves and the evergreens to twist and undulate in great circular motion. If the branches are not supple and yielding, they break. We are much like trees. While I believe we must bend and trust to the will of God, I have also noticed that the trees with no leaves have fewer attachments. The wind passes through them with little effect. They are not as affected by tumultuous change. It is good to be able to bend, but also to be able to withstand the strongest gale. After sheltering in the lee of a giant oak for a short time, we resume our walk as the wind finally dies down.

I do not have many attachments. While I respect, and in return, have the respect of most of my fellow sisters, Eawynn is my only attachment, my heart and my breath. Between us, we will tackle this problem by opening a search for an acceptable candidate for this position. If an adult of sound mind and body approaches me who sincerely wishes to fulfill this duty, I will no doubt allow it, but I will not allow someone to be forced into doing so. The idea that we must find and convince a person to fill this role is coercion at best.

7 December 1454

The Warning

Brother Edward walked over to Lambley shortly after noon yesterday. Stopping by my study, he asked if he could sit for a moment. It appeared that he was out of breath. I wondered if he was ill, as he is a few years younger than me. He must have seen my questioning look. He apologized for his demeanor, saying that exertion of any kind seems to tire him. He went on to suggest that we need to take one more load of supplies, enough that we might use two pack animals, to the needy families we serve. His reasoning is that we might not be able to get through again if the snow starts early. I agreed to leave early the next morning, while the weather stays clear of storms. Leaving him to find his way out, I went in search of Eawynn and stopped by the kitchen to request supplies be packed and readied: root vegetables, cabbages and grains.

This morning, Brother Edward arrives with an additional pack horse and supplies from Lanercost almost immediately after Prime. Eawynn grabs some bread, cheese, and apples for our journey as I help to load our packhorse and prepare our horses for departure. Although we had not visited the abandoned cottage recently, we decide to check on it first as we ride up to the Roman wall. The cottage is situated about one-half mile off the Roman wall, out of sight of from our position at the Roman fort. Turning to the north to follow the path toward the cottage, we can smell smoke. Nearing the cottage, a visible stream of smoke wafts into the sky. A horse whinnies as we approach, but there is a noticeable lack of farm animals or gardens. A tall man steps out of the door, dressed in dirty clothes, brown britches and boots, with the sleeves of what was once a fine silken shirt rolled up to his elbows. His reddish-brown hair is tied back in a queue with a leather cord. He demands to know what our business is in a low, raspy voice. When Brother Edward explains what we are about, the man strides forward to examine the contents of the saddlebags on the pack horse, rudely taking out several bunches of vegetables and grain, more than we would have given one person. When I inquire if he lives alone, he simply glowers at me and then stops suddenly, as his eyes light on Eawynn. He retorts that who did or did not live there is not our business, as his uncle is the lord of Thirlwall, and the property is his by rights. He then bids us to be on our way with an unpleasant leer, never taking his eyes from Eawynn.

We leave in measured haste, trying to maintain some semblance of being in control, and continue the rest of our journey in a somber mood. The other families are grateful for the supplies and seem well enough prepared for winter. They all invite us in for hot tea and, except for the last family, we decline the invitations. By the final visit, the reality of what could have happened has settled in, and I need to rest for a bit. Sitting by the hearth to warm ourselves in front of their fire, I realize just how shaken Eawynn is. Her normally rosy cheeks are white with a mixture of disgust and fright. The ride home seems to take forever, and I keep glancing over my shoulder.

7 December 1454

Evening

It is late evening when Eawynn knocks and enters my study, where I am still documenting the supplies that had been given out, what supplies and exactly how much to each family, including the hostile man in the first house after the Roman Fort. Ignoring my protests to continue with my work; she motions to me to take a walk. It is dark outside and there is a waxing gibbous moon in the middle of the sky. It is also very cold, and I am already chilled from the ride home. She grabs my hand and pulls me toward the small, forested area on the side of the children's learning room. When she feels that we are far enough away from the convent so that her whispers cannot be overheard, she informs me that she is certain she has seen this man before. She has tried hard to remember where, perhaps in the village or on one of her trips to Carlisle with the abbot. She has seen him and remembers that he stared at her. Clearly, the man frightens her. I try to reassure her. I promise that we will never go back to that house again. This seems to mollify her a bit, until she reminds me that he was probably the one that had followed us during the summer. That night she crawls into bed with me like a frightened child seeking its mother and sleeps with her head on my shoulder until dawn.

12 December 1454

The Anchoress Situation

The longer I consider the idea of establishing an anchoress for the purpose of raising revenue for the Church, the more appalled I become. Should we then burn her body when she dies, so that the bones can be used as relics that can be sold, a practice that I have heard takes place in Spain? Evidently, we are not bringing in enough revenue for the diocese of York and the Catholic Church. How was I not aware that our primary mission was to provide revenue for the Church?

I will not allow some young, naive girl to spend her life imprisoned in a cell, to be a pawn of the Church in order that said church has a "living saint" in residence. With Eawynn's input, we decide to accomplish this in a rather underhanded way. We will keep a detailed record of our efforts, including our interviews with incoming novices and all present oblates, novices, and sisters at Lambley. A suitable candidate will not be found. Perhaps Abbot Walton will have better luck finding a suitable candidate for the position of anchorite instead.

13 December 1454

Miracles

I wake this morning to a cacophony of glorious birdsong, and the hint of the sun rising with the emergence of pink ribbons of clouds in the eastern sky. What a miracle each day is, each second of life in this incredible, unfathomable universe! Jesus Christ proclaimed love, unconditional love for all of creation. He called us to be like him, to grow in this marvelous energy of creation, and in this way, to become Christlike. I do not understand from His message in the Gospels that he ever wanted us to worship him. If we are made in the likeness of God, then we must accept our shortcomings and failures as well as our successes. We are allowed to have feelings of fear and anxiety, just as we are allowed to have feelings of love and compassion. What matters is how we treat ourselves and others. We are all part of this marvelous creation. So many, including the early Church fathers, have perverted his simple teachings with messages of guilt, fear, and damnation in the quest for power and control. My confession is that I am sometimes very attached to my humanity, to my worries and my prejudices. All we can do is forgive ourselves and renew the practice of kindness and compassion that Christ taught every day.

17 December 1454

Beatrice

A month has passed since our ultimatum to Beatrice. I call her into my study and provide her with a small sum of money. She takes the money and leaves my study with her head held high and a very unrepentant attitude. A month of solitude has had no effect. She still blames everyone else for her misfortune. She leaves in a carriage to travel south to York. I do not know what her future will be, but I fear for her just the same.

We have received word from Avice's family that they will not take her back. Sister Mathilde speaks with me to vouch for Avice's behavior when working with the children. Avice has been diligent about all other duties. Avice meets with me and requests to stay on to be fully trained as a novice. I agree, conditional upon her continued diligence.

25 December 1454

The Birth of Our Lord

How marvelous that the birth of a special child is a cause for such celebration, much like the pagans celebrate the death of the old god and the birth of the new god at winter solstice. I have often wondered if this is why the Church proclaimed the birth of Christ near the time of the winter solstice. When was the time of the census for Rome? It is difficult to imagine a census in the middle of winter. Like so many of our Christian holy days, it occurs to me that these are celebrated at or very close to the times of the ancient pagan holy days.

There is an older woman, reputed to be a healer, who lives on the outskirts of Brampton. I think that she professes to be a Christian, but I am not sure. It would be unwise not to do so, but I suspect she follows some of the old ways. She has already given advice and suggested herbal remedies to some of our convent community. It was she who advised the former abbess to use the elderberries that grow wild in great abundance as a tonic for sickness. I am intrigued by this. I would like to make her acquaintance and speak with her, although in such a way that I do not endanger her.

THE YEAR OF OUR LORD

1455

JANUARY

3 January 1455

A New Year

A new year! Winter is upon us in full force. A recent blizzard keeps us all inside except for shoveling a path to the livestock barns and trying to keep paths open to Lanercost Abbey and Saint Mary Magdalene Church. The livestock are put up, sheltering in our great barns. The challenge is to keep their water unfrozen. There is a well close to the barn that is covered. The men told me that it must have been dug from a natural spring as the water level is constant and it rarely freezes. Still, the task of carrying unfrozen water to so many animals is daunting. The sheep with their shaggy coats are usually fine in the snow. Their pasture has a fast-moving stream that flows through it. There are always shepherds on watch for any who are in distress. Luckily, there have been no lambs born this early. The hay harvest was adequate, with enough fodder to keep us until spring.

In the convent, the stores of winter crops still hold. I think we will be tired of cabbage and turnip soup soon. There is an adequate supply of grains for porridge, but not a surplus, so we must be judicious in our use of them. The supply of apples is running low. They are beginning to look a little wrinkled, but they are still sweet!

At last, the sun is shining! We will see to digging ourselves out a little later this morning from last night's additional accumulation of snow. Sometimes being isolated is a blessing. I am filled with gratitude, for we have had no sickness yet this winter, although care must be taken for the occasional travelers that stop here. I ask for volunteers to make up a rotating schedule of nuns who will be responsible for admittance to the convent. Interestingly, Avice is the first to volunteer for two shifts every day. She is still a novice. If she stays, she will profess her initial vows when the bishop visits in the fall. Those in charge of admittance are instructed not to admit any strangers, or even those who work in our community, if they appear to be ill. All strangers must be isolated until we know they do not carry disease. We have heard rumors of the flux in other communities. It is good to see the sun. Our Lady and Mary Magdalene, watch over us.

10 January 1455

Thomas

A small boy of about three was left on the side of the foundling wall early yesterday morning. I heard the foundling bell as we were at morning prayers, and Mathilde left us to check the foundling box. She came back to report that there was no baby present. I went back with her to look outside. We exited the convent by the main door and walked around to the location of the foundling box in the main wall. There we discovered the child, sitting against the wall, all bundled up in shabby blankets. He was fast asleep. Despite the cold, he was still warm. Likely, he was asleep when he was abandoned. Mathilde gently picked him up and carried him into the kitchen where it was warm.

He awoke as we brought him inside. At first his eyes filled with tears, and Mathilde hugged him to quiet him. He relaxed when he realized we were not going to harm him. We offered him some warm porridge and a glass of warm milk, but he ate very little. He knows his name, which is

Thomas, but speaks with a slight lisp as some small children do. He is a beautiful child with almost white hair and sparkling, big, blue eyes. I sent a novice to bring some toys from the room where the very young orphans play. As we showed him the toys, he smiled and laughed delightedly. He appears to have a sunny disposition. Mathilde and the novices who care for our children will be very pleased to have him. It is evident that someone loved him very much. What circumstances could have caused the abandonment of such a child? We will check the families in the surrounding communities to see if anyone knows what family he belongs to.

We will make every attempt to make his transition into our establishment easy for him. I have every confidence that Mathilde will take excellent care of Thomas. This evening, we will offer special prayers to Our Lady to guide us in finding his family, and in aiding this precious little one to the best of our abilities.

16 January 1455

Traditions

Now, in the quiet of winter, in the time between Advent and Lent, when the Church reflects on the life of Jesus of Nazareth, from his humble birth to his crucifixion, we pause to consider his teachings. We will focus on the Gospels during our daily times of reflection. It is the work of Jesus and his message alone that are important for humanity. I have often wondered how the simple teachings of a carpenter from Nazareth developed into the Church of today, a political force evolving for its own glory and power. I requested at Christmas that Sister Yvonne and Eawynn research the history of the early Church to find when and where all the traditions came from. After reading the Gospels, I find little to predict this ostentatious development. The teachings of Jesus should be the light that guides us forward, not the teachings of his disciples or the founders of the early Church. Paul of Damascus is one of the best examples of this. I often think the title Christianity is a misnomer. Paulianity would better describe all the rules and traditions of our current religious state.

From Eawynn's research, with the aid of Sister Yvonne, we discover that different versions of the Gospels were oral traditions until centuries after the death of Jesus. Throughout the centuries, theologians and members of the ruling clergy have chosen and discarded which texts they deemed valid, and which they did not. While the truths the Gospels teach are eternal, the stories are questionable. There is a game of passing a phrase quietly around a room of people to see if it remains the same at the end. As novices, we would often sit in a circle and play this game, usually when the sisters were not present. The results were often hilarious. The phrase would come back distorted, wildly embellished, or utter nonsense almost every time. Every religion, including the ancient Roman and Greek religions, had a virgin birth. Do I discount all the miracles? Absolutely not! Life is a miracle. That the sun rises every morning and that a great tree grows from a seed are miracles. Let us not be sidetracked by the trappings of Christianity that serve to further the power of individual sects or charismatic preachers. Love and tolerance, and the care of all creation are the messages of Jesus.

18 January 1455
Paul of Damascus

Our scriptural passage yesterday was a reading from the first letter of Paul to the Corinthians. It both concerns me, but also explains much of the attitude toward women that we experience from members of the clergy. I have written it out so that I may explain myself.

"Brothers and sisters: I should like you to be free of anxieties. An unmarried man is anxious about the things of the Lord. But a married man is anxious about the things of the world, how he may please his wife, and he is divided. An unmarried woman or virgin is anxious about the things of the Lord, so that she may be holy in both body and spirit. A married woman, on the other hand, is anxious about the things of the world, how she may please her husband. I am telling you this for your own benefit, not to impose restraint upon you, but for the sake of propriety and adherence to the Lord without distraction."

All the four possibilities herein involve anxiety, so his first statement about being free from anxieties is false. In my experience, limited as it is, most unmarried men are much more anxious about women than they are about the Lord. Their natural state seems to be to attract women. The same is true of unmarried virgins. Many of our young postulants and novices are not here at the convent by choice. They are much preoccupied with the young men of the village who work on the abbey grounds. In fact, it is sometimes all I can do to keep them separated.

Why should we not be anxious about the things of the world? God created us to live and thrive in the world. We are the caretakers of this incredible paradise, and it falls to us to care for those who need our assistance. The attitude that Paul has toward women indicates that he has little understanding of them, and values them far less than men. Unfortunately, his teachings and prejudices are the cornerstone of Christianity. Let us turn back to the teachings of Christ alone.

20 January 1455

Thomas

We now understand why little Thomas was left with us. When he urinates, there is blood in the urine. His lower back is tender to the touch. I asked one of the brothers from Lanercost, who is more knowledgeable than most about healing, to examine him. His medical evaluation of Thomas was that Thomas had bad humors in his blood, and he suggested putting leeches on him. I have seen this practice make an adult much weaker. I would not allow this for a small child. Instead, we have given him elderberry tea and willow bark tea to relieve the pain, but it has not helped much.

21 January 1455,

Inventory

Yesterday, Eawynn agreed to inventory our cat population at Lambley and brought me the results. We still have four cats that live inside the convent. One male cat had to be relocated to the barns, but other than that, they are all well suited to their respective areas. Two cats are encouraged to stay around the kitchen and the pantries. I have a black fluffy female, whom I feed in my study to keep her nearby. She does like to go outside for a short while each morning. I am sad to say that she is quite the hunter and kills as many birds as she does mice and moles. Still, I am very attached to her. When she is not in my lap, she spends the remainder of her time sleeping in a patch of sunlight on the floor. There is also a multicolored cat that eats in the kitchen but tends to stay closer to the children's wing during the day. I suspect that she likes all the attention and possibly food scraps from the children.

The convent cats do very well with goat's milk and meat table scraps. They tolerate and even tease the dogs. Our two females, which includes my black cat, appear to be pregnant. I guess that is to be expected. I hope to find other homes or establishments to take a few of the offspring later. They are such useful and charming little personalities. I wonder about the problem of inbreeding though. It can eventually produce weakened offspring in livestock. It is wise to introduce new blood into the any animal population from time to time. Then I realized that because litters of kittens are often found near the abbey, inbreeding should not become a problem.

Cwenhild has three cats in the barn. She habitually places one of them in the grain room every night and lets it out in the morning. These barn cats are only fed goat's milk, so they must hunt for their suppers. When I encounter one of them on my walk, they are always friendly, and they do appear to be healthy. Cwenhild says she sees very little evidence of rodents.

Cats are regarded with suspicion by the priests of the Church, who in turn influence their congregations. It seems cats are often kept by older, solitary women as companions.

These women are often also viewed with suspicion by the Church. I do not understand this attitude.

22 January 1455

Gisela

I finally meet with the woman, Gisela, who is a healer in the community of Brampton. I ride to visit her small cottage, which is about a mile to the east of the village of Brampton, near the Milton Beck. I travel with two of our novices, Judith and Eugenia, who regularly stop there for advice and herbal remedies to help with the pain of their monthly menses.

Her recommendations include warm compresses on the stomach while lying down, and exercise, specifically stretching and walking. She also suggests willow bark tea, which we already use for pain of any kind. Even more interesting is the construction of a holder for the folded rags the girls use, which is easily held in place and very easy to wash. I will pass these instructions on to Sister Rosamund, who oversees sewing.

Gisela is surprised to make my acquaintance. She thought the novices and sisters who came to her for help did so in secrecy. Even so, she is a gracious woman of middle years, and quite observant about the community she serves. She is indeed a marvelous font of knowledge about herbal medicine and a very knowledgeable midwife. The shelves in Gisela's kitchen hold many containers of the herbal mixtures and the tinctures she makes. When I mention that I have little use for the practice of using leeches, she corrects me by saying that leeches can be useful to reduce pressure in a wound if it has become too filled with blood. She also mentions a discovery she has recently made, that the small white worms that form on spoiled meat are effective in cleaning out a pus-filled wound where the body tissue has decayed. Apparently, these little worms eat only the decayed flesh. She explains that she puts out meat to spoil when she needs these worms, indicating that they only take a few days to appear. She adds that meat kept in a closed container is less likely to develop worms and speculates that there is a connection to the flies on the meat, but she does not understand how this can be so. Glancing around her kitchen, I notice that cleanliness is of utmost importance to her.

Gisela has an adult son and grandchildren who live close by in Brampton. I will continue to ask her for advice when needed. She has been much more helpful to the local community in times of illness, and has produced better results than the local physician, whose remedies often make no sense to me at all. Incidentally, she has three cats, and no mice or rats anywhere.

23 January 1455

More Cats

Three abandoned kittens have been found by the wooded areas behind the meadow where the children play. A few of the older girls said they had been outside looking for the early wildflowers and heard them mewing. They had no trouble catching them and brought them to my study. I sincerely doubt the tale about looking for early wildflowers in January, but I chose not to question it. All three kittens are now in the barns where they will receive a daily ration of goat's milk, along with some meat scraps from the kitchen until they are old enough to hunt for themselves. Kittens do not thrive on goat's milk alone.

24 January 1455

Thomas

Thomas has developed difficulty breathing and has had several bouts of convulsions. It is difficult to watch such a beautiful child in such agony. I am almost praying for his release from this life if the pain does not subside. Fortunately, he also has some good days. The sisters have devised a small chair to carry him. They take him along with the others in our care to the barnyard every morning when the weather is nice. Thomas has a strange obsession with wheels and asks to see all the carts and wagons that have wheels. I have asked if a chair with wheels might be constructed so he can be pushed on walks. I have also asked the healer, Gisela, to look at him.

29 January 1455

Philosophizing

Walking outside to the barns this evening, I see the sun low on the horizon causing a sharply delineated display of light and shadow on the trees, bare of their summer leaves. Extraordinary, this spectacular display of duality, light and dark. Each half of a tree is the opposite side of the same coin. One side of a tree cannot exist without the other. Likewise, what is light without darkness? Other dualities of creation come to mind: sound/silence, joy/sorrow, success/struggle, good/evil. This path of thought also poses questions. Is evil the opposite of good, or is the opposite of good only its absence? I think that evil comes from some energy of emotion: anger, fear, hurt, greed; but perhaps the opposite of good is apathy.

My faith in a benevolent creator is challenged when I observe the pain and hardships creatures endure, but without struggle, without pain and adaptation, growth would be difficult, both for the individual and humanity. The tree of knowledge in the garden was essential for growth. The history of Christianity has used this tale to assign blame to a woman, as this was and still is the easiest explanation; however, without the knowledge of good and evil, how would humankind evolve? Humans are shaped not only by their experiences, but also by their responses to those experiences. There are always choices that can be made. One cannot choose rightly without adequate knowledge of the consequences of a particular choice or path of action, or the choice of no action at all.

This is not to say that what a person experiences in life cannot be beyond bearing. I have heard it said that people are never given more than they can bear, but often see circumstances beyond imagination that destroy humans. The year before we dug out the secret cellar rooms to store our root crops and grains, the harvests all over the countryside were much less than normal. The summer had been colder than usual, with little rain. When autumn came it rained constantly. Crops and hay rotted in the fields. During that year, the bishop required that the abbeys give the same amount of produce as the previous year. We did not have enough grains and root crops left to feed ourselves through the winter, let alone help the starving people in the surrounding area. By early spring, we were rationing our grains. People came from all over to beg at our doors, and we had to turn them away. One family lost four children to starvation before the husband hanged himself. I later saw the mother with her remaining infant sitting alone near the church of Mary Magdalene. Cwenhild and I had walked over to see why she was there. She stared at us blankly and did not respond when we tried to get her out of the cold. We succeeded in moving her inside the church where it was warmer. In the morning, she was gone. We found her body with the child frozen by the cemetery.

So many died that spring. The frozen ground was too hard to bury the dead, so they were left piled up outside the cottages, frozen. It was a macabre sight, and the frozen children were the worst of all. I never thought I would be numb to such misery, but with so many deaths we became like sleepwalkers. Every day there were more. When the weather warmed, the villagers burned them. The Church condemned them for doing so, and they were made to do penance, but few of the survivors bothered. There were even survivors who cursed God and the Church. Is this how one survives the horrors of plague or war, or constant abuse during childhood? If the Creator truly is a loving God, I can make no sense of this kind of hopeless existence. I have been told repeatedly that what I cannot understand, I must accept in faith. I think that is rubbish.

FEBRUARY

1 February 1455

Wisdom

Today, the wind is strong and from the west, probably ushering in a storm soon. Walking outside from the kitchen to the meadow where the children play, the wind propels me along at an almost uncomfortable rate of speed. It will be necessary to walk back to my study inside the convent, through the corridors. Without assistance, I could never walk into such a strong headwind. Feeling the wind is like feeling the very breath of God. From the book of Wisdom in the Old Testament, the Hebrew people felt that the breath of God was feminine. In Hebrew and Greek, Sophia, (σοφία) means wisdom. The Hagia Sophia (Sofia) was constructed in 537 AD in Constantinople to honor her. I have seen illustrations of this great cathedral. I also learned from the research done by Sister Yvonne and Eawynn that

Sophia was worshiped by first century Gnostic Christians as another face of God. The Gnostics were later persecuted as heretics by the Catholic Church. The Eastern Orthodox Church still believes the Holy Spirit is feminine. I rather like to feel that God has a feminine side. The comforter.

I stop by the children's area to check on Thomas. I have been doing so every day, although I have come to dread watching the slow decline of his body, yet, his cherub face lights up as I enter the room. He holds out his arm and I hug him, gently, so as not to cause more pain. Thomas has great need of the comforter, and yet she does not come. It is difficult to keep my faith.

5 February 1455

Winter Sickness

The sweating sickness has reached our community. I had hoped we would be spared this year. Several villagers have become sick. Two children in the village have died, and now three of our novices, who are often in the village on errands, are affected. The latest snowfall has made sending for the brother at Lanercost, who also has supplies of healing herbs, impossible. Those known to be ill are isolated, but we cannot isolate those attending them. When the illness began, I reached out to Gisela for advice. She said there was no sure cure, but recommended rest, herbal teas, broth, and plenty of fluids. As long as there are enough of us well to tend to the others, we will get through this.

Guda has provided hearty soups and bread for those of us who are not affected. Eawynn is still searching the manuscripts for advice on how to deal with these sicknesses. She found references to a medical book by Jan Yperman, a Flemish physician, but it is not a manuscript that we have. We do have the Latin copy of The Canon of Medicine by a Persian physician, but there are no references to this specific sickness. Perhaps it was not prevalent in the holy lands. It does not seem that Hippocrates addressed this issue either. Eawynn has found nothing so far.

How this disease has come here is a mystery, as few travelers have stopped here in the past month. Believing that disease is spread by ill humors or bad air makes no sense. From past observations, I think there must be contact with someone who is ill. I am also rather grateful that the local physician from Brampton is unable to attend us at this time.

I expressed my opinion of him to Gisela. We have had much better results following her advice.

11 February 1455
A Wheeled Chair

Timothy, who works as a carpenter for both abbeys, was given the task of designing a chair with four wheels so Thomas could be pushed around instead of carried. Timothy worked with a blacksmith from the village to construct the chair for Thomas. He loves to be pushed along the lanes, but the pain is ever present, and he has lost more weight. He must be handled carefully as I can feel that the upper bone in his right leg is broken. It is as if something has eaten through it. How he bears this pain is beyond me. We pray for him daily, but I do not know if I am praying for his recovery or his death. His death must come soon. This is too much for anyone to bear. I cannot understand how a loving God can permit this unspeakable pain in such an innocent child.

Gisela visits when we are sure that the sweating sickness is gone from the abbey. She smiles at Thomas as she looks over him carefully, and gently feels the broken bone in his leg. We have been giving him willow bark tea for the pain, but it is obvious that it upsets his stomach, and he hates the taste. Gisela gives us something stronger, a tincture that she mixes from the sap of poppies, which she grows in her flower beds. She has kept the seeds for years, saying that the seeds were originally brought back from the holy lands by crusaders. Her family have been healers for generations and they have kept and cultivated these flowers since then. She draws me aside to say that she has never seen such a heart-wrenching case of the wasting sickness. She lets me know that there are options to end this suffering when it becomes too great to bear. We have enough of this tincture to last a few days. She says she will bring more soon, as that was the last that she had made. She has the milk of the poppy flower in bottles but must mix the tincture fresh for each use. She only uses it when the case is hopeless.

13 February 1455

A Time of Industry

The sickness has finally disappeared from Lambley, although there are still a few cases in the village. I now have my suspicions as to how this last disease spread. Our novice, Kendra, who has recovered well enough to relate the story, told me that she and Bernia were sent by Guda to bring some herbs to the home of a sick child. The mother, who made them some tea, also appeared to be sick, although she declared that she was not. The child recovered. We have just learned that the mother did not. We will continue to be vigilant until there are no more cases.

Winter is the season of intellectual productivity. Several sisters have been trained to scribe by Sister Yvonne, and she continues to work with novices who show an aptitude for this kind of work. She has taken Maud on as a special student even though she is still an oblate, because Maud was already proficient at reading and writing when she came to the abbey. It takes intense concentration, so the library where they work is unusually quiet. They often work by candlelight as the days are still very short.

Sisters Joan and Eleanor are now busy copying the notation of some of the old music that was found in Lanercost's library and passed on to us. Their specialty is the copying of ancient musical notation. They are both quite proficient at reading music, as they learned to play musical instruments before entering as novices. Sister Joan is my elder and plays the harp beautifully. Sister Eleanor professed about ten years after I did. She plays the dulcimer and sings.

She has a lovely contralto voice and often harmonizes. Unfortunately, we do not have a dulcimer at Lambley. Sister Yvonne works with Eawynn to copy texts of herbal lore and husbandry. The supervision of this is Eawynn's domain. I often wonder how the inadvertent incorrect placement of a note in a copied piece of music will affect the music for future interpretations. I am certain these errors must occasionally occur. We are especially fond of and careful about copying the scores of Hildegarde of Rupertsberg Abbey from the 12th century. I find her music to be most inspirational!

A new litter of five kittens has been born in the hay barn. They have been removed, along with their mother, to a safe room in the cloister away from the other cats. Hopefully, they will survive. That makes a total of eight more cats at the abbey. We will need to find homes for some of them. We also had our first lambing. This is very early, and Sister Rosamund has made little woolen jackets for the lambs that are born this early. The ewe and her lamb are in a stall in the barn with lots of straw. I pray that the rest of the ewes, as well as the nannies, wait awhile before birthing. It is still very cold.

As an aside, I tell Eawynn that the systematic way of signing with hands that she developed while at Lacock Abbey should be codified so those who are mute can easily communicate with others. I am not sure she appreciates this challenge, but she accepts it. It would be a service for those who cannot speak to be better able to communicate with others.

14 February 1455

Eawynn

I have managed to have an adjoining room with Eawynn since her return from Lacock Abbey. Last night, she crawled into bed beside me, the first time in many days. It is very cold at night! We regularly slept together when we were younger, many young nuns do and no one thinks much about it, but as we have grown older, it has become less frequent. We both have aches and pains that cause us to change position often, and this disturbs the other's sleep. Also, I snore. She usually comes in and leans her head on my shoulder for a short while, then returns to her own bed. Our beds are not big enough to accommodate two people, although that did not stop us when we were young. Last night we both slept through the night, and I woke up curled around her this morning.

15 February 1455

More Arrivals

A few more lambs have successfully entered into life, and yesterday twin kids, both bucks, were born. Male sheep can be castrated and will produce wool, but there is no real use for more than one male goat in a herd, two at most. Usually enough are born for the Easter day meal, lamb and kid being the favorites.

All but one kitten has survived. I cannot tell this early on whether they are male or female. They will be moved back to the barn as soon as the weather warms. Fleas are a problem with cats who stay indoors, well, fleas are just a problem, and we have found no solution except to keep those areas where the cats hunt very clean. Bathing cats kills the fleas on them, but the fleas return shortly. Anyway, bathing cats is not easy.

This morning, I spied little snowdrops and crocuses beginning to peek through the snow in the garden. Spring will come soon.

16 February 1455

A Foundling

After Vespers, the foundling bell to the Abbey rings. I walk outside with Sister Mathilde to check the foundling wheel where a newborn infant swaddled in rags is sleeping. Mathilde lifts the child and carries him to the rooms where our babies and very young children stay. As she gently places the child on a changing table, the child wakes up and begins to root around, as though looking for a breast to suckle on. Mathilde unwraps the sodden rags and we discover the baby is a boy. Thank goodness he was not outside in the cold for very long in these wet rags. The tiny boy seems healthy, but a nursemaid will need to be found immediately, as there is not one at the convent at present. Mathilde wraps him in fresh, dry blankets and leaves to go to the kitchen to warm some diluted goat's milk. Tomorrow we will search in the surrounding area for a woman who is nursing. Eawynn comes in just as Mathilde is leaving. She picks up the child and rocks him gently. I watch with surprise. I have never seen Eawynn pay much attention to any of the children. She stays with me until Mathilde returns. At least the baby does not appear to be undernourished, but then, it cannot be more than a day or two since his birth, as the umbilical cord is still attached. I will ask Gisela if she knows who might have given birth to this little one.

I despair at the circumstances that result in the abandonment of infants and children. Most come from conditions where the mother is unable to care for them. Inquiries will be made to see if there are families who might have lost a child and would like to adopt this little one. I always make sure the families that adopt are good homes that will care for the child. We will not name him until I am sure there is no alternative but to raise him here. If he stays, we will care for this tiny boy until he is five. While girl orphans, like Margy, stay with us at Lambley, the boys are sent to Lanercost to be raised by the brothers at age five. Girls like Margy, Lynet, and Odelyn are given whatever training they are capable of handling. They grow up to be cooks and servants, some marry, some stay to become novices. The brothers at Lanercost are very good at raising and educating the older boys.

For some time, I have been considering the establishment of an orphanage with a formal school, and a hospital for the surrounding area, both within the confines of Lanercost and Lambley Abbeys. This will require more resources than we have at present, and a larger building with multiple classrooms. We will need to find some wealthy donors. I must approach these ideas carefully with Abbot Alexander Walton, as he is slow to adopt changes. When I first suggested that he allow Eawynn to accompany him whenever he needed someone who could record details and transactions, as well as discretely keep a close watch on all proceedings, he balked at the idea having of a nun along with them. Of course, Eawynn and I had a personal motive, access to Lanercost's records. He finally allowed Eawynn to travel with them on a trial basis on a trade mission to Carlisle. Apparently, she noticed that a wool trader was trying to cheat him. He has requested her presence at all important meetings since that time. Abbot Alexander may need time to get used to the idea, but I am certain he will come around.

18 February 1455

More Treatments

Watching over Thomas has become a full-time job. Mathilde can no longer take care of him and care for the other children at the same time. We have set up a schedule to follow with various nuns and novices taking turns in a room that is close to my study. We have tried treating Thomas with tinctures of henbane and hemlock in very small amounts. He cannot keep them down. The only thing that works is the tincture made from poppies that Gisela sends every few days. It takes very little for the tincture to work. Thomas is now sleeping or unconscious a great deal of the time. That is a blessing. It seems this tincture also dulls the pain. We no longer put him in his chair and push him about. We tried spooning broth into his mouth, but he could not swallow it. He has lost interest in all things. There is a dark pall over him. This is the wasting sickness, and it is terrible to watch in an adult, but even more so in an innocent child. It is heart rending.

20 February 1455

Bleating

The quiet of winter is waning. Birthing season is upon us, both for lambs and kids. It is always a jolt to go from a time of silence, of reading and meditation, to the eruption of bleating from the barns which can be heard all over the convent grounds. We are singing the psalms and listening to the readings at Prime when the noise interrupts our meditations. The music of the final psalm falls apart when Brigitta's voice begins to shake, and she starts to giggle uncontrollably. The giggling spreads among the novices, and the psalm stops abruptly when Judith stops singing. It is her lovely voice that carries us all along with her. It takes more than a few moments for everyone to gain their composure again, although I feel the laughter probably did our hearts good. We finally resume the song and limp along until the end, when I dismiss everyone.

At the morning meal, I advise the use of wool balls stuck in the ears for any whose work needs quiet concentration. The racket from the barns usually subsides at night and resumes in the early morning hours. As if that is not enough to disturb the peace, some of the hens are broody, which results in a racket of clucking. They are hiding their eggs. Next it will be the geese and ducks.

22 February 1455

Joyful Noises

I am in a quandary as to what to do about the singing at offices. Everyone sings. I cannot complain about the lack of enthusiasm. Perhaps it is because we are quiet so much during the day that the heavens open with joyful noise during the chants. While I do appreciate the heartfelt spirit of our sung prayers, I cannot help but wish that a few of the sisters would simply mouth the words. How uncharitable is it of me that I do not, cannot, encourage their unmelodious efforts? God may appreciate a joyful noise, but it makes my head hurt. I would almost rather hear sheep bleating. I need to find a solution to this problem. Perhaps only a select few to sing, a choir? Sometimes I rue the day when I agreed to keep Eawynn's secret. She has a lovely voice. I have heard her sing a few times when we were riding out, far beyond the range of anyone hearing her. Somehow, I do not think I will solve this to my satisfaction anytime soon.

23 February 1455

Thomas

S omeone has been at Thomas' side at all times. He had not awakened at all for the past day. Father Kenric came by yesterday afternoon to pray over him and anoint him. I sit in a chair beside him throughout the night. I doze for a few moments but remain vigilant most of the time. Eawynn comes in several times to check on us. As the sky begins to lighten, I behold a shadow which descends and hangs over his bed, and I know I am watching the Angel of Death. I have seen this apparition above dying patients before. As the sky turns a rosy pink in the dawn, his breathing stops. It is over. I am too exhausted to cry. He is beautiful in death. More importantly, he is no longer in pain.

Thomas' funeral mass will be held tomorrow. He will be buried in the chapel cemetery. A small grave has already been prepared. Thomas was such a sweet little soul and was loved by so many. Indeed, he was a favorite of several of the novices and sisters, so much so that I had to remind them not to neglect the feelings of the other children we care for, as that is an easy thing to do when one child is terminally ill. What is the message that we can take away from watching this small child die? Is it to make us aware of the impermanence of everything, the continuous change that is pervasive in all of creation? I have no answers.

25 February 1455

Vineyards

March is almost here, and with it, spring will come in all its glory. With luck and the blessing of Our Lady, we will have some bright, sunny days to begin the pruning of the grape vineyards before the sap rises. The vineyards were planted several years ago, and last year was an adequate harvest. I have seen in the records that it is only in recent times that it has been warm enough to grow grapes in England. Grapes could be a very important crop for all in the Irthing River valley.

Our first labor is to repair damaged trellises and cultivate the ground around each vine. We begin the day with knives and twine. As we work, we also trim each grape vine and loosen the soil around it with a hoe. The trellises are made of hemp rope and have two horizontal levels. The old growth is cut back so only four new buds can grow from each vine, two at the midpoint and two at the top of the vine. Grapes clusters only grow from new growth. We listen as Guda explains how it is done, a speech I had heard for more than twenty-five years. It is really addressed to the novices who assist us. I notice that Cwenhild is nodding her head in agreement. It always amazes me what a wealth of information that young sister carries in her head. Although it is still quite cold, we are out in the sunshine. As soon as the cane growth is long enough, we must return and tie the canes to the trellises with hemp twine.

MARCH

3 March 1455

War

The weather has been cold, rainy and blustery for several days, making it very unpleasant to venture outside. Much needs to be done outside, but little is being accomplished at present. The vineyards have been pruned and the trellises repaired. Now the garden must be tilled for spring crops, but the continuing rains make tilling in mud almost impossible. Today we spend a few hours outside, and then come in and huddle near the fireplaces for warmth. Spring and warmer weather, return soon! Thank goodness for the hot tea and soup.

News has been received that there is increasing support for the York branch of the Plantagenets, especially as our Lancaster king continues to experience bouts of mental instability, which are increasing in frequency and strength. Edward Beaufort, the Duke of Somerset, was recently killed in a battle between the two factions. Beaufort was a Lancaster who supported the king and, as such, was the main rival of Richard, the Duke of York. Both Lancaster and York have legitimate claims to the throne as they are all descended from Edward III. Our support has been requested by both the Lancasters and Richard of York. As with all the churches of the north, both large and small, we must tread carefully. While the abbeys have always fully supported the Lancasters, the Yorks reside in very close proximity, practically in our backyard. Henry VI could dissolve our abbeys, but Richard of York could destroy us utterly. We need to be as quiet as mice, hopefully not to be noticed by either faction if we are to survive.

4 March 1455

Eawynn

Being inside during such inclement weather always gives me time for reflection. Several sisters are sitting close to the fireplace with me, sewing and mending garments. We rarely dress in full habit in the evenings when the abbey is quiet, and we have no visitors. Eawynn is across from me in her chair, always careful to keep some distance between us when we are in the company of others, even now, especially now, as there are women who would happily replace me as abbess. Every year since I became abbess, there have been wealthy widows and other nuns who have appealed to the Archbishop of York for my position. Abbot Walton keeps me informed about these inquiries. Making me aware of other applicants is the archbishop's way of informing me that I can be easily replaced. Giving others little to gossip about seems prudent. The firelight reflects gloriously off Eawynn's reddish gold locks. She is still as stunningly beautiful as when she professed at the age of twenty.

As I sit there, the feeling comes over me that Eawynn and I are being watched and judged this evening by Sister Riona, a dour, middle-aged widow who chose to profess two years before I became abbess. It is the feeling I sometimes get when I am on my walk and turn to find one of the laborers watching me. When I glance up, she looks away. I know she dislikes my authority. She joined the abbey when her only alternative was to remarry. She and Sister Helena, who is three years older than I am, have formed a pact of sorts by refusing to do any work whatsoever that dirties their hands.

They sit in the sewing room or the gardens all day working on embroidery and sewing. Their monetary contributions upon entering the convent were such that they expect to be treated like duchesses, and often require the novices to wait on them. I know that Sister Riona has been asking questions about Eawynn's friendship with me. Sister Yvonne has warned me that these two often have their heads together gossiping. As devout as Yvonne is, she still has a fine sense of humor. She refers to these two as the Spider Sisters, after the venomous widow spider. Thank goodness, Sisters Riona and Helena are not very popular with the rest of the sisters. Their questions about Eawynn and me have remained unanswered, not that there is anything to tell. The two nuns are generally avoided by the novices. Still, they are troublemakers. I have considered that they might prefer the weather at Lacock Abbey in southern England to the cold, dreary moors of North Umbria. It might mean a bit of bargaining with the abbess at Lacock, but it would be worth it. I would need the approval of both the abbot and the bishop in Carlisle to pursue this course of action.

4 March 1455

Evening

After Compline, as I am readying myself for bed, Eawynn opens the door between our rooms and comes to sit in the straight-backed chair by my small desk. She is already dressed in her night robe, with her hair down. Silently, she looks up and smiles while handing me her hairbrush. This has become a ritual between us. Taking my time, I slowly brush out the knots and tangles and continue to brush until her mop of hair shines like polished brass. In turn, I sit on the edge of the bed while she rubs a liniment that Cwenhild had recommended on my twisted leg. It eases the muscles and prevents spasms in my calf and foot during the night. I have refrained from asking Cwenhild what it is made from, as I am sure that I do not want to know. The ritual of brushing hair in the evenings before retiring to bed began shortly after Eawynn returned from Lacock Abbey. While most nuns keep their hair short for expediency's sake when wearing a veil, both Eawynn and I had longer hair when we were younger. Growing older, I have joined the ranks of nuns with short hair that is easy to care for. Eawynn has insisted on keeping her locks long.

The depth of our friendship increased due to Eawynn's actions when she was fifteen and I was twenty-one, already a fully professed nun. On a night of terrible storms and cold temperatures, she simply snuck into my room during the night and crept into my bed. I awoke in the morning to find her asleep beside me. Waking her, it was obvious that she was terribly distraught. She had received a letter from her family that her future husband was anxious to complete the wedding. They would be coming to fetch her home soon. She had never expressed any real desire to become a nun before, but now she was frantic to do so. Although she had never shown any interest in becoming a religious, she wished to become a novice and so forth, as quickly as possible. Her reasons were twofold; she did not want to marry a horrible old man, and she did not want to be separated from me. At the time, I did not know how much our friendship meant to her. It was only when I realized that I might lose her, that I also realized how dear she had become to me.

5 March 1455

Fasting

It is the beginning of Lent, and with it comes the practice of fasting. The purpose of fasting is not to become physically weak or lose weight, but to create a hunger, a spiritual void that only Christ can fill. Coincidentally, Lent occurs in the early spring, a time when our supplies run low, and hunger is often our daily companion. The abbeys at Lambley and Lanercost are Augustinian. Our diet at Lambley is simple. Very little meat is consumed, as most of the animals are more valuable for other things. However, the occasional kid goat or chicken that has stopped laying has lost any purpose other than as nourishment. Fish are eaten at the evening meal a few nights during the week. Luckily, the convent is near the river where fish are plentiful, and fish are not considered to be meat. Grains such as barley, wheat, and oats are staples that are used for porridge, ground for bread and, of course, barley is used to make beer. During the winter, root crops, nuts, and dried fruits supplement our meals, as well as dairy and eggs.

Augustinian orders require some dietary changes for Lent. Occasional fasting during the week is one of them. During Lent, all meat, dairy, and eggs are prohibited. We also fast more often, which means bread and water, and sometimes only one meal a day. For myself, fasting causes me to be lightheaded and shaky, which is problematic when there is so much to be done in the spring. Guda oversees tilling and planting the herb and vegetable gardens. Specific chores are assigned to everyone, while she watches over us with hawklike attention to detail. Our laborers use the plow horses to till the fields for grains. We tie up our skirts and go barefoot through the rows to plant the wheat and the barley. I find that making myself part of the working group always improves everyone's attitude. There is less complaining. We sing and have competitions to complete the work. Margarethe and I supervise the trimming of fruit trees and grapevines, as well as the tying of grape canes when they are long enough.

The problem is that all this labor happens during Lent, when food supplies are already scarce. I tend to ignore the practice of fasting when I think it is necessary. I especially ignore these restrictions for children and young adults. They are growing, and these severe restrictions seem quite unhealthy. Whereas we do forego meat, the children are allowed limited amounts of dairy such as goat's milk and cheese, as well as eggs. I also ignore these restrictions for any pregnant and nursing mothers, or infirm that we are caring for. While I understand the reasons for fasting, good sense must prevail.

10 March 1455

Eawynn

Today marks thirty years since Eawynn professed her wish to become a nun of the Augustinian order to the Abbess at age fifteen. When Eawynn received a letter from her parents on the fourth of March 1425, she panicked. She knew they had betrothed her to an older man, a widower whom she disliked intensely. She brought the letter to me for advice. Her first impulse was to run away. Not wishing to be parted from me, she begged me to come with her. Knowing we had very limited time to conceive a plan, her desperation made us daring. I suggested that Eawynn not inform the abbess, Isabeau Sysson, of her family's wishes, but instead tell the abbess that she had received a calling from God to enter the holy order and become a Bride of Christ. I accompanied her to the abbess and suggested that Eawynn might take the vows of a novice immediately, and then travel temporarily to Lacock Abbey in Salisbury, which was under the direction of Abbess Elena de Montfort, until such time as her final vows had been made. Our plan worked, as novices often visit other abbeys during their training, although I was surprised when the abbess did not question our haste.

A letter was sent by messenger to Eawynn's parents to inform them that Eawynn had taken vows as a novice and had left with an escort to receive the remainder of her training at Lacock Abbey, after which time she would return to Lambley. I have no idea what took place when her family arrived from Carlisle to take her home. I made myself very scarce indeed during that visit, but I heard that her parents were quite angry. Eawynn's father protested her decision to join the Augustinian order as a nun. He went so far as to appeal to the Bishop of Carlisle to stop the process and make Eawynn return home, but to no avail. Eawynn had already taken vows as a novice. The bishop felt he could not stand in the way of someone who has decided to devote her life to God.

The next five years were the most difficult of my life, but also possibly the most important. It was during Eawynn's absence that my determination to be the mistress of my own life at Lambley began to take shape. Having no idea until the moment she left how strong my attachment to her had grown, she had become the friend of my heart. Although I mourned her absence, I was determined to learn all that I could about the management of a convent and, at the same time, become indispensable to the older sisters who oversaw various aspects of convent life, as well as to our abbess, Isabeau Sysson. I have never considered myself to be ambitious, but I felt I had no choice. I worked very hard to prove myself as a devout, hardworking, and very capable Sister of Saint Augustine.

11 March 1455

The Unthinkable

As I step outside after Prime to check the weather, the cold wind almost knocks me down, although the sun is dazzling, more like a November morning than one of earliest spring. I sent word to Brother Edward two days ago to join us this morning. It is time to resume our regular visits to four poor families along the Roman wall toward Gilsland, near one of my favorite spots, the waterfalls by the gorge of the River Irthing, which are usually thundering in spring from the snowmelt in the hills. It was last December when Eawynn, Brother Edward and I checked on these families.

The family with a newborn baby is of special concern as they had few resources for food and firewood when we last visited.

I am surprised when Brother Edward is not already waiting for us in the courtyard. The stable boy loads a packhorse with supplies, and Eawynn and I mount our hoses and ride to Lanercost Abbey to ask Edward to join us. The brother who greets us at the gate motions us to stand back. He informs us that Edward and quite a few others are experiencing a stomach ailment, possibly due to something that was served at the evening meal yesterday. This means we must either go on our own or wait until Edward has recovered. We ask if there is another brother who can accompany us, and he shakes his head, sadly. Although uneasy about making the journey without Edward, we feel it is necessary, especially since the supplies have already been packed. We set out and manage good time on a path that follows the River Irthing. Keeping our pace at a quick trot until reaching the Roman Wall, we stop at the old Roman Fort for a few minutes to catch our breath and take in the scenery. We stand in the lee of a wall to stay out of the wind and look out at the brown heather and gorse bushes that cover the hills. The occasional tree stands in the distance, still devoid of the leaves that will bud out in the next few weeks. If we pass this way again in two months, the hills will be blanketed with yellow gorse and purple heather. A few ravens drift overhead and perch in a nearby leafless tree. The sight is depressing.

As the sun peaks out from behind a cloud, we turn from the fort and remount, trotting downhill toward Gilsland in the direction of the river gorge. We avoid the path leading to the deserted cottage where a very unpleasant and intimidating man had made his residence the last time we were here. A feeling of unease tickles the back of my neck, as if we are being watched. I keep glancing anxiously over my shoulder until my horse trips and I almost fall off. Laughing at my near mishap, Eawynn warns me to pay more attention to where I am guiding my mare. We bypass Gilsland, intending to visit the families as we ride back toward Lambley Abbey. The thundering waterfalls can be heard before we reach them. Picking our way carefully through the rocky slope down to the waterfalls, spray forms a cold mist above the river. We stop several feet away to keep from getting drenched, dismount and sit down on our coats to eat a meal of cheese, bread, and cold tea, ground tying the horses to allow them to graze nearby.

After, I remain seated, watching the horses by the edge of a copse of trees, while Eawynn walks toward the falls for a closer look. The footing to the falls is rocky. I have attempted it once, only to discover that I am unable to navigate it even with my cane. Standing with my hand held above forehead to shield my eyes from the sun and with my cane on the ground beside me, I turn as I hear a sound behind me, expecting to find that my mare has wandered closer. The last thing I remember is something hitting my head.

The muffled sounds of screams slowly pierce through my consciousness, and I gradually realize the sound is coming from close by. Turning onto my side and opening my eyes, I can see Eawynn lying on the ground with a man brutally forcing himself on her. Holding both of her hands in one of his above her head, while the other covers her mouth, the forceful stabbing motion of his hips makes me realize he is raping her. Time is suspended. It seems to take forever for me to struggle to my hands and knees. All the while, Eawynn writhes beneath the man as he continues to brutally force himself on her. Standing unsteadily, I hear him groan and watch as he half collapses on her. Taking advantage of the few moments that they struggle; I steady myself with my cane and stumble toward them. She takes advantage of his inertia to try to get away, but he quickly lifts himself up on one arm and punches her, which causes her to fall back to the ground, unmoving. All the helpless anger of my childhood floods through me as I totter unsteadily behind him with my cane and swing the top of it, which is carved as a ball to fit my hand. Putting all the force of the hatred I had felt as a child into that swing, I hit him on the head. To my surprise, he falls sideways off Eawynn, who is making gagging noises. My rage overwhelms me as I hit him again and again, not even noticing when he stops moving. I continue to pound him, even when my cane splinters and breaks, until Eawynn, who has raised herself to her feet, grabs me from behind. Swinging around in my rage to break free of what is hampering my movement, I stop at the sight of her. Her face is swollen and bruised, bruising is appearing on her wrists and throat, her riding habit is torn, ripped away from her legs, and a streak of blood is visible on the inside of her thigh. I grab her as we collapse to our knees.

The remainder of the afternoon passes like a nightmare, from which I am unable to wake. I slowly get to my feet, then help Eawynn to rise. Approaching the man cautiously, I check to see if he is simply unconscious, or worse. One look at his open-eyed stare tells me all I need to know. While there are few punishments for rape, as it is difficult to prove, the punishment for murder is death. He is well and truly dead. I am a murderer. Surprisingly, Eawynn acts before I do. She motions for me to help drag the body into some bushes where it will not be easily spotted by anyone riding by. Making sure first that the site is cleared of all the items from our meal, she helps me mount my mare. With difficulty and a great deal of pain, she manages to scramble up onto her gelding and indicates that we should not return to the convent, but instead travel to the healer's cottage.

The ride to Gisela's cottage is dreadful, as my head throbs and every step the horse takes produces new agony. Leading the packhorse with Eawynn riding in front, I can see that her situation is much worse. We cut across the country and through some forested land to avoid travelers. Although it seems to take forever, it is only about six miles, and we travel at a fast walk. As we approach, gratefulness floods through me when it appears that Gisela is at home by herself. Having heard our approaching horses, she meets us in the front yard and carefully helps us dismount, first Eawynn and then me. She makes Eawynn lean on her as they walk into the cottage where she sits Eawynn on the side of a bed. I tie the horses to a post and limp painfully into the house behind them.

Gisela has undressed Eawynn and is already sponging and cleaning the cut and dirt from her face, arms, and thighs as I enter. She bids me to rest in a chair until she finishes with Eawynn, then makes a cool cloth soaked in some tincture to hold to the side of my face as she examines me. Other than a loose tooth on the bottom right side of my mouth, nothing appears to be broken. She makes us rest while she readies herself to travel to the convent, which is about a quarter of an hour by horseback. Eawynn, signing to me to speak for her, pleads with her to speak only with Cwenhild, and to bring Cwenhild back with her.

Having galloped most of the way on her dun gelding, Cwenhild rushes in the door within the hour. Relief shows on her face that we are alive, which turns to anger as she sees the damage done to us. She pulls up a chair and sits to hear our story. Of particular importance to her is a description of the man. I note that his clothing, though filthy, marks him as landed gentry, and I describe his reddish-brown hair drawn back in a queue. He appeared to be taller than average and of middle years, such as we are. Eawynn indicates that his eyes were brown and his face freckled, and he was very strong, such as a soldier. Describing where the attack took place and exactly where we had hidden the body, I note

Cwenhild's look of consternation, as if she might know his identity. She says she will go early the next morning and take Timothy, Alaric's son, to help her, as she trusts him completely. She suggests that Eawynn and I return to the convent tonight and tell that we had been attacked, nothing more, at least not until Cwenhild has dealt with the body and possibly identified him. If asked for a description, we are to feign being in too much of a state of shock to respond.

13 March 1455

The Morning After

Despite Cwenhild's suggestion, we do not return to the convent that evening but tell Cwenhild to let everyone know that we are safe, that we accidentally lost control of our mounts and fell on a rocky hillside near the Roman fort, from which it had taken us a long time to catch our horses and the packhorse. There is to be no mention of an attack. The less people know about this incident, the better. I ask her to tell Margarethe that we will stay another day under Gisela's care and then return. Meanwhile, we will await Cwenhild and Timothy to tell us how they have managed.

Cwenhild arrives at Gisela's just before noon the following day. She relates that they found the body easily enough. Taking care that no trace of Eawynn's clothing remained on the dead man, she and Timothy dragged his body to the waterfalls and threw him over the side onto the rocks below. She also retrieved my splintered cane, which I had left on the ground in my haste to be away from that place. Timothy found the dead man's horse tied to a tree a little way back in the woods and set it loose with a broken bridle. Cwenhild is sure the man is the illegitimate son of the Earl of Thirlwall Castle, which is close to the hamlet we were to visit. Evidently, he is very well-known and has a reputation for violence.

After Cwenhild has departed, Gisela informs us that she knows Eawynn is not mute, as she cried out and muttered in her sleep last night. I remember hushing her and holding her until she quieted, but Gisela comments on it to both Eawynn and me this afternoon. Gisela seems both impressed and amused that Eawynn has never been found out. Although both Eawynn and I look much worse today than we did yesterday, we both feel better. Keeping compresses to our faces and other sore places, we spend another day here.

14 March 1455

Recovery

We ride back to the convent this morning, leaving our horses with Cwenhild in the stables and making our way through a side door to speak with Sister Margarethe. Eawynn goes to her room while I speak with Margarethe, asking her to make excuses for us for the next few days. Wishing for a few days in solitude, I request that no visitors other than her or Cwenhild bring us meals. We will also see the healer if she drops by.

16 March 1455

Healing

Although my jaw is still swollen, I feel much better. Eawynn continues to rest, and her body is healing well. She refuses to talk about her feelings but sits in a chair and stares out her small window. Flourishing a new cane made by Timothy, Cwenhild drops by this morning to my study, as I have finally emerged from my room. Cwenhild is listening for talk of a man gone missing, but there is no news so far.

I try to coax Eawynn to talk to me, but she says she wants to forget the whole ordeal. Meanwhile, we will send Brother Edward out with Cwenhild and Timothy to take the supplies to the families that we were scheduled to visit. Tomorrow, Eawynn and I will both return to our duties, acting as if we are still recovering from nothing more than a bad accident.

17 March 1455

Lent

I am making a poor attempt to write as though our mishap never happened. Over the years, Lent has become my least favorite season, as the dietary restrictions leave everyone so cross. Even the children, so often free of adult worries, become irritable. Grumbling from everyone is becoming audible at mealtimes, which in turn upsets the kitchen staff. When a sheep gets caught in one of the fences, breaks a back leg, and must be killed, I almost ask that it be butchered immediately so we can have a nice stew! Eawynn quickly makes me realize what a bad idea that is. My anger at these Lenten rules only increases when sheep is butchered, but the meat parts are fed to the dogs, cats, and fowl.

We conduct our days quietly during Lent, supposedly to promote communication with God in our time of hunger. I am reminded lately, that communication with God is a two-way path. Listening to God is as important as talking to God. I confess that I am much better at talking. I spend a lot of time talking to God, mostly, I am embarrassed to say, to complain, and sometimes, more concerning, I find I talk to God to criticize.

I remind God that His earthly design could use a lot of improvement. Hunger for any reason should never be an issue. Unfortunately, His plan allows for those who take more than their share, leaving many people lacking basic resources. Greed and the desire to accumulate wealth promote unhealthy and cruel competition. Basic human character traits seem to lean heavily toward greed, hunger for power, and control of others. Natural disasters that destroy innocent souls do not seem very nice, and if God is a God of love, He might consider making a few changes, such as revising some of the absurd rules that His Church inflicts on His people.

I do spend some time listening. There is voice in my head that whispers that humans need challenges and struggles to

176

grow, and that growing to become more like Christ is really the point. While I accept this, I still feel the cards are unfairly stacked against us in a game where the rules have not been disclosed. There are some born with no chance at all. What can a child who dies of starvation or disease, or a young girl who is misused until she dies or takes her own life, possibly learn? Sometimes none of this makes any sense to me. I sincerely hope I have not offended Him. Actually, today, in this season of Lent, I do not care.

18 March 1455

Faith

I have often heard that with enough faith, one can move mountains. How does one get this faith? Where does it come from? There are mountains that we need to move! There are conflicts that we need to avoid. I worry that while the English are at each other's throats, the Scots would find this an excellent time for raiding south of their borders. Has there ever truly been a time of peace on this island?

Brother Edward, Timothy, and Cwenhild are visiting and supplying the four remaining households that we look after, that Eawynn and I had been unable to visit. After finishing,

Edward reports nothing out of the ordinary as he stops by, apologizing for not being with us the day we had the unfortunate accident. When he leaves, Cwenhild drops by to say that they had stopped by the falls to rest, and Timothy had checked over the side of the falls for a body, but it was gone. Possibly, the water has carried it downstream.

Eawynn has taken to sleeping with me at night. She does not want to be alone, but also does not want to talk about the rape. Giving her the time to work out her feelings has been difficult for me. We have always been able to discuss what is on our minds, but she has shut down like a locked book. I encouraged her to talk at first, but I no longer press her. Hopefully, she will process this and come out of it in her own time. I will be here, waiting.

20 March 1455

Treats

Sister Mathilde comes to my chamber early this morning to discuss the possibility of building a small room that would be attached to the door leading out from the children's classroom to the grounds where they play. The purpose of this room would be a place where they can hang their outer garments and store their muddy shoes or boots. Evidently, cleaning up the classroom after their morning lessons are over has become quite a chore when the grounds are muddy or covered with snow. Eawynn is sitting in a chair beside my bed reading. She does not look up except to greet Mathilde, but I know she is listening. As Mathilde makes ready to depart, she stops and adds that since Lent has begun, she has noticed a lack of spirit in the children. She wonders if they are getting enough to eat. The food has been very plain and not much to their liking. Even the morning snacks of hard crackers are lacking in appeal. She is worried about their health. I tell her that I will try to find a solution.

Later in the day, I walk to the barn and find young Timothy, fixing a stall door. I ask him to accompany me to the door that opens to the grounds from the classroom. Working here since childhood, helping his father and grandfather, Timothy has developed a wonderful talent for carpentry. I want his opinion and ideas regarding building a room for coats and boots at the side entrance to the classroom. We walk to the lawn where the door to the learning room is located so he can visualize what is needed. As we discuss the project, the door opens and the children come running out, followed by Mathilde and two novices.

Timothy and I finish our discussion, confident that the project will be completed successfully, and he departs. The children play for a few minutes, then suddenly they become quiet and line up in a row by height, smallest to largest, facing Mathilde and me. To my astonishment, I turn to find Eawynn and Avice, who has joined the kitchen staff, walking toward us on the path beside the convent while carrying two large baskets. When the towels are removed from the top, they contain large, delicious cheese rolls. There is exactly one for each child with five left over. How did Eawynn know I would also be here? What a treat! I will not ask if this will become a Lenten tradition, but I somehow think that it will. At least I hope so.

21 March 1455

Laughter

This morning, we begin planting in one of the cultivated vegetable gardens that we have been preparing. As usual during Lent, we begin our work quietly. Silence is not one of the rules of the Augustinian order, but I instruct the rest that by clearing our minds from distraction, we may listen more attentively to God. I feel like a hypocrite because listening to God is the last thing I want to do now. Of course, we can communicate quite effectively without speaking, and the morning is filled with birdsong, which is worth listening to.

It rained yesterday evening, and the fields are muddy and full of small puddles of water. We tie up our skirts and go barefoot through the rows to distribute the seeds. I imagine we look quite the sight. Kendra, one of the novices, slips and goes down into a puddle. She signals that she is unhurt and turns to get up, but slips again, completely covering her habit and legs with mud. Her friend, Bernia, attempts to extricate her, but falls as well. At this point, Maud bursts out in loud, almost hysterical laughter. As you may well imagine, we all lose our composure as the two crawl to a less muddy spot where they can finally stand. The hilarity is contagious. I do not think I have ever laughed that hard. My ribs ache. I expect that we should all perform some small penance for such unruly behavior. Laughter is not a usual part of our daily routine. After today, I think perhaps we should incorporate it at some point every day.

Eawynn was not with us as she is working on a difficult translation of some text in the library with Yvonne. I wish she could have shared our laughter, as she has become very serious lately, and I worry about her. I have stopped asking her to talk to me, because she becomes very annoyed when I do. I fear the incident will destroy her peace if she does not deal with it, and I do not think she is taking the steps to heal.

23 March 1455

Remorse

Why do I not feel more remorse over killing the man who raped Eawynn? This lack of remorse over taking another's life has been plaguing me. I have confessed to God, but I dare not confess to a priest. I do not even trust Father Kenric at Lanercost, and he is as devout a man as I have ever seen. My guilt is that I am not sorry that I killed him. Should I be sorry? I cannot trouble Eawynn with this. Last night she broke down and sobbed herself to sleep as I held her. I can only hope that breaking down like this is helpful in processing this kind of trauma.

This morning, she mentions that she would like a few others that she trusts to know the truth of what she experienced. She names Mathilde, Margarethe, Rosamund, and Yvonne. It is surprising to me that she trusts Rosamund and Yvonne, but she claims that she does. Timothy and

Cwenhild already know. She indicates that we would just say the man left us there and not mention the killing. If she is comfortable with this, I will agree, especially if this helps her to heal. One thing is for certain. Secrets do not stay secret if more than one person knows, so I told her that there is danger in letting others know. She must understand the risk, not only to herself, but to me.

27 March 1455

A Meeting

Mathilde, Margarethe, and Yvonne meet with Eawynn and me this evening. Cwenhild declines to join us, saying that she already knows the whole tale and does not wish to inadvertently give away details that might cause uncomfortable questions. Rosamund also does not attend, giving no reason at all. Addressing the others, it is clearly difficult for Eawynn as she signs for me to speak of the rape. She breaks down several times, then bravely bids me to continue, tears streaming silently down her face.

I relate the ordeal in some detail, finishing the tale by explaining that the man was gone when she and I regained consciousness, and that Eawynn remembered little of his appearance except that he had dark, unkempt hair, and was tall and very strong. At first, Mathilde and Margarethe are silent with horror and shock. Eawynn signs, requesting that they tell no one, and they nod agreement. Giving her hugs and reassurances, they depart. Yvonne is quiet for a long time. She sits bent over with her elbows on her knees and her head down. Finally, she peers up at Eawynn and me, looking back and forth between us. In a soft voice she asks, "Is that the whole of it?" She continues, "It seems unlikely that a man would rape someone, especially a nun, and then leave them alive to tell the tale." At that point, I am glad Cwenhild has decided not to attend. When neither I nor Eawynn replies to her question, she shrugs, walks to Eawynn, hugs her, and turns to go. At the door she turns back. Lowering her voice she whispers, "Any deed of revenge against this man, that might have been committed, has my approval." At that, she opens the door and goes out.

APRIL

6 April 1455

Easter

Easter is a quiet and somber celebration. The usual Masses have been observed for Holy Week. This morning, Father Kenric says two Masses for the day of Our Lord's resurrection. All at Lambley and Lanercost Abbeys attend the sunrise Mass at the church of the Blessed Mary Magdalene. It will not hold a great many people, so a later mass is said for the surrounding communities. A few close neighbors do attend the earlier service, mainly the ones who also attend the early Sunday Mass. Our midday meal is roasted kid goat and roasted duckling, with such vegetables as can be found this early in the Spring, mostly foraged greens with boiled barley mixed with honey and walnuts. I have little appetite, due to the recent stress of our ordeal. Eawynn does not attend, neither the mass nor the meal. She makes no excuse. Surprisingly, no one inquires about her. It seems the news of her ordeal has spread. Although Eawynn has received much attention and compassion, and I am grateful for her care, I have received little. Very few know that I killed a man. I try to put it out of my mind, but the knowing resurfaces at odd times, causing me to tremble with fear. I am not sorry for the deed, as I believe he would have murdered both of us. It is the fear of being found out that troubles my thoughts and sleep.

9 April 1455

Piglets

Good progress has been made in identifying those who are in desperate circumstances this spring. Food can be hard to find this time of year. No one is allowed to hunt deer or wild boar on the landed estates. Indeed, they are not even allowed to hunt pheasants. The penalties for doing so are dire indeed. Households with a cow or goat and some chickens manage much better than those without, but the landowners still take a share. Even the Church charges tithes. It is a wonder these folk survive at all.

Cwenhild stops by to inform us that three sows have all had large litters of piglets. If they are all healthy and survive, it is a sure thing that the bishop in Carlisle will claim quite a few for his palace this fall. Eawynn signs that she thinks we should distribute a piglet to each household that needs one as soon as they are weaned. She will alter our records to show that fewer piglets were born. A grown pig can survive on table scraps and provides a large quantity of smoked meat for the winter. A sow is even better, as she can provide more piglets. Any household that is given a breeding sow needs to agree to pass on a few piglets to their less fortunate neighbors.

I am not sure we can get away with this, but it is worth the effort even if we get caught. It depends on who is keeping track of the number of piglets. I think we might just be able to pull it off. The bishop will not miss what he never knew we had! Why does it always lighten my mood when I feel that we can help the poor at the expense of the rich. By rich, I mean large landholders and the Church. We may have to teach some families how to feed and care for pigs. I will leave that up to Cwenhild, as I know very little about this.

16 April 1455

Solutions

Today, I finally ask Guda to come speak with me. I cannot put this off any longer. It has been months since there have been any serious problems in the kitchen, and Guda has openly admitted to her kitchen staff that she requires help. She is still in charge. It is obvious that only her inability to see well hinders her, as her mind is as sharp as ever.

When she arrives at my study, she is understandably upset about the possibility of having to give up her position as the head of the kitchen. Her distress is visible, but she holds her head high and stubbornly attempts to stare me down. Most religious who have served under her as novices can attest that Guda can be very intimidating. Trying to put her at ease, I ask her to sit and share a glass of mead. She makes a gesture of resignation and sighs. Sitting, she places her square, worn hands in her lap, as a tear slides from a clouded eye. We speak at length about Guda's time at the abbey. She tells me that she started working at Lambley as a kitchen maid at the age of 13. By the time I arrived at Lambley, she was in complete charge of the kitchen, the herb gardens and the vegetable gardens. I reassure her that she is still very much needed at Lambley, that the convent will always be her home, and I ask her to think about what she would like to do next. Guda pauses and stares out the window of my study for a few moments, lost in thought. Then, she turns to me and softly replies that what she would like most would be to sit outside in the sun and warm her old bones. While assuring Guda that time to rest, time to sit in the sun will be in her future, I also endeavor to make clear how deeply those of us who live at the abbey value her, as well as her knowledge of cooking, and of preserving foods and herbs. It will be difficult for the abbey to continue as a strong and healthy institution without her. Preserving Guda's vast and valuable knowledge is essential, so I determine that it must be written down, a task Yvonne has volunteered for. I ask if she would mind being available to speak with Yvonne, especially if anything happens in the kitchens for which we might need to rely on Guda's expertise and experience. Delighted, she asks if she can remain in the kitchen to answer questions and give advice when it is required. Replying, I say that she can do so, as long as she makes certain she has enough time to rest. For the time being, we will proceed in this manner. Hopefully, things will continue to go smoothly.

Sister Margarethe, who is presently in charge of the novices, has requested that she be Guda's replacement in the kitchen. As a young nun, assisting Guda in the kitchens was her favorite duty. Of all the sisters, Margarethe is the most knowledgeable about the job. She chose to work as Guda's assistant until she was appointed to replace Sister Gertrude as mistress of novices. Further, Margarethe is very capable. However, this means that someone else will need to oversee the novices' training. I have Sister Agatha in mind for this position, but I haven't spoken to her yet. She presently helps Mathilde with the older children. Prayers to Our Lady that the transition is not difficult.

Tomorrow, we begin work in the grape vineyards. Tying grape canes while the weather is nice is something I look forward to every spring. Each vine has been trimmed so that four arms (canes) have grown from it. Two arms or canes are tied with twine to both the lower cord and upper cord on each side of the grape vine. It is peaceful work, and something I enjoy. We each work on a separate row, maintaining quiet conversation as we go. Sometimes, someone starts a song and the rest join in. The work should be completed in a week if the weather remains pleasant.

18 April 1455
Schedules

A schedule has been worked out for Guda. First, she is still in charge of planning the menu for the meals for the near future and will discuss this with Sister Margarethe. Second, she is to meet with Yvonne for a couple hours each day to relate the knowledge that we seasonally need to know with regards to cooking, baking, planting, and so on. The topics that need to be notated are as follows: planting and care of both crops and herbs, recipes for cooking and baking, drying of herbal medicines, formulating medicinal tinctures, and preserving fruits and root vegetables. We will tackle this season by season. I am sure I have forgotten something, but we will add needed information as we go. In short, this will be a practical treatise on the running of a convent. Accepting the challenge with growing enthusiasm, I think Guda is now welcoming her new position.

Spending three to four hours each day tying the grape canes keeps us busy, as our work in the vineyards continues. The weather has cooperated so far. Last year we sold most of our grapes to the brothers on the Holy Isle of Lindisfarne, where they were made into wine and mead. We received a percentage of the wine returned for our use. I would like to establish a winery and cellar of our own eventually, so we are not as dependent on the brothers of the Holy Isle.

25 April 1455

More Secrets

This evening at the gloaming, Eawynn pesters me until I agree to take a walk with her to the river as she has something she wants to discuss with me beyond the hearing of anyone else. Shining brightly through the trees, the moon is almost full, and we can see the path well. Silently, so as not to attract attention, we walked across Lanercost's grounds down to the forested area beyond. Entering the woods, Eawynn suddenly stops me, abruptly flinging her arm in front of me and putting a finger to her lips. Faintly, as we stand quietly, I can hear rustling and moaning sounds. Approaching slowly and with care, we behold two figures, one holding the other up from behind to a great oak tree. I recognize them as old brother Alfred and one of the younger brothers. I quickly realize that this action is consensual, and we carefully and slowly back away. I am not sure if we are seen, although they are so thoroughly engaged that I am not sure they would have cared. I will certainly not be the one to cast a stone.

We backtrack and decide to sit in the moonlight on the walkway by our own gardens, where several benches are set up. The topic that Eawynn brings up is her monthly menses. She is usually very regular and keeps track of them on a calendar. She is worried because she is two weeks late and fears that she might be with child. I respond that the trauma might have affected her. My own monthly periods have been irregular for the past two years, and I believe I am going through the transition to being barren, which for me will be a blessing. As she is only a few years younger than me, might it also be a possibility that she might be beginning to go through the change? She rejects that, stating that her breasts seem tender and that she knows this is also a sign of pregnancy. The question is, what should she do now? What are her choices? We will keep this quiet until we know for sure. We will go to visit Gisela and find out what her options are.

29 April 1455

Brigitta

Brigitta has been with us for almost six months. Arriving disguised as a dirty urchin, she refused to give us any information about her previous life. I do fear there must be someone looking for her, but she has found her place working outside, gardening and tending the animals. Preferring to be outside rather than inside in the kitchen, cleaning. or working with those who card the wool and sew, she seems to be thriving. Eawynn and Yvonne have been giving her some lessons in reading and computation in the afternoon. Unfortunately, Brigitta's progress is slow, as she has had very little training in either of these areas. I try to explain to her how very important it is for women to be able to keep accounts. At most large estates, the mistress is in charge of financial matters. Women are believed to be better at these skills, but I think the real reason is a more practical one. The lord of the estate is often absent for long periods of time, either fighting in wars or required to be in attendance at the court of the king. The reality of running the estate often falls to the lady of the estate when her husband is gone.

Brigitta has only expressed an avid interest in working with Sister Cwenhild, tending the chickens, geese, and ducks, and the baby lambs and kids. Although she resists our efforts to provide her with well-rounded training, she will eventually have to learn the household tasks as well. Even so, she is very diligent about attending all services and loves to sing. However, I might be wrong, but I do not think she has a calling to be a member of the religious community.

30 April 1455

Honor to Our Lady

The first of May is the day we honor Our Lady, Mary, the mother of Jesus. Today, as I stand with Sister Agatha and watch, the novices begin tying long ribbons to the poles that have been used long before I became a novice. There is no difficulty in attaching the long, colorful ribbons to the shorter maypole used for the children's dance. I continue watching as they attempt to attach the ribbons to the taller pole used for the novices' dance in the evening. The two novices who try to climb the tall ladder get halfway up before they come back down; their faces ashen with fear. I send one of the younger girls to find Timothy, in the hope that he can accomplish the task. Instead. she returns a short time later with Brigitta, whom she had seen at the barn. Brigitta, dressed in baggy woolen britches and boots, takes a handful of ribbons and scampers to the top of the ladder as if it is something she does every day. By this time, she has an audience. The children have come out with Mathilde to play and are watching with fascination. As two novices hold the ladder for her, she attaches what ribbons she is holding in her hand and climbs back down for more ribbons. Eawynn has appeared by my side and draws a sharp breath as Brigitta climbs up for the second time. At one point, she makes the ladder sway back and forth a little and laughs as the novices holding the ladder gasp with fright. When she is finished, she climbs down laughing and dares the frightened novices to go to the top.

A silence ensues, so quiet that we can hear a rooster crowing in the distance. I am about to intervene when Odelyn, our very quiet and studious orphan, makes her way from the group of children with Mathilde to the ladder. Without a word she begins a slow climb, placing each foot carefully on the next rung of the ladder before pulling herself up. Brigitta speaks only once, immediately asking Odelyn to come back down. Odelyn ignores her. I watched with my heart in my throat, hardly daring to breathe as Eawynn grips my hand tightly. The girl continues to climb, slowly, step by step by step. The sides of the ladder grow closer together at the top and the ladder seems to sway slightly as she approaches the top. Timothy and Cwenhild have appeared and stand with Brigitta and the novices holding the ladder. I had not even seen their approach, so intent was I on the small girl. Reaching the top, Odelyn holds out her small arm and gingerly pats the top of the pole. Without glancing down or even looking at the crowd below, she begins to make her descent. A collective sigh is heard from the crowd as she nears the bottom, turning into thunderous applause when she finally steps down. With eyes lowered, she marches straight over to Sister Mathilde, grasps her hand and hides her face in Mathilde's skirt, from which she then peeks out with a slight, embarrassed smile. I turned to hear Cwenhild, walking back toward the barns with Brigitta, giving Brigitta a tongue lashing for allowing the child on the ladder. Turning back, I see Mathilde herding the children away from the pole, Mathilde walking after them, still holding Odelyn's small hand, and stopping to give her a hug.

MAY

1 May 1455
May Day

The children's maypole dance occurs in the morning, with Odelyn participating in the dance, smiling the whole time. I cannot remember ever seeing her smile before. It seems that everyone has come out to watch and join in singing the maypole song, as the children weave in and out in opposite directions until the ribbons are completely wound around the pole and tied off at the bottom. After the dance, they are fed sweet cakes and tea sweetened with honey.

Following tradition, we sing the lovely hymn by Hildegard of Bingen in the late afternoon, after our supper, to honor Our Lady. As we sing, the novices, dressed in white with their hair bedecked with woven flowers, walk solemnly up the garden path, two by two. Picking up a ribbon, each novice waits until all are ready. Then they began to dance, weaving their way around the tall maypole where Brigitta had attached the ribbons. Following that, they gather in a semicircle around the statue of Mary, which is in a small grotto of stones near the rose bushes, as one of the novices places a crown of woven flowers on Our Lady's head. Throughout the ceremony, I notice Brigitta looking on wistfully, until Cwenhild walks up behind her and places her arm around the girl's shoulders. As the ceremony finishes, they walked away together, arm in arm, both holding a sweet cake from the table where treats had been set out for everyone. Eawynn grabs a few sweets from the table and brings one to me as we make our way back to my study to await Vespers.

Hail to you, O Virgin!

You overflow with glory,
you pure creation.

Hail to you, chastity's darling,
foundation of all sanctity,
God's pleasure.

For the power of the Most High flowed into you
because the Word of God in you put on
the garment of flesh.

Gleaming white are you like a lily,
because God beheld your face
before any other creature.
O beauty, love's incomparable delight,
God was so enraptured with you
as to place deep within you
fire, heat, and tender love.

So the Son fed from you.
Then your body sprang with joy
as the symphony of heaven
sounded forth from you,
because you, O Virgin,
bore the Son of the Father.

Now may the dawn arise,
joy for all the earth.
And may a symphony break forth
in praise of you, Mother of God,
full of love.

Hildegard of Bingen

4 May 1455

Spring Endeavors

Tying the grapes canes is finally completed. Brigitta, alongside Bernia and Kendra, (novices who work in the kitchen), are gathering honeysuckle flowers to dry for tea and tinctures. The flowers grow on the edges of woodlands and by the stone fences where there is sunlight. They go out early in the morning, before the bees are active. I continue to help Sister Margarethe and Sister Avice with planting the herb and vegetable gardens for short periods of time. Unfortunately, I cannot bend over for a long period of time before my back begins to cramp. Once planted, we will await the arrival of sprouts.

Apple and pear trees are in full blossom in the orchards. The unopened blossoms are pink and open to white flowers, with both colors intermingled on most trees. Blossom petals cover the ground under the trees like a carpet. There are no leaves on the trees yet, but the buds of the leaves are visible. The scent of the blossoms pervades the air all the way to the barnyard. This morning, as I walk out to check the blackberry bushes, I watch Mathilde take the children out for a walk in the orchard to see and smell the blossoms. She allows them each to pick a sprig of blossoms off a tree. They will take their sprigs back to the learning room where they will be put in jars of water. The lovely scent from the blossoms can last up to a week.

Last fall we had a gift of two fig trees, brought back by some travelers from Spain. They have been in pots all winter. We recently planted them in the orchard. I am hoping they will thrive here, although I have my doubts.

Eawynn's period still has not come. Early this morning after Prime, she tells me she is sure that she is pregnant. Since we were not absolutely certain before, we have not yet spoken to any of the others. Tomorrow, Eawynn and I will ride to visit Gisela so Eawynn can be examined by the healer, who is also a midwife. If she is pregnant, then we can decide what will be done next. It will be Eawynn's decision, and I will support her however I can. I have noticed a change in her lately, as though she is resigned and has accepted her fate. Nothing has been heard about the man, so I assume his body has not yet been discovered.

5 May 1455

Confirmation

The visit to Gisela's cottage this afternoon confirms my worst fears. Eawynn is pregnant. Gisela examines her thoroughly and asks her many questions. Gisela even volunteers information about taking herbs that will cause a miscarriage, stating that the pregnancy is still in the early stages when the herbs are most effective, but also warning Eawynn that doing so can be dangerous, both for mother and babe. Eawynn replies that she will need time to consider everything. She is very quiet on the way back to the abbey and asks if I will bring a plate of food to her room and make the excuse to everyone that she is not feeling well. I finish eating and make a plate for her. Upon entering her room, I can see that she is fast asleep on her bed, so I put the plate down on her small writing table and leave. I will check on her again before I retire for the night.

7 May 1455

Adelheid

Sadly, a woman from one of the nearby villages arrives this morning to drop off her eleven-year-old daughter,

Adelheid. The woman is very distraught. It seems that Adelheid's father has turned her out. The child is pregnant, although we do not know who is responsible. I suspect it might be one of her older brothers. The child clings to her mother, sobbing, as the woman attempts to leave. She shushes the girl and gently pushes her away. The girl crumples to the floor, hugging herself and rocking back and forth, as her sobbing continues. Mathilde and I attempt to stand her up, but she is limp, her legs give way. We gently pick her up, each holding a side, and carry her to a chair to sit down, but she slides to the floor again. Margarethe hurries in and assists Mathilde to help her stand. She and Mathilde take the child, half walking and half carrying to a room in the children's quarters. We will take care of her as best we can. I fear for her. She is a small and timid child.

I have yet to speak with Eawynn. When I checked on her last night before retiring, she was asleep, but I could see that she had woken up at some point and eaten most of the food on the plate. She has avoided me most of the day today, as she spends her time in the library, only showing up for the liturgical hours and at mealtime but keeping her distance from me. I spend most of the day with Mathilde, getting

Adelheid settled. When I finally retire for the night, Eawynn is asleep again.

8 May 1455

Decisions

Upon waking this morning, I realize that Eawynn has crawled into bed with me sometime during the night. Sleepily, she apologizes for seeming to ignore me for the last few days. She murmurs that she has made a decision and wants to meet with me and a few other sisters so she can find support for the next few months. She has decided to have the baby, has, in fact, grown used to the idea. I hug her and say I will gather Cwenhild, Margarethe, Mathilde, and Yvonne in the library after the Vespers.

Hesitating to put Adelheid with the rest of the orphans, Adelheid has been placed with Cwenhild for the next few days. Cwenhild and Brigitta have been asked to give her some small tasks, but also to make sure she eats and to let her rest as much as possible. Cwenhild and Brigitta both have rooms in a small building by the barn. They will make up a cot for her there and monitor her at all times. It is the best we can do for now.

10 May 1455

A Meeting

Eawynn and I meet with the sisters, as she requested. I explain the ordeal that we had been through again, continuing to exclude the part about killing the man. Of course, Cwenhild shows surprise, and in no way indicates that she has been involved. Using hand signs, Eawynn explains that she is now pregnant with the rapist's child and that she intends to carry it to term. I add that we recently visited Gisela, and Gisela has confirmed the pregnancy. I do not add that a miscarriage brought on with herbs is an option. A silence follows, until Mathilde stands up from her chair and walks over to Eawynn. Placing her hands on the sides of Eawynn's head, she gently kisses her forehead, the embraces her and hugs her for a long moment. Eawynn begins to cry, softly, which brings the rest of us to tears. Yvonne brings us back to the matter at hand by recommending that we keep the pregnancy a secret as long as possible, as it will be quite easy to disguise a pregnancy under a habit. She also mentions the possibility of Eawynn traveling to a different convent while still in the early stages, delivering the baby there, and returning after. Eawynn shakes her head, visibly shaken at the suggestion. She will not leave. I agree with her. She needs our support. It is unthinkable for her to endure this ordeal with strangers, especially those who might not understand what she has endured, or that she is the victim of a crime. Margarethe agrees, hugging Eawynn, and reassures her that she will be well cared for here, with healthy food and lots of rest. It is agreed between us that she will remain working in the library as long as she is able, as that is not strenuous.

12 May 1455
Knowledge

I am frustrated by my lack of knowledge of medical herbs and treatments. I am sending two girls, Ellie Dalton and Maud, to Gisela. Ellie is a novice and young Maud is still an oblate. Both are dependable girls who can read and scribe. Their job will be to assist Gisela for a period of months, yet to be determined, to learn from her about healing tinctures and herbs. They are also tasked with writing everything down. Hopefully, six months should be long enough. Gisela is surprised by the offer but says she would welcome the help. The girls will still follow the breviary or canonical hours each day, except for the ones we usually skip at night. Besides focusing my spiritual energies, I find that following the hours breaks up the day and is beneficial for concentration. The girls will come back to the convent on weekends, and we will visit with them often to make sure they are staying on task.

I am not sure Gisela agrees with all the religious trappings, but she wisely does not comment on any of them. I suspect she may follow some of the older beliefs. If so, she is wise to keep it to herself. I would like to learn something about the way people worshiped before Christianity was brought to these parts, but I am concerned that asking might be frowned upon by the Church. Rumors abound that women have been burned at the stake for any hint of religious differences, particularly in Scotland. Gisela has been a great help with illnesses and child birthing in the past. We need to keep records of her knowledge that has been handed down through generations of women.

15 May 1455

Rain

Torrents of rain have poured down on us for two days drenching the ground. The sloping path between the chapel and our kitchen is a stream, flowing halfway to my knees this morning as I attempt to walk to the chapel. I am forced to turn back. Our morning prayers are held in the dining room of the convent while the children are breaking their fast at one of the back tables. It is most definitely not quiet. Mid-morning, as I watch from the window in my study, the sun momentarily breaks through heavy gray clouds, then is swallowed up again. It appears the deluge is slackening. My resolve to build covered walkways between the buildings, especially to the chapel, is greater than ever. We were soaked to the skin yesterday evening at Vespers. Unfortunately, I forget about this project when the sun is shining.

It will also be necessary to hire a thatcher to attend to several places where the roofs are leaking, especially the two leaks in the kitchen and the one in the sitting room where we like to spend our evenings in quiet conversation while we knit or sew. The sound of water dripping into pans on the floor seems to grow louder the longer one is forced to listen to it. As the drips continually change their location on the ceiling, we must also change the pans that catch the water. Perhaps the entire building needs to be re-thatched. That is an undertaking that I do not think we can afford.

16 May 1455

Adelheid

Adelheid has been at the abbey for a little more than a week. We have learned very little about the child. She seems quite unwilling to disclose the details of her circumstances. She is in poor health and sleeps a great deal, which is probably for the best. She is still spending her time under the supervision of Cwenhild and continues to sleep in the small house Cwenhild shares with Brigitta. After consulting with Cwenhild, I assigned Adelheid two tasks, which she began a few days ago. She must help Brigitta with feeding the chickens, ducks, and geese both morning and evening. She seems to have already formed a bond with Brigitta. She must also watch little Henri for a few hours every afternoon, which means she must walk by herself to where the smallest children are situated. Mathilde has agreed to supervise this interaction. Henri is the orphan foundling that was left for us this past winter. He has learned to sit up, likes to feed himself, and is quite an active and amiable little fellow. He will be crawling soon. I made this decision by considering that Adelheid will need the experience of taking care of an infant. As she has taken to caring for Henri with complete confidence, I believe she may be familiar with this task already.

This evening, I ask Cwenhild to allow Brigitta and Adelheid to accompany Eawynn and me on a walk through our orchards in the morning, out towards the grazing pastures, in the hope of learning more about her past. I also need to survey what damage the storms may have caused and this will be a good time to become better acquainted with Adelheid. I tell the girls that we older women would like to enjoy their youthful company, and that they are to come to my study as soon as their morning chores are completed.

17 May 1455

Blame

Brigitta and Adelheid arrive at the open door to my study and tap softly to announce themselves. I send Brigitta to the library to fetch Eawynn while I gather my coat, gloves and cane. We meet Eawynn and Brigitta, who are waiting for us by the side entrance to the kitchen. Eawynn has snagged some hot rolls from a basket on the counter as she passed through. This morning, the rains have ceased, and the air is cool and thick with the scent of flowers. As we walk, I notice that there is little damage to the crops, just a few broken tree branches. We continue walking until Brigitta stops. Turning toward Adelheid, she pleads with Adelheid to disclose the details of her situation. Apparently, Adelheid has already confided in Brigitta. With a look of pure misery, Adelheid confesses that she feels she is to blame, indeed, her brother and both parents seemed to think so. She has received unwanted attention from her brother since she was four. He threatened to hurt her if she told. Regardless, she did tell her mother, who refused to believe her. Hearing her story brings back awful memories, that make me feel angry and helpless all over again. I have heard this tale so many times before. It is an all-too-familiar tale. With no protection from her mother, Adelheid tried to avoid her brother's advances, but often failed. She had been unaware of what the consequences would be. When her father found out, he believed the brother, who said the child seduced him. She feels such shame, that somehow, she is to blame, that she is a sinner with no hope of redemption.

When I ask her how many children are in the family, she holds up ten fingers plus two and indicates that three are younger than her. Seven are boys, and these receive preferential treatment. The mom is also quite often indisposed and is unable to care for herself during endless pregnancies. How can the conditions in a community that cause such misery be resolved? If we are to follow our Savior's admonition to feed the hungry, a charity should be established by the Church to do just that. There is also a need to help women who bear child after child until they are worn out. I will speak with the abbot to see if our abbeys could join in such an effort in the surrounding community for those who are in need. I worry that the problem will be to accurately identify which families will participate, which husbands will allow their wives to participate.

Consider a family where there are so many children, so many mouths to feed, that some children are given more favorable treatment than others. This is often the case when a young mother has been forced to bear child after child until it ruins her health. This is not the norm, but it is common enough. Family size is usually controlled by the childhood sicknesses that periodically ravage our communities. When there are too many children, particularly girl children, they are disposed of somehow. Adelheid is fortunate that her mother brought her to us. If she had been turned out of the house, she would have been a pregnant child, begging on the streets. There is no way of knowing what her fate might have been, but it does not bear thinking about. She would not have survived long.

20 May 1455

Foraging

The village midwife, Gisela, arrives to examine little Adelheid this morning. As I watch, she feels the child's abdomen and checks her throat under her chin, her eyes and ears and her breasts. The child is embarrassed, placing her thin arms across her breasts and staring at the floor in dismay. I feel for her, being treated like a horse up for auction, but Gisela is just being thorough. Patting the child on the shoulder to reassure her, Gisela tells us that, despite her diminutive stature, Adelheid is in her sixth month. Although she is being well fed for perhaps the first time in her life, Adelheid is still undernourished and very thin. Cwenhild and I had thought she was only about four months along. After the examination is over, and Adelheid has left to return to the barn, the midwife also tells me in confidence that she fears greatly for Adelheid. The child's hips are as small as a boy's. This bodes ill for an easy birth.

This afternoon I walk out with Sisters Margarethe, Cwenhild, and Yvonne, to forage in the meadows and woodlands around the abbey for berries and wild greens. Our stores from winter are depleted, and the greens in our garden are not yet ready for harvesting. Hoping to find lambs quarters, purslane, chick weed, dandelion, plantain, wild garlic, and onions, each of us takes one or two novices with us so that they may learn to identify these important plants. There are some ripe wild strawberries in a meadow by a small woodland stream that are picked. It takes great restraint from all of us not to eat them right there on the spot, but we resist. I will make a note of the spot for next time. As it rained yesterday, we are also hopeful of collecting some chanterelles to dry. I will send out Cwenhild with Brigitta tomorrow, as Cwenhild is familiar with mushrooms. I am very careful about who gathers the mushrooms!

On the way back to the kitchen, Cwenhild and I stop in the orchard to check on the trees. The apple and pear trees are still in blossom and some tiny fruits are beginning to develop on some of the limbs. We will need to trim them soon, or perhaps have some laborers from the barn do it, as the limbs are tangled from last year's growth. Trimming fruit trees and thinning the fruit when it sets allows for larger, healthier fruit and preserves a healthy tree. If two apples grow together on a tree, they are often small and misshapen. Knowing that I should not, I picked some small sprigs of apple blossoms to put in water glasses on the tables in the dining room. At least we did not come back entirely empty-handed.

21 May 1455

Singing

I continue to work with those who can sing, although I have had no real formal training. Singing the psalms at the different offices during the day is something I have always enjoyed. Since we have had no real choir master, I had appointed myself. As a child I learned to read musical notation while learning to play the lute and harp. I am so grateful for the voice of Judith and now, the lovely voice of Brigitta. Judith has begun to make harmonies for some of our chants. She often directs the singing of parts. Despite her youth, the older nuns recognize her talent and follow her advice. She has even composed music for a few psalm settings. Slowing, I am relinquishing the job of director to her. Together, Judith and Brigitta have raised the level of our musical praises to God and Our Blessed Lady. In fact, I have heard that our choir is becoming well known in the surrounding area.

23 May 1455

Blessed Rain

Another rainy morning. God's tears! Yesterday, Eawynn insisted on going out foraging with Cwenhild and Brigitta. She said she needed some fresh air and someone to talk to other than Yvonne. They found a few chanterelles in a wooded area under some large oak trees. They will check this area again after the rain lets up. The edible greens were not numerous, so they only gathered a few, taking only the leaves off some young lamb's quarter and plantain, but now they know where these greens are located. The plants should be much larger next week. I saw many blackberry and blueberry bushes in full bloom on my short walk. I think we will be able to pick enough for drying in about a month. It takes so much work to adequately prepare for winter, but this is not really work, as those of us who forage really enjoy it. The weather is so delightful this time of year that I want to be outside every morning, but not when it is raining.

We will all stay inside today, and hopefully finish carding the remaining stack of wool. The wool has been compressed into a large wooden crate in a corner of the sewing room. Strangely, a few little pieces of wool have been found in odd places. The mystery is solved as Rosamund notices a cat raiding the box of wool and pulling out pieces of wool to play with. This particular cat is now banished from the sewing room. We card the wool and put it aside. In the winter it will be dyed and spun into yarn by the sisters, by Alfred, who works with Sister Rosamund, and by the novices who are learning. Alfred is Sister Rosamund's very special assistant who has been with her for several years. All will take place under the watchful gaze of Sister Rosamund. That area is her specialty. She knows what to use to make many different colors, and how to combine colors to produce others. I admit, this knowledge is beyond me. I only hope there is a novice who has the interest to learn and expand on this knowledge of colors. The blankets and rugs we weave are beautiful, a good source of revenue, and the work keeps us busy during the winter months. I am sitting here with Eawynn, finishing my tea and watching the gentle rain on the herb garden, where the small sprouts are just struggling up through the soil. What a blessed day! Mary, Our Lady, has smiled on us today,

24 May 1455

Eawynn

I have pressed Eawynn a few times to tell me more about her years at Lacock Abbey. I knew her first few years were difficult, but she does not like to talk about them or dwell on them. Perhaps the reason she is so opposed to continuing her pregnancy in another convent, where she has no friends or support, is that she fears a similar experience to Lacock, only she would be even more vulnerable as a pregnant woman. Since her pregnancy, she has become more willing to discuss her time at Lacock Abbey, to justify her reason for not wanting to leave us.

She shows up at the door to my study midafternoon with Sister Yvonne, a pot of tea, some biscuits, and three cups. I close the door so that we will remain undisturbed. Signing, she begins her tale of her years at Lacock Abbey, until Yvonne holds up her hand, laughing, "I know you can speak,

Eawynn. You mutter and cry out when you fall asleep in the library. I try not to draw attention to it, but I am sure there are others who have discovered this since your pregnancy began. You must be more careful where you nod off if you expect to keep up this pretense any longer. I am amazed that we are only learning of this now."

Eawynn bows her head, embarrassed, and quietly begins, "The abbess at Lacock was quite put out when she discovered that she had to deal with a mute. She gave me tasks that are usually left for a common laborer, cleaning out the chamber pots in the nuns' quarters, as well as those in the large room where the novices sleep. I was made to sweep and wash floors and clean up the dining hall after meals. I have never been clever at spinning, or sewing, or knitting, and she scoffed at my attempts. She called me a stupid child, and said she had no idea why the likes of me could even dream I could become a novice. The first months were so difficult that many times I wished I had just married that horrible man. But I refused to complain and busied myself working on a system for using hand signals to communicate during my free time in the abbey's library. The librarian, Sister Katherine, noticed my work and asked Abbess Elena de Montfort if I might be allowed to work in the library. The other novices avoided me at first, but a few became intrigued when I demonstrated how to use hand signs to communicate. Other novices began to include me in their conversations, especially when I taught them my signs, and the use of hand signs became a means of communication between the novices during the times when silence is observed. They would ask me the symbol for something, and sometimes I had to make up a sign on the spot, and then remember to record it in my notes." I laugh as I imagine the surreptitious use of hand signs to communicate when the mistress of novices was not watching. Eawynn never fails to surprise me.

She continued, "My last two years as a novice were much improved when Abbess de Montfort was replaced by Agnes Frary. I do not know why she was replaced, but these positions are often political and can change when money changes hands with the archbishop. When I made my initial profession as a sister of Saint Augustine, my friends, because many had become my friends, asked me to stay on. It was tempting, but I knew in my heart that I had to return to Lambley." At that she glances over at me and smiles, shyly. I have never known Eawynn to be shy, so this is a new development. Or perhaps she is just embarrassed.

We were steadfast about writing to each other while Eawynn was at Lacock Abbey. It seemed that a letter arrived from Eawynn around the second week of each month with much detail about the events since her last letter. Both her letters and mine were more like reports than anything of personal interest. I had to learn to read between the lines to discover how miserable her life was under Abbess de Montfort and how much improved her position became when Agnes Frary replaced de Montfort. I would reply with descriptions of the events at Lambley in great detail, usually within a week, although devoid of my opinions on anything. We knew these exchanges would be read by others. We had agreed to keep in contact and knew that voicing our opinions on any matter political or religious could bring trouble. My heart yearned to know how Eawynn really felt, and if she missed me as much as I missed her, but I did not dare to ask except in person.

26 May 1455

Rodent Control

The Sabbath was a quiet one, as I felt we all needed a rest yesterday. This morning, I walk out with

Cwenhild, Brigitta, and some novices to check the spots where Cwenhild located wild greens last week. I am hopeful of finding more greens to go with the grains we have left from the winter. It will be nice when the garden crops begin to produce. At least, the chickens have finished molting and started laying again. There are plenty of eggs and goat's milk to see us through, and there are always fish.

I will walk over to Lanercost Abbey tomorrow to speak with Abbot Alexander. I have not been there for some time, and it will be nice to visit as well as to discuss future plans for both our abbeys, especially the establishment of a community pantry for those families who have difficulty finding enough food. While the abbeys can provide some of the supplies, there are those in the community who will also be encouraged to help. I will take Adelheid with me, along with Brigitta. I think a change of scenery would do them both good, and they seem to get on well with each other. Lanercost Abbey is not far. Adelheid's pregnancy does not show if she wears loose clothing. That is one situation we will not disclose until we must. Since her family is part of the local community, I am not sure how the abbot will react. There is an ulterior motive for our visit, I wish to find homes for our ample supply of kittens, and the girls will peddle this idea much better than I can.

We will pack three or four kittens in baskets to carry with us, as there are no cats at Lanercost Abbey. The previous abbot was convinced that cats were creatures of the devil. Meanwhile, their grounds and buildings were overrun with rats and mice. I have noticed that a few of our grown cats occasionally make forays to the grounds at Lanercost, but the brothers do not encourage them to stay. I am hoping the girls can change their minds. We have had three litters of kittens that we are aware of at Lambley. Some of the kittens died of the sickness that is prevalent with young kittens. The ones that survived are healthy and very friendly. They will keep the girls busy for the journey. Observing kittens and their antics gives me great joy. If the abbot approves, the kittens will grow to provide rodent control at Lanercost

28 May 1455

Strangers

As we walk to Lanercost this morning, the girls are having a wonderful time picking wildflowers, and singing as they carry their furry charges in baskets with lids that close. They are acting as if they do not have a care in the world. We stop near a small, cold stream that runs into the River Irthing to watch a family of squirrels chattering in the trees around us. They scold as we pass by. It may be my imagination, but I also think the squirrels are throwing things at us, left over acorns and twigs. Is this even possible? I have never heard of such a thing. We also watch a long striped, brown snake slither through the underbrush into the water, the harmless kind that is found in our barns and feeds on rodents.

As we approach the Abbey, there are travelers by the side of the road, a Jewish family that is traveling eastward towards the coast, and a few farmers with laden carts. I try to speak with the Jewish man who is driving the horses pulling the wagon, but he refuses my attempt to stop him and seems to be in a hurry to move on. I want to see if we can offer aid in any way, but I also understand why he is cautious, as our archbishop has recently denounced these families. I have also heard of trouble for those of the Jewish faith in both Spain and France. Many families have chosen to travel toward Eastern Europe beyond the German provinces. Their position in England is precarious and depends on the good will of the current king and the archbishops. I certainly do not understand the persecution of an entire race of the people, who were once the chosen people of God, for the crimes of the few that crucified Christ. Sometimes we forget, our Savior was a Jew.

I spend a great deal of time speaking with the abbot, discussing plans for a community pantry. He is intrigued by the idea and indicates that he thinks it is worth pursuing, especially if we can find wealthy donors to assist with the costs. Abbot Alexander also tentatively agrees to try keeping the kittens on the grounds. While I am meeting with the abbot, the girls are busy outside, watching the kittens, where they draw quite a bit of attention from some of the monks. While a couple of the brothers cast dark looks at the kittens, quite a few are curious. They gather around Adelheid and Brigitta and begin asking questions. They also request to hold the fluffy little darlings. The girls allow the kittens to be passed around, and a couple of the brothers begin playing with them, dangling their belts for kittens to bat at with their paws and cuddling them to their chests. One brother laughs uproariously as a kitten crawls all over his shoulders and neck. At that point I am sure our quest will be a success. We spend the last fifteen minutes of our journey explaining about their care. The head cook arrives in a rush just before we depart and demands that he have his pick of the kittens for the kitchen. Leaving the brothers to sort out where the kittens will reside, we set out shortly before sunset to return to Lambley. The sun is low over the treetops, and a cool breeze had sprung up when we finally take our leave. It is a clear, cool evening with much birdsong. Despite that, I want to make haste, as dark clouds are moving in from the west, and I expect rain.

As we arrive at the convent, I am surprised to see that our young novices have all abandoned their veils and are waiting for the evening meal with their hair down. Is this a rebellion of some kind? It is certainly a new development! Thankfully, there are no visitors at the evening meal. I am immediately suspicious that Eawynn might have had a hand in this. I will not take the girls to task for this until I have spoken with them and given it more thought. They are testing the boundaries, as many of their age tend to do. I see no reason why consecrated virgins in the shelter of the cloister should hide their beauty, after all, they are not married. Still, if it turns out that I allow this to continue, I am sure there will be trouble, if not from the abbot at Lanercost, then from the bishop himself.

When I speak with Eawynn about it, she threatens to let her own hair down if I do not allow the younger girls to continue. Eawynn argues that by allowing them a tiny bit more freedom to express themselves at certain times, I will prevent worse behaviors in the future. It makes me wonder if Eawynn might have been consulted by one of the girls, and then have encouraged or even instigated this change in behavior. I am not sure I agree. It seems harmless to allow this, but only at times when there are no visitors. Besides, Eawynn's threats are never idle, and her blazing mop of red hair would certainly be seen by someone. This could indeed focus unwanted attention on us.

JUNE

2 June 1455

Eawynn

It is evening, and we have retired to our rooms after Vespers. Eawynn returns with tea fetched from the kitchen and joins me to sit by my small fireplace. The night is chilly, and I have lit the fire. We have been together for such a long time; we are like two pieces of a puzzle that interlock. We are very different from each other, but we fit.

When Eawynn returned from Lacock after being away for five years, it was as if we were strangers. Our conversations were awkward. Neither knew what to say, or how the other felt. It seemed impossible to find an opportunity to speak to her alone. We circled around each other for a few days at this strange dance, until I asked her to accompany me as I rode out to deliver a message from the abbess to the shepherds in the summer pastures. This was not an unexpected request, as we had often ridden out together for various duties before Eawynn had departed for Lacock. We mounted our horses and rode into the countryside without speaking. As we approached a meadow, she looked sideways at me and called out, "Race me." Just like that, we were girls again, tearing across the field until we skidded to a halt at the tree line, with Eawynn a full horse length ahead. She dismounted with a leap and pulled me from my mount with a hug so fierce I thought she would crush my lungs. I did not pull away. Since that day, no matter the minor disputes or disagreements, we have never lost each other or been separated for any length of time again.

Now, we face a new challenge. What will Eawynn's options be when the truth of her rape and subsequent pregnancy can no longer be hidden? If she is forced to leave, I will go with her. If she decides to raise the baby, I will help. I will give up this vocation in one beat of my heart if I must make the choice of remaining a sister of Saint Augustine or having Eawynn by my side, no matter the circumstances.

15 June 1455

Trouble

Picking and preserving garden vegetables and herbs has kept everyone very busy the last few days. We have all retired to bed in the evenings tired to our very bones, too tired to even write in my journal. This morning, a letter is delivered to me from Joan Sevenoke, Prioress of Haliwell. She writes that she has heard rumors that our virgins stand in church with unbound hair, clothed in white, and that they adorn themselves with jewelry. She admonishes me, quoting Saint Paul in his first letter to Timothy, "Let women comport themselves with modesty, not with plaited hair, gold, or pearls, and costly attire." I remember telling Eawynn that there would be trouble over the decision to allow the novices this little freedom. Still, I am just amazed at how quickly the details of that decision have spread. I find that I need to organize my thoughts so I can be ready to defend my decision if that occasion should occur, as I am sure it will.

First, I have always thought the passage Joan Sevenoke refers to is about married women, not virgins. Second, I have always suspected that Paul had issues with women. He often refers to women as though they are not real thinking beings with emotions, but only objects that obstruct men's relationship with God. Paul was not one of our Savior's original followers, did not in fact even know Jesus personally, and elevated himself to an exalted rank as one of the heads of the Church after his miraculous conversion on the road to Damascus. I place a great deal more importance on the teachings of Christ than on the tediously detailed admonitions of Paul. Why is it that disciples so often take it upon themselves to unnecessarily elaborate on their master's simple teachings? I worried that allowing the girls some small freedoms would cause trouble, and now it has come. Well, we shall see!

16 June 1455

Death and Pregnancy

It has been a little over three months since that dreadful incident by the Gorge of the River Irthing. Today, Timothy and Cwenhild, who have taken over the business of bringing supplies to those four remaining families, stop by my study to inform me that the body of a man has been found several hundred yards downstream from the waterfalls, caught up in some brambles and bushes by the side of the river. A man who was fishing in a small boat saw something which did not look natural and rowed over to investigate. The local constable was called. He was able to identify the dead man by his clothes and a ring on his finger. The body was badly decomposed and partially eaten by wild creatures. So, we finally know who he was. Our assailant was the illegitimate son of the Earl of Thirlwall. Timothy tells me there is to be an investigation.

I hesitate to give this news to Eawynn. She is at a stage in her pregnancy where she is always tired. While I cannot excuse her from attendance at the liturgical hours, because that might raise too many questions from others, I request that Yvonne let her take naps when she needs them. Yvonne comes to me to say that Eawynn has been found asleep at her desk several times, so they have worked out a plan for her to take naps so that her absence is not so noticeable. Her pregnancy is not showing, but she does look different somehow.

17 June 1455

The Serpent

Our Bible reading this morning is from Genesis, the tale of Adam and Eve in Garden. All day I have found myself questioning the narrative. I am in a quandary about the role of the serpent. The serpent in the garden of Eden is associated with snakes. God reinforces this association when he said he will place enmity between women and snakes. I quite appreciate the snakes we have in the gardens and meadows of Lambley Abbey. The long brown ones with stripes do not cause much harm if they bite, and they only bite in defense if someone tries to pick one up. The grass snakes and corn snakes are very useful in keeping the mouse and moles populations under control, more useful sometimes than cats. There are also adders, whose bite can be serious, but we rarely see them. There have been reports of sightings of these venomous snakes being eaten by the smooth snakes in the garden. But I digress from my original thoughts.

Does mankind's unreasonable fear of snakes come from God's admonition? These questions whirl through my mind at night until I cannot sleep! What was an evil serpent doing in the garden in the first place? How did it get in? Was not the great Archangel Michael guarding the gates? Was not the garden supposed to be a safe place? One can only wonder that perhaps this temptation has been planned by the Almighty, and if so, for what reason? Is it possible that the presence of a tree of knowledge that is off limits to mankind, and the presence of a serpent who calls God's bluff, has been intentionally set up? I will have to assume the snake got in regardless of Michael's presence and the safeguards that God put in place. Eawynn just laughs at me when I get like this. She says there are no answers and no way of knowing, so I should stop troubling myself.

18 June 1455

What is the Truth of the Tale

Drinking my tea outside this morning seems like a good idea. It is cool and quiet. The only sounds to break the silence are the birdsong and the tiny frog chorus coming from a small pond behind the barns. Everything has gone as expected the last few days. The sprouts in the gardens are flourishing. The flocks are secure. Grass for grazing is abundant. The few kittens remaining are either playing on the wall outside the kitchen, or fast asleep in a patch of sunlight. Eawynn is a picture of health and even little Adelheid has lost the look of someone who has been starved.

Grappling with the story of Adam and Eve in Eden continues, although I have decided to just let the issue of the serpent in the garden go unchallenged. Evidently, God created serpents along with all the other creatures that he tasked Adam with naming. Still, as I reread the story, I realize that the serpent is not referred to as Satan, although our Church leaders assume that this is so. The serpent had arms and legs before being cast down by God, which puts me in mind of a dragon. Is that possible? The mighty Archangel Michael is supposed to have slain a dragon. Might it have been this one? I am also not sure where the tale of Michael slaying the dragon comes from, as I cannot find it in the sacred texts. I must ask Eawynn to research this further.

The blame for being evicted from the garden has always been reserved wholly for Eve. It is considered to be Eve's sin. Adam does not share any of the responsibility. I have been examining this pretext carefully and find it somewhat contradictory. She was told there would be two very different outcomes for choosing to eat the fruit of the tree of knowledge from two different sources. From Genesis, chapter two, God tells Adam that he will die on the very day that he eats or even touches the fruit of the tree of knowledge of good and evil. In chapter three of Genesis, the serpent speaks with Eve, telling her that she will not die from eating the fruit, but that her eyes will be opened, and she will know good from evil. Human nature, also a trait endowed upon mankind by the creator, should also be taken into consideration. It is human nature to be curious.

Life in Eden is wonderful. All of Eve's needs are met. Day after day, the same. Is she bored? Does she long for a challenge, something more? Eve listens to the serpent and takes a chance. She chooses to eat the fruit. She chooses to eat the fruit that is on a tree, placed in the garden purposely to tempt her, given her very human nature, by the Creator that designed the garden, the tree, the humans, and the serpent. Does this all add up to an accident waiting to happen? Or is this the intended outcome? As an aside, I often think Heaven might be a bit like Eden, with non-stop singing and praying, much like our days in the abbey. Thank goodness, we also have many other varied tasks and daily challenges to deal with that keep us occupied.

The result of Eve's decision to eat the fruit from the tree of knowledge? She lives to give birth to children with great pain, to fear snakes, and she, along with Adam, is forced to leave the garden of Eden. Neither Adam nor Eve dies immediately from eating the fruit, as God had warned. I have often wondered what would have happened if she had not eaten the fruit? Perhaps she would have lived forever, in Eden, with only Adam, and no children. I think I would have chosen the apple as well.

19 June 1455

Solitude

Determined to have some time to myself, I retrieve my walking cane and set out by myself this morning, immediately after breaking my fast. I am only a few steps out the door when Eawynn joins me. Lambley is always so busy, and although the nuns mostly maintain a quietness as we go about our daily tasks, there always seems to be a problem that I must solve or a question that must be answered immediately, even when it is obvious that I am quietly meditating. I have even been disturbed while praying in the chapel. It is a cool morning, with just a hint of the warmth that foretells the coming of summer heat. I always enjoy Eawynn's company. I also realize that she objects to me taking walks any distance from the abbey by myself.

I fear the practice of the novices at Lambley going about with unbound hair is causing more than a little stir. Word has gotten out. I have heard that the novices and young oblates at other convents have been influenced to imitate these practices. I do expect some consequences for this eventually.

My thoughts stray to the question of the purpose behind the temptation of Adam and Eve. What could the purpose be if not to give humankind the knowledge to choose? Can that be considered original sin? Placing the blame for the eviction from the garden on Eve is the very precedent for the treatment of women since that time by those in authority in the Church. Blaming Eve for the downfall of mankind has enabled men to view women as untrustworthy. Women are often labeled as temptresses, especially if they do not comport themselves according to the standards of the day. At least Eawynn is keeping her hair bound up under her veil.

20 June 1455

Humility

The last few days have been very difficult. I have been in bed with terrible pain in my twisted leg. I will need to stop my daily walks for a while. Eawynn helps me as I limp into our chapel for our morning service. I request that we have only a short service today. No one objects, so we sing a psalm and read the passage from the Gospel of Luke about the Prodigal Son. I am relieved when it was over, but the reading gives me pause. Was I given this deformity to keep me humble? My deformity puts me in mind of biblical persons who were placed, or intentionally placed themselves, in positions to experience great humility. It must have been very humiliating for the Prodigal Son to return home, begging for food and shelter, after spending his inheritance on gambling and harlots. It is a story of the ultimate love that God has for all humankind. No matter what we do, God will always love us and welcome us home. It is comforting to know this.

21 June 1455

The Prodigal Son

I spend time with Adelheid this morning, weeding the herb garden behind the kitchens at Lambley. We pick wildflowers for the table settings in the dining hall and gather wild blackberries this afternoon. Blackberries are preserved by drying. If the sunshine is strong enough, they are dried outside on cloth that has been laid on tables. Margarethe is afraid we might lose too many due to the rain, so she is drying them in the still house this year, with a fire that burns with very low heat. When dried this way they retain some flavor of the smoke. Depending on our supply of honey, a jar can be filled with berries, and they are covered with honey and sealed. This year, the bees have produced an ample amount of honey. That is my favorite way to preserve them. Of course, we eat them freshly picked as well.

There are a few showers in the afternoon when we seek cover under the trees, as it is important to keep the berries from getting wet, which causes them to rot faster. Adelheid soon tires from stooping over and rests on the large branch of an oak tree that has grown close to the ground. I fill our smaller baskets with berries and bring them to Adelheid when they are full. She carefully pours them into a bucket that she keeps under the branch and out of the rain, and then returns the baskets to me to fill again. Adelheid is well into her pregnancy and appears healthy. I pray daily to Mary and the Magdalene for her safety. Adelheid indicates that she still blames herself for her present condition. Her remorse and humility are palpable. If her circumstances had been different, she would never have had to make these choices. Even though I find her guiltless, she repents daily while kneeling in the chapel each morning.

My thoughts turn once again to the character of the Prodigal Son. He was repentant when he returned home, penniless and starving. His father, who thought he had lost this son forever, was overcome with joy, dressed his son in fine robes, and killed the fatted calf for a feast. I wonder what would have happened next if this story had continued, knowing what human nature can be like. Would the son have been truly repentant and remained dutiful now that he was given a second chance, or would he have taken advantage of the situation and tried to replace his older brother in his father's affections? Would he have felt enabled to swindle more money out of his father, only to return to a life of debauchery? I have only witnessed a few instances in my life where people have truly changed, and many more where they have not. Perhaps I am too much of a skeptic.

And what of the older son, the son who remained constant? Do the angels truly rejoice more over the one sinner who repents than the ninety-nine who remain faithful followers? I have a great deal of difficulty believing that. Concerning the ones who have always remained faithful, have they never questioned the meaning of their existence and always just followed all the rules? Is it better to just accept the beliefs that we are just expected to accept, or is it better to question them? It certainly is easier to follow along without questioning, but I have never taken the easy way. Perhaps I tend to overthink things. Tomorrow I will spend some time outside sitting with Eawynn and a few of my trusted sisters, Yvonne and Rosamund, who are both quite conservative, and of course, Margarethe and Mathilde. Yvonne and Rosamund were novices at the same time as I was. Both also took their initial vows in 1423. Unlike me, they sought the sanctuary of a convent voluntarily and appear to have great devotion to God. I value their conservative input because they are honest and kindhearted, and they often put my feet back on an acceptable path. I need to give voice to my questions about the scriptural passages that concern me, and my sisters will provide me with their honest, heartfelt thoughts.

25 June 1455

Contrary Advice

Receiving both supportive and conflicting opinions from our group discussion, at least Margarethe is in total agreement. She and I are often of the same mind about biblical interpretations. Eawynn sits off to the side recording notes of the conversation. I am sure she will have much to say later this evening. Mathilde supports my opinions, although she feels that people can and do change for the better as they are faced with life's trials. Sister Rosamund surprises us all by standing up and pacing, as she tries to communicate her discomfort about questioning the scriptures. She stammers, "I do not understand why you cannot accept that these Bible stories are the actual word of God, Isentrude. I feel strongly that the parables and stories of the Bible are teaching tools that are meant to be taken literally, that the message of God's infinite forgiveness in the story of the Prodigal Son is of the utmost importance at all times in history." Tears of frustration fill Rosamund's eyes and slide down her face. I am ashamed for upsetting her. I apologize for making her feel uneasy. At that moment, Yvonne raises questions about another biblical parable that we also take literally, specifically, the story of the bridegroom and the wise and foolish virgins. This causes Rosamund to excuse herself and leave the room.

While I feel that I need to reread that parable, I also must consider that Rosamund may be correct. Perhaps I should take these parables at face value, teaching tools at a time in history when that was what was needed. With all this commotion, I also need to find some quiet time to clear my mind. Perhaps I will help with the carding of that last batch of wool tomorrow, working with my hands in silence, and using that practice to silence my thoughts.

26 June 1455

The Tale of the Bridegroom Who Was Late

With the aid of my cane, I complete a short walk in solitude this morning after we break our fast. For me, this summer is a time of introspection. The more I think about the message that Christ will return, and that we must always be ready and prepared, the more I believe that Christ is already present, in all the totality of creation. The spirit of God is in all things, and we must treat all things with love, humility, and compassion. I reread the parable of the bridegroom and the wise and foolish virgins. The obvious truth of this parable is that we must always be prepared for the second coming of Christ, but, if we are always mindful of the spirit of the creator in all things, we maintain preparedness. God/Christ is already here. I would like to discuss this further with Sister Yvonne.

My issues with this parable are focused firstly on the virgins. Virgins are very young girls, either too young for marriage or just old enough. They have been instructed to wait for the bridegroom who will come at a specific time for the wedding feast. Some of these children have ample oil for their lamps, and some have just enough. We might ask why some have just enough. Perhaps those with "just enough" are foolish, or perhaps they are poor. When the bridegroom is late, the "wise" virgins will not share their oil with those who have brought just enough oil. Their lamps are going out, and they have no option except to leave to find more oil. The girls who are adequately prepared are so focused on the bridegroom that they have lost all compassion for their sisters' plight.

The bridegroom is late. He is late. I cannot stress this enough. The cause for all the heartbreak in this parable is that the bridegroom is late. When the foolish maidens show up late to the feast, they are turned away, but it is really the lateness of the bridegroom that causes the "foolish" virgins to be refused entry from the feast, from heaven. And so, the foolish, or possibly poor, girls are punished, while the selfish maidens are rewarded. There are no consequences for the late bridegroom. Is there any doubt that this parable was written by a man? I cannot believe our Savior would even tell such a tale. Is our God so lacking in compassion as to turn those away who are not properly prepared, possibly through no fault of their own? I truly cannot reconcile myself with this belief.

Eawynn expressed her thoughts yesterday evening after our meeting, when we had retired for the night. She is quite skeptical about all of it, and thinks I am wasting my time and energy by questioning these parables, as she does not think there are really any answers. She also thinks it is not wise to upset the more conservative sisters. Eawynn believes in living in the present. While she shows great compassion for the plight of those who suffer through no fault of their own,

247

she also does not put up with foolish thinking. She asked to be excused from these meetings if we have more in the future.

27 June 1455
Summer at Last

Summer has truly arrived, and with it long, warm days. We are careful to wear our full habits in the parts of the convent where guests are allowed, but we are sometimes down to our under-shifts in our private apartments. Otherwise, the afternoon heat can be unbearable. If we are lucky, there will be a shower to cool things off. I like to spend time outside for an hour or so with Sister Cwenhild and Brigitta when I am able. I do tasks that do not take a great deal of walking. Carrying a feed bucket in one hand and my walking cane in the other allows me to throw feed to the chickens, geese and ducks. I can gather the chicken eggs in a basket as they are laid in boxes that are built high enough off the ground to be out of reach of some of our predators. However, I let a lad from the stables carry the eggs to the kitchens, as I do not trust my ability to carry them any distance without dropping them. Gathering duck and goose eggs is beyond my abilities, and is left to Brigitta, who is very agile. She and Cwenhild milk the goats and cows. The sheep will not return until late fall. The horses that kept for traveling stay in the pasture behind the barn, where there is plenty of grass, shade, and a good stream.

We have had more visitors than is usual lately, pilgrims on retreat from various parts of England. They come mostly to hear the singing during the offices of the day. The music is lovely, thanks to the musical talents of Judith and Brigitta. Judith has a lovely soprano voice which is complemented by Brigitta's alto. Judith also taught Brigitta how to read music. Judith's talent for arranging the music is far beyond mine, so I have given her the task of planning our rehearsals. She has composed the music for several psalms. She and Brigitta work diligently to help the rest of us learn our parts. Word of the lovely singing has spread across Northumbria, from York to Carlisle. Still, it is very brave for anyone to travel at this time. Travel is precarious at best, especially in the north of England where our abbeys are located. I am disturbed by the rumors I have heard about several clashes that have recently taken place between the king and those who follow Richard, Duke of York.

28 June 1455

Eawynn

I am watching Eawynn this evening as she sits reading in the chair by our fireplace. The book keeps slipping from her hands onto her lap as her head tilts slowly forward. With a small start, she recovers the book and begins to read again. Then the pattern repeats itself. Her eyes close as her head nods forward again. I need to wake her, and either send her back to her own bed or tuck her into mine.

I remember the first time Eawynn came to me after returning from Lacock Abbey. It was the night after our wild ride. She waited until the convent seemed asleep and quietly made her way to my room where she entered, crept into my bed, curled up around me, and fell asleep. It was awkward getting her out of there in the morning, as we no longer had adjoining rooms. I needed to contrive a reason for such an arrangement again with the abbess. At that time, we were both fully professed nuns, although both still in our twenties, and I was fast approaching thirty. What reason could I come up with other than the fact that we had spent our youth sleeping together, as close to each other as two sisters?

Since birth, my leg has periodically caused me great pain. There are times during the night when I really do need someone close by to assist me. I petitioned the abbess to allow Eawynn to sleep in an adjoining room, so I would not disturb the others if I needed assistance during the night. After watching me limp around worse than usual for a few days, the abbess finally agreed. This is the reason we have adjoining rooms now. My leg does occasionally trouble me still.

29 June 1455

Refugees

There is more news of Jewish refugees fleeing areas all over Europe. They usually travel east toward the Holy Roman Empire and beyond. We have seen families making their way from Carlisle toward the east coast to board ships for the Netherlands. Occasionally, they stop by the abbeys to rest for a few days before traveling on. Word must have spread that we are a haven. We are just careful to keep them isolated, in case they carry diseases.

The belief is almost universally held that Jewish quarters in a city acquire more wealth than is acceptable, mostly by means of usury. The never-ending conflicts between England and France, and the ongoing wars in the holy land have caused rulers to evict the entire Jewish population of a city in order to gain their resources to further national ambitions. Their status in England is precarious as they have recently been evicted from London. Other cities may soon follow this example. My heart goes out to them. Giving aid to these refugees is frowned upon by the Church. In some of the dioceses, aiding them is forbidden. So far, the Archbishop of York has not taken this extreme position, so we give what aid and shelter we can at the abbeys, while trying not to draw attention to our labors.

The way nations and peoples treat each other causes me great distress. What can be done? I often spend time praying to Our Lady to give me guidance in these matters. Will nations never learn to respect and accept each other, and live in peace? All nations and factions claim to be supported by God. Which faction of the present conflict in England does God support, the Lancasters or the Yorks? They both proclaim rule by divine right, that God stands behind them, that God supports them. What hypocrites humans are! The message of Christ has truly been ignored, from the highest levels of government to the smallest shire. If we do not lead forward in love, we will be lost.

JULY

3 July 1455

Despair

I am beside myself with grief. Adelheid went into labor two days ago. Gisela came to assist us. She was confident that Adelheid was not full term, but we really did not know when her baby was due. Eawynn and I stayed with Adelheid, holding her hands and wiping the sweat from her brow, relieved occasionally by Brigitta and Cwenhild. We tried to have her drink sweetened tea to keep up her strength, but she could not keep it down. She struggled in labor for two days, but never reached a point of dilation where she could pass the baby. The labor took all her strength. She is only a child herself. Childbirth is difficult for a grown, healthy woman. Even so, Gisela said a great many mothers and babies who appear healthy do not survive.

This morning, Aldelheid fell into a fitful sleep where she awakened only slightly during the contractions. Toward the end, she lost consciousness, which was a blessing. Finally, she stopped breathing. In a last effort to save the baby, Gisela cut into her and brought the baby out, a tiny girl child. The baby never breathed.

The lot of girls and women, especially the poor, is so terribly difficult, and that difficulty is caused by men. I do not believe, cannot believe that this is somehow God's will. I cannot believe this! This is a cruel joke indeed. This is our lot because there are men who are allowed to be cruel. Poor girl children have no value. Girls from wealthy families at least have the value of being a broodmare for their family. I must not dwell on this. I must somehow find the strength to see this through.

6 July 1455
Adelheid

This morning, we watch as little Adelheid, and her child are buried in a copse on the very edge of our consecrated cemetery. It is a pretty place, with wildflowers among the trees, and the sunlight filters to the ground in places. Eawynn insisted that Adelheid be buried here, even though she has not received supreme unction. We will make sure the spot is not recognizable as a place of recent burial. We never divulged her condition to the abbot at Lanercost, as he would not have approved of this burial. As women who are menstruating or in childbirth are considered unclean, she would not have been allowed to be buried in hallowed ground. Furthermore, the Church will not give the last rites to a baby that has never taken a breath. I believe Adelheid would have wanted to be buried with her child, two children together.

The tradition of impurity of women under certain circumstances stems from the ancient Hebrews, not from Christ himself. Jewish men who even touch impure women must then undergo a rite of purification. Although I do not know for certain, my guess is that this belief springs from Eve's sin. If God is indeed merciful, he will welcome these two blameless children with open arms, despite the absurd, detailed prohibitions of the Church. I must lock this deep sorrow and anger away in my heart until such time as Our Lady can help me heal.

7 July 1455

Comfort

Sensing my sorrow and grief at the death of a child, Eawynn appears in my chamber to comfort me as soon as I make my way there to retire for the evening. Sitting on the side of my bed, I can see that she is not herself. Perhaps it is her pregnancy. She is tired and despondent. When I last spoke to Cwenhild, she remarked that Eawynn has been lacking her usual sense of humor and mischief. Eawynn always visits the barn a few times every week to see Cwenhild and Brigitta, often for some prank or mischief. Cwenhild reported that Eawynn has not been out to see them in at least a month. When I ask Eawynn if anything is wrong, she indicates that she is just tired. When I ask her too often, she becomes annoyed with me. She spends most of her day in the library overseeing the copying of texts and aiding Sister Yvonne. I must try to get her outside more, hopefully to help raise her spirits. We both questioned Gisela about the dangers of pregnancy in an older woman. Gisela replied that pregnancy in older women is not unheard of but could be more difficult than pregnancy in younger women, especially if it is the woman's first pregnancy.

Tonight, Eawynn and I hold each other for as long as we are able. Adelheid's death has affected us all. I think I need to be comforted as much as Eawynn does. Her pregnancy is visible now when she wears her night shift. Between my old bones, that must change position often during the night, and her pregnancy, which also makes some positions uncomfortable, the bed does not easily accommodate two middle-aged women, even though we are both still slender. Eventually, she leaves me for her own bed.

It was Eawynn who showed me what it is like to truly love another person. I was surprised at the depth of feeling and completeness one could feel when loved by another. While nothing has ever been said, I feel quite certain there are others in our community who are suspicious of the depth of our friendship. Our bond is more than friendship, it is as strong as any marriage. I sometimes feel that we love each other more than we love God or His Holy Church.

8 July 1455

Acceptance

This morning, I rise from sleep hearing birdsong and take my tea in the herb garden. Everything is wet with dew. It is possible that we had a shower during the night. I often wonder how the world seems to go on despite the tragedies we experience. The sun appears every morning. The stars come out at night, and we watch the moon as it passes through its phases. Death is a part of life. Adelheid is with God. I am sure of this. Perhaps she was sent to us to teach us about love, and about the complete acceptance of those less fortunate. She is no longer tormented about her past, or in pain. Our Lady cradles Adelheid in her arms. It is our lot to carry on the best we can, to spread love and respect for all. Our Lady has imparted the following wisdom to me. Love, compassionate love, is the answer. The most important thing we do is look in the eyes of every being we meet and know we see the face of God.

This evening, I watch as at least a dozen swallows flit around in the gloaming. They appear to be playing, but I think they are hunting insects. Eawynn walks out and sits with me. We watch together as stars appear, one by one. There is no moon now, perhaps it will rise later tonight. Fireflies sparkle in the tall grass. I put my arm around her shoulder, and we return to our chambers for the night.

9 July 1455

Heavy Burdens

My mood swings back and forth, alternating between despondency and acceptance, making it difficult to find the energy to do anything. The last few days have weighed heavily on all of us. Despite the reassurances that she is just a little tired, Eawynn can hardly be roused this morning. I leave her to attend Prime and return to see if she will eat or drink anything. I offer to fetch some herbal tea, which she refuses at first. She indicates that she has blinding pain behind her eyes. We keep her room dark, and I give her willow bark tea. She detests willow bark tea, but she swallows it sip by sip. I look in on her regularly and try to continue the day's activities.

Our first big crop of root vegetables was harvested yesterday; cabbages, parsnips and turnips, as well as some peas, green beans, and kale. It is raining this morning, so we clean the root cellar to make it ready to store the root vegetables for consumption this winter. I expect we should have at least one more harvest of turnips, leeks, and parsnips, possibly two if the weather holds, from fields that received a second planting. I try to supervise this job because

Margarethe does not like being in the cellar. There are the usual spiderwebs to be swept away. It was not popular with everyone who needed to go into the cellars, but Guda never removed a spider web that was occupied by a spider. She claimed they ate other insects, particularly roaches. I follow her practice regarding spiders and snakes. Today, there are also several piles of tiny bones, the remains of rats either eaten by snakes or vomited up by owls. A few mice scamper away as we clean the corners. I see the head of a snake disappear into the wall. I did not mention the snake to the others. Margarethe goes along with me in allowing spiders and snakes, but she is terrified of both. She usually sends a novice to the cellars to fetch supplies.

In the afternoon, we aid the farm laborers, as well as several brothers from Lanercost, who are cutting the hay with their scythes, by bringing water. It is truly a sight to behold, as they strip down to their waists. I try to keep from smiling as I watch the novices sneak glances at them. Hopefully, there will be two days without rain so that the hay can dry in the fields. Wet hay produces mold, which sickens the animals. Anyone that can be spared from both abbeys assists in forking the hay onto wagons to be stored in the haylofts of the barns. The rest of us continue to supply water to the workers, as well as bread, cheese, and fruit for the midday meal. The wheat and barley will ripen soon. The process of harvesting the grains is much more complicated as they must be thrashed first to remove the grains. The grains of wheat will be ground into flour at the gristmill in Brampton.

Sister Rosamund has begun the process of dyeing the carded wool. She and Alfred spend a few hours each day supervising the novices and any nun who will assist her, which excludes Joan, Riona, and Helena. There are vats hung outside over fire pits that are filled with water and brought to a boil. The water is boiled with woad, weld or madder, as well as combinations of these plants. All of this is done under the watchful eyes of Sister Rosamund. Fresh woad leaves yield blue dye, while the roots of the madder plant produce a brilliant yellow. Red is made from flower spikes and leaves of weld. In turn, combinations of these can be used to produce green, purple, and orange. I think Sister Rosamund likes to experiment with other dyes as well, such as walnuts and beet juice. Regardless, it is a hot and arduous process, and probably the least favorite of the novices. The actual spinning, knitting, and weaving are winter chores.

11 July 1455

A Spiritual Practice

Others have fallen ill with the same symptoms as Eawynn, intense pain behind the eyes, especially when exposed to light. Eawynn has recovered somewhat but is still very weak. I manage to have her sit up in a chair for a bit each day. I try to assist her to walk outside, but she only makes it as far as the door. She has little appetite, but I insist she eat something to get her strength back, for herself and the baby. I send word to the abbot at Lanercost. He replies that several of the brothers are experiencing these symptoms as well. It is a curious malady. Those of us who are well continue our daily tasks, even as we care for those who are ill.

Today I am determined to truly look at and see everyone, every creature I encounter. This takes concentration, as my mind tends to wander, and I am easily distracted. We have a stray dog that has been adopted by the kitchen staff. He is black and white with a black patch over one eye. His eyes are light brown and have such a look of intelligence that I am certain he understands much of our language. He makes it his job to protect the back door of the kitchen from the cats.

I often meet him on my walks. When I speak to him, his presence is such that I feel a soul is present. I feel the same way about the small black cat that I have in my private quarters. She is very vocal and extremely demanding when she needs attention. However, she is also quite particular about whom she allows to pick her up. I only wish there were some way to keep her from having litter after litter of kittens other than locking her up inside, which I now do.

16 July 1455

Fever

I have had a fever for the last two days, and the pain behind my eyes was such that I could only bear being in a darkened room. I experienced dreams of incredible and awful beauty, but also terrible. The dreams occurred during sleep, but also when I was awake. I dreamt of a woman clothed in darkness but surrounded by light so bright that I had to shade my eyes. Her eyes blazed. She was glorious while in mourning and was standing on a high precipice. Her sorrow bathed the earth in her tears, weeping for the pain and suffering of those born into circumstances from which there is no escape. Her awful anger at the tyrants that perpetuate these horrors on innocents was frightening. I can only pray that there is redemption and restitution in some future time for the multitudes that suffer from the divisiveness and prejudices fueled by those in power.

Was this a vision or just a fever dream? Was the woman an avenging angel, or a deity of some other realm? Humans can be so very cruel. I question the need for such cruelty and suffering in this life. In truth, humans are not the only creatures who receive enjoyment from the suffering of others. I have watched a cat play with and torture her prey for hours before killing it. Did God design creation this way? For what purpose? My belief in His Holy Church is sorely shaken at times like this. Thankfully, the horrors of this dream fade as the hours pass.

19 July 1455

Dreams and Visions

The fever comes and goes. Although the fever has broken by the time I wake in the morning, it often returns throughout the day. The dreams have continued. Why am I having these awful dreams? I am no visionary. Last night I saw a woman looking on the earth and weeping, while gray ashes covered her hair and garments. Multitudes of people were moving in migration from chaos and famine, as polluted waters ran with blood and the fertile lands turned to desert. Pestilence and famine amidst the horrors of wars and persecution were orchestrated by those who remained in power. Even the Holy Church had turned its back on those true followers of Christ; those who preach love, tolerance, and compassion of all; those who see the earth as our mother, to be tended and cared for. The splintered sects of Christianity no longer followed the teachings of Christ, but warred amongst each other for power, position, and riches. The air had become fouled, the land barren, and the waters polluted with poisons and the refuse of an overrun and overburdened planet. This unmitigated greed is insanity. Our precious earth and everything in it is a manifestation of God. I cannot believe this is the future of mankind!

22 July 1455

Psalm 8

Gratefully, the horror of my visions has lessened, and I have not dreamed at all the last two nights. Yesterday, I was able to get up and walk around a bit. This evening, I am sitting outside in the cool night air with Eawynn by my side. She puts my hand on the small roundness of her belly and smiles. She is now reconciled to this pregnancy. I do not know how this situation is normally dealt with, as she was not made pregnant by promiscuity, but by rape. I can feel the faint movement of her child. It is a clear night, which is unusual in the summer. I can see multitudes of stars and those celestial bodies called wanderers by the ancients. I am in mind of Psalm 8.

"O Lord, our Lord, how excellent is thy name in all the earth!
who hast set thy glory above the heavens.
When I consider thy heavens, the work of thy fingers,
the moon and the stars, which thou hast established;
What is man, that thou art mindful of him?
and the son of man, that thou carest for him?"

I am in awe of the magnitude and magnificence of the night sky. I can almost hear the celestial music that attends this spectacular sight. Is it possible the Creator fashioned the Heavens with music, with sound? Could primal sound be the source of healing, for ourselves and for our world? I would strive to find the tonalities and progressions that would accomplish this, but I fear my abilities are inadequate.

As we sit close together, gazing at the night sky, Eawynn falls asleep on my shoulder. I fear for her health. Since the sickness, she is still unable to stay up for any length of time. Although she tries to be cheerful, I think she would rather be left alone to sleep. Despite the pregnancy, she has also grown terribly thin. I check on her several times during the day. She is never far from my thoughts.

25 July 1455

Heaven

As I grow older, I find I am less attached to worldly things. The practice of being in a state of total awareness in the present takes a lot more concentration than it used to. I spend time wondering what Heaven will be like, or Hell for that matter. I am worried that Heaven may not be somewhere I would like to be, especially if the duration of my stay is eternal. If Heaven is a place where angels sing unceasingly, and there is no more sorrow or strife, or even challenges to overcome, I find myself thinking how depressingly boring it might be to spend eternity like that. I like to solve problems. I like challenges. As much as I may think that the celestial music of creation is beyond words, I am not sure I want to listen to it all day.

There are people that I have known in my life that I did not or do not like. What if these people are also in Heaven? Of course, I loathe my brother, Daibhidh, but I sincerely doubt that he will be in Heaven. There were a few tutors and nurses in my childhood that were quite unpleasant and condescending that I would probably avoid in Heaven, if they were present. I learned not to ask Sisters Riona and Helena to any meeting that I called as they would argue interminably about the pettiest thing, which made it difficult to accomplish anything. They have resented me ever since and the dislike is mutual. Can I avoid them in Heaven? Do I have to converse with them and be nice to them, because it is Heaven, after all? What if the friend of my heart is not with me? I would prefer to cease to exist altogether than spend eternity without her. Also, if Eawynn is there, there will never be a dull moment. I sincerely hope the afterlife is another place where humans can continue to challenge themselves and grow.

31 July 145

As Summer Passes

The days of summer pass, one much like the previous. There is peace in the certitude of a quiet sunrise, an afternoon shower. I take refuge in the Beatitude, "Blessed are they that mourn, for they will be comforted." The Creator and the energy of creation are around us always. One only needs to stop, breathe, and listen, to feel the all-encompassing healing of God, and to allow that healing to begin. Some days I feel such faith and gratitude. On the days when I feel as if I will drown in the depths of despair, I remember this prayer to Our Lady.

Our Lady holds you in her embrace,
Evil cannot touch you.
Sorrow cannot conquer you.
Hold fast to the hem of her garment.
She will show you what your path should be,
What road you should travel.
Travel the path of love.

AUGUST

7 August 1455

Harvest

Another harvest of hay is ongoing, along with the gathering and preserving of fruits and vegetables. Cwenhild is organizing a group of girls composed of novices and oblates, as well as Brigitta, to work on a rotation, carrying water to the field laborers in groups of two. The heat has not been unbearable, but harvesting hay is hard work and the laborers must have a continuous source of water. I walk out to watch the ongoing parade of ten girls carrying water as well as some flatbread and cheese from the kitchen. The hay has already been cut and has been lying in the fields to dry. It must be stored before it rains. With some surprise, I notice that Brigitta has opted to join the men who are forking the hay into the wagons. Sister Agatha arrives shortly after me. I ask her to take over the supervision of the girls, as

Cwenhild has already joined the men to drive a team of work horses pulling a large wagon to deliver the hay back to the hay barns where it will be stored. Timothy is driving a smaller wagon with only one work mare hitched to it. There are laborers who have been hired to perform the task of unloading the hay into the haylofts. The skills needed to make this endeavor run like a well-greased wagon are impressive. Cwenhild, Timothy, and Brigitta have grown into this vocation as a team.

8 August 1455

The Meek

My reflection for today is to discern the meaning of the word "meek" as it is used in the following beatitude, "Blessed are the meek for they shall inherit the earth." I believe that Christ was referring to Psalm 37, verse 11. "But the meek shall inherit the earth." What does it mean to be meek in this context? Being meek does not imply weakness. It does not imply submissiveness, except to God. The meek have learned to listen. They know that God will provide for them here, in this lifetime, if they have faith. The meek are not easily provoked. They can easily let go and walk away from situations that would otherwise vex them.

They do not need to control others. They realize that confrontation is futile. The meek can view those who would agitate them with detached compassion. In this way, meekness imparts a quiet strength to deal with all of life's challenges in due time. Meekness is not a trait I am naturally gifted with. Nor am I trusting. Not even of God's mercy, despite the reassurances.

The challenge for me is to have patience and, in doing so, reduce my anxiety about the future. This is a message I need to hear repeatedly, as I worry about things that I have no control over when I am supposed to be trusting our Creator. That said, there is always a part of me that doubts, that does not trust. I remember too well the tale of Job, whom God allowed Satan to misuse in order to win a bet. Are we just playthings for the Almighty? Like a mouse is to a cat?

9 August 1455,

Eawynn

Although managing an abbey takes most of my time, I spend some time each day sitting with Eawynn. The last illness left her so terribly weak. She has returned to her work in the library with Yvonne, but still needs periods of rest during the day. I consider the possibility of sending her away to a Benedictine monastery that specializes in healing, but I am not certain she would go, especially with the pregnancy. She is almost five months along according to our calculations, and the pregnancy is beginning to show. I ask Sister Yvonne to require Eawynn to take time in the afternoons to rest. Eawynn objects, but it is obvious that she is grateful. I will also ask Gisela to come and see her.

13 August 1455

Travelers

A small caravan of travelers is passing through this morning. I ask Sister Margarethe to walk out and stop them, as she can walk much faster than I. When I see that their group of three wagons had stopped, I go closer to speak with them, keeping some distance between us. Sister Margarethe and I offer refreshments of cool herbal tea and some bread. The men driving the wagons are grateful for a short rest, as are the few women who come out to speak with us.

I am ashamed that our archbishop in York has decreed that those of the Jewish faith and those who are travelers, landless tinkers, are to be refused entry to any village. I inquire if they have any news or needs. Indeed, they tell me they have just been through an epidemic and still have two very sick men in one of the covered wagons. They have only lost one elderly woman to the sickness. Sister Margarethe and I offer what assistance we can without making direct contact with them. We allow them to camp some distance from the convent itself for a few days to rest and offer some supplies for their journey. In exchange, they give us the news of the area west of Carlisle and offer to mend pots and pans. They are not Jewish. They say that everywhere they go, they are asked to move on. Townspeople have called them names, but otherwise, they have received no ill treatment. Apparently, it has been worse for Jewish families. In Carlisle, the houses of the Jews were ransacked, and their men were beaten. We are fortunate to have met these tinkers as their work with kitchenware is excellent. They even sharpened the knives. I pray for their safe journey.

14 August 1455

A Visit from Gisela

Gisela stops by to examine Eawynn early this morning. She brings Maud and Ellie with her and tells them to go find something useful to do. Evidently, she does not trust them enough to leave them at her cottage by themselves. I lead her to Eawynn's bedroom where we can have some privacy. She feels for the baby and says it seems to be fine and developing normally, although she reiterates that she is always concerned when a woman in her forties gives birth, especially if it is her first child. She also examines Eawynn, feeling around her throat, under her arms and around her breasts, and looking carefully at her eyes. Eawynn laughs and asks, "Do you wants to check my teeth, like a horse's teeth are checked before it is sold?"

Gisela responds, "That is a very good idea," and proceeds to peer into Eawynn's mouth with a flat stick holding her tongue down. Eawynn gags so hard I think she may throw up.

Finishing her examination, Gisela tells us that she thinks Eawynn's tiredness stems from the pregnancy and recommends lots of sleep, slow walks, and sitting outside in the shade. She instructs her to drink dandelion tea, which I know Eawynn does not like, so I will have to sweeten it with honey. Gisela also instructs her to eat three meals every day, whether she feels hungry or not. She thinks Eawynn should not be working any longer, at least not until her health has improved.

We leave Eawynn to rest. As we walk outside, Gisela draws me to one side. She says she is very worried. Just because she can find no distinct cause does not mean everything is well with Eawynn. Gisela cannot determine the cause of Eawynn's weakness, but believes it is a sickness of the spirit. She does not think spending time in a Benedictine healing center will help. Gisela is concerned for both the mother and the child. To lift Eawynn's spirits, Gisela urges that every effort should be made to show Eawynn how truly valued and needed she is in the community, despite the mishap that has befallen her. Gisela stresses that Eawynn needs the support of those who love her, now more than ever. With that, Gisela asks in the kitchen where her two apprentices might be. Margarethe informs her that she thinks they might be with Sister Agatha and sends one of the novices from the kitchen to find them. I leave her there and go back to check on Eawynn, who is fast asleep on her bed.

17 August 1455

Divine Right

Today my prayer is a short, but earnest one, a prayer for the leaders and rulers of the Church and the realms. I am not sure prayers are effective, but still, I make the effort. There are many who have prayed daily for relief from inescapable misery to no effect: a dying child, more nutritious food, the health of a husband or wife. I do not think God hears all those prayers, or perhaps he does not listen. The prayers that are answered are those where the answers are wrought by the hard work of our hands, and sometimes even that is not enough. The rulers of our country and the leaders of the Church certainly cannot be relied on for aid. They only take. There is something very wrong with the idea of the divine right of kings. Being born into a royal family does not make one fit to rule! Those who seek power in whatever form do so for their own selfish reasons, certainly not for the good of their subjects. The horrors of poverty, slavery, wars, and persecution are in evidence all around us. The good services provided by the Church come from our small local establishments, not from the leaders who live in luxury far removed from the misery of the world. Such hypocrites!

22 August 1455
Fasting and Health

As religious, we are often called to fast. There are many holy days throughout the year where fasting is required. Just as it is important to know and understand the treatment of illnesses of the body, it is perhaps even more important to understand how to keep the body in good health. Fasting of any kind and for any reason should only be in moderation, and never for the purpose of self-denial. The body, like all creation, is a manifestation of God and should be treated with great reverence. Fasting is never for children because it would cause harm.

A healthy diet that is varied, with abundant grains, fruits, and vegetables, dairy cheeses and occasional fish, fowl, or meat will promote vitality. Just as important is sustenance for the spirit, time every day set aside for contemplation or even simply a break from labor. This is as important for lay people and workers as for religious people. It is especially important for women, as I have noticed that wives and mothers often do not seem to have any time in which to renew their spirits. Often, all they would need are a few quiet breaks throughout the day, away from their duties with a cup of herbal tea.

I am adamant that the physical and spiritual needs of everyone at our convent are well taken care of (and well deserved), from the most important nuns to the lowest kitchen or barn laborer. We have made a start, scheduling at least two breaks during the day built into their daily schedule, each lasting one quarter of an hour. We also allow a half-hour break for the midday meal. It is up to the nun who supervises each area to make certain this is implemented. I have required those nuns who oversee different areas of the convent to keep a journal of how this is progressing. Yvonne, Rosamund, and Margarethe readily agreed. Only Mathilde and Cwenhild have put up any resistance to this idea, saying they agree with the concept, but are much too busy to journal its implementation. I have advised them to have another nun or novice in their area charged with that duty. All employers, in whatever capacity, should do the same. There is nothing more important than seeing to the health of all. Only when these needs are truly satisfied can one be free to experience God fully.

23 August 1455

Solitude

While community and friends are so very important, never underestimate the value of learning to be alone. Beyond our fears and loneliness is the immense quest for self-knowing that can only be accomplished when we are forced to stop and really see ourselves. Few would volunteer to be alone, but learning to be alone is so, so necessary for spiritual growth. Growth is almost always uncomfortable, and sometimes even painful.

I considered sending Eawynn to the Benedictine monastery at Westminster that is devoted to healing, but I have decided against it. She is too weak to even ride a horse. Cwenhild, Brigitta, and even Yvonne and I are taking turns being with her so that she is not alone. We make sure she eats, and Cwenhild assists her to take short walks, a little longer every day. I sit with her outside in the shade for an hour in the afternoons.

24 August 1455

The Word Was Music

"In the beginning was the Word, and the Word (logos)
was with God, and the Word was God."
John 1:1

The Word implies sound. How astounding that the Word, the source of all creation, is sound! The sound from which the energy of the universe sprang forth in all its melodies, harmonies, unison, polyphony, and discord. Indeed, the Word is the celestial music of the spheres.

Through my ignorance and humble talents, I try to recreate this beauty, though my representations are mere reflections to be sure. Judith is far more gifted than I am. I believe she is truly connected to the creative source in such a way that the music flows from her. Music is the life water of the soul, and it surrounds us. If only we would stop and listen with stillness in our minds! Music, the Voice of God.

SEPTEMBER

5 September 1455

Grapes and Hell

Autumn is nearly here. I can almost smell it. There are already some leaves beginning to color. Cwenhild is busy with farm laborers repairing the enclosures for livestock before the flocks are brought in. Most of the hay and silage has been stored, but Cwenhild thinks there may be one more cutting of hay if the weather stays warm. Every nun and novice that is physically able is picking grapes to make wine and mead. I find Brigitta and Cwenhild to be exceptionally fast at picking the grapes. They have been in a contest with each other all morning. The bulk of our grapes is sold to Lindisfarne. The remainder is used to make wine and mead for us. This will be the first year that Margarethe has been in charge of making the wine and mead. She has

283

assured me that she is very nervous that it may not turn out well.

Mathilde and her novices are exempt from this duty as they must care for the children. They walk the children out to the vineyards to watch us work and let them pick a few grapes to eat. While they are here, a large group of noisy, honking geese flies over in a V-shaped pattern, heading south. The children are thrilled to see them, as the pattern of their flight changes constantly, with small groups of geese filtering in and out of the pattern in smaller formations.

While there is no connection between grapes and Hell, picking grapes gives me a great deal of time to think. Lately, I have been thinking about Hell, perhaps because I am reaching that stage of my life where the options of either Heaven or Hell are inevitable. Will the fact that I question so much of the Catholic faith determine where my soul goes after death? Despite this, I will not stop questioning in my quest to understand what meaning life has. I am most unrepentant about my search for answers. The idea that sinners who do not repent will spend an eternity in torment in Hell is unconscionable. I really cannot see how this judgement can be considered justice for the sins of such a short time on earth. Is this the judgment of a merciful and loving God? Does God consider the special circumstances of our lives? So many are born into and live in squalor and poverty. I think there must be some misunderstanding or error in this translation of the Gospels. Did Our Lord really mean that any who did not follow Him, even those who had not heard of Him, would be eternally damned? I do not accept this. God is a God of love who loves all of creation.

7 September 1455

Eawynn

Eawynn's health has improved a bit under the special care that Gisela insisted she follow, although she is still tired, and very thin. She is given a special diet and spends much time sitting outside in the warm sunshine. She is taking a short walk with me when the abbot intercepts us as he passes by on some errand, and kindly inquires about her health. It is good to have his support in this difficult matter. She is almost six months into her pregnancy. Despite trying to contain the knowledge of the events that led to her condition, word has gotten out and I think almost everyone knows. If anyone blames her in any way, I have not heard of it.

Gisela comes by weekly to examine Eawynn, with Ellie and Maud in tow. She puts on a smile of confidence when she talks to Eawynn, but I see the worry and fear in her eyes as she leaves. She has confided in me that she fears Eawynn might not be healthy enough to carry the babe to term. I pray to Our Lady daily. Knowing that I must trust and let go of my fears, I try to trust, but trust about personal things never comes easily for me.

9 September 1455

Worry

Every task I undertake during the day is an effort to stop my constant worrying about Eawynn. Aside from participating in the hours with the other sisters and novices, I set aside time to write and practice new sacred music. Even so, there are certainly days when I am relegated to just practicing the songs I already know. Inspiration often does not come, nonetheless, the very act of writing every day is important. Tending the vegetable and herb gardens, just being outside, helps to momentarily bring me out of my dark thoughts and worries.

Today, Eawynn comes to my study and speaks with me at length. It is the first time she has acknowledged and given voice to her fears and feelings about her condition. She laughs at the way Gisela keeps up a positive attitude around her. Eawynn knows she is ill, with a sickness that cannot be cured. She is trying to stay healthy as long as she can, for the baby. She makes me hush when I protest. She asks me to be honest with her about everything. She says that death is not something she fears. She worries about me, about how I will cope without her. As much as I want to deny everything, I will do as she asks. Her request is that I spend as much time with her as I can, knowing that her time is short.

11 September 1455

Acceptance

With all the great wisdom and learning of the Church, with its many trappings and traditions, with all the abilities of humans to analyze and solve daily problems, I am quite often reminded of how simple life really is.

We have in our community a young male adult, Alfred, who was left as a baby at our convent over twenty years ago, presumably because he is very different from most humans.

I have seen this condition before. Because of his condition and sweet disposition, it was decided that he would not be sent to Lanercost, but instead be allowed to remain in a place where he is truly comfortable and valued. Humans born with this condition have faces that are rounder with slightly slanted eyes. Their dispositions are usually quite happy, and they seem content to do the most menial, repetitive tasks with such good will, taking such pride in their work! He has been working under the supervision of Sister Rosamund for several years now, carding, dyeing, and spinning wool. Rosamund has often said he is like a loving son to her. He helps her immensely, and always with such good cheer.

When I have had to make a complex decision and have analyzed the problem from every possible outcome or approach, until I have thoroughly confused myself, I have learned to ask Alfred for his thoughts on the issue. I have often been surprised at the quality and simplicity of his response! I asked him if he had ever lost someone that he loved deeply. He replied that he had. Then he turned and regarded me with a searching gaze. He said, "I know about Eawynn. She will be well, because she is already part of everything. You do not ever need to worry about her." Life is so simple, and I inevitably make it more complicated. Love is always the answer. Love and acceptance.

20 September 1455

Dark Thoughts Indeed

How do I love?
How do I love the man who beats his wife?
How do I love the mother who abandons her children?
How do I love the landowner who turns out a tenant family
      on a winter night and they freeze to death?
How do I love the evil rulers, both secular and sacred,
      who fleece those in their care of all they own?
How do I love those who revel in their evil deeds?
How do I love a mother who sells her younger daughter to
      a convent to provide for the resources of other
      siblings?

This is my struggle. Every new day I arise faced again with the opportunity to love; the kitten playing with my shoes, the sad, old barnyard dog, the cook in the kitchen, yelling at her helpers because she is not feeling well. How do I love those who are hateful and cruel? Our Savior bade us, "Love your enemies and pray for those who persecute you." I love because I must. I must separate the person, made in the image of the Creator, from that person's deeds. I find this very challenging indeed, as challenging as forgiving my enemies an infinite number of times. I resolve to love, and yet, I am often unsuccessful. Often. Every day is a new beginning, to look into the eyes of those who commit evil and know that they too are beloved of God. Then, I wonder if the Almighty is even aware of our deeds, good or evil. If we are to become like Christ, we must learn to look with infinite compassion on all. At this I am failing greatly.

24 September 1455
On Growing Older

As I grow older, I find the need to be more mindful of how I move. The wrong move can cause pain in the hip or the neck, and a wrong step can cause a fall and possibly a broken bone. It takes a special kind of effort to remain vigilant to my body's movements. I have been taught this lesson the hard way, with falls that left me in pain for several days. Despite this, I cannot say that I have entirely learned this lesson!

There is a special kind of stepping, of walking, when kittens are underfoot. It is like having eyes in one's toes, a sliding motion that is never quick and always controlled. When I am mindful, I can do this quite well without tripping or losing my balance. If I forget, the consequence is that I either step on the kitten that is underfoot or lose my balance trying to avoid it. This only happens when my mind is occupied with something else. Being constantly aware of my surroundings, my thoughts, and my actions is good training for all situations in life. At the moment, I am seated in Eawynn's room, thankful for her presence which fills me with such joy, and grateful for the warm, fluffy black cat that is curled up on my lap!

26 September 1455
Gratitude

It is the season for picking and drying elderberries berries. Margarethe, Bernia, Kendra, Avice, and Brigitta are picking elderberries, cleaning them, and laying them on fine meshed cloth to dry after they are cleaned. I help with the cleaning task because it allows me to sit down. Blessed Mother, forgive me, because I really dislike cleaning elderberries. It takes forever. They are a wonderful tonic in the winter for all kinds of ailments, and we never seem to have enough to last until spring, so we are diligent about preserving as many as we can.

The dried berries are boiled with honey to make a syrup that must be used soon afterwards, because it does not keep well. With our honey, we also produce an elderberry mead that does preserve very well. I prefer not to keep too much of this readily on hand as it is a favorite drink of some of our community, and I find that it mysteriously disappears. Mead is also a wonderful tonic for winter illnesses. After the last bout of illness, most of us are finally blessed to be busy and healthy again.

27 September 1455

Chickens

Kendra and Brigitta make a fascinating discovery this afternoon. Chickens love elderberries. Chickens become so excited when some elderberries are tossed on the ground. The girls spend a great deal of their time throwing handfuls of elderberries around the barnyard instead of working. I must admit, it is interesting to watch our chickens squabble over the elderberries, but even more entertaining to watch the girls! It is a pity that I finally must put a stop to it. We never have enough elderberries to last the winter. Also, I do not know how the berries will affect the birds as a source of food. We will need to check on them.

Regarding chickens, I was walking by the hen houses this morning with Cwenhild, trying to find out what caused an ungodly racket last night. We found that at least two of the hens are missing. We are trying to find out where the hen house was breached but have failed to do so. I was very worried about our broody hens and their little charges, but they are fine, as they are kept in a separate enclosure.

The flock of hens and two roosters roam the grounds by the barn in daylight. There is almost always someone around to keep a watch out for predators, of which there are many, mostly foxes and badgers. At dusk, the chickens go willingly into their hen houses that are equipped with perches and baskets in which to lay their eggs. I suspect this was the work of a badger. A fox would have indiscriminately killed many more chickens. Life is never dull here. Sometimes I wish there was a bit less drama.

Every evening is spent with Eawynn, relating the events of the day. I did take a short walk with her after the midday meal, after which she returned to her room to rest. She tries to remain interested, but I can see how much the effort of listening tires her. Mostly we sit in a companionable silence and read, or doze.

29 September 1455
The Bishop's Appeal

The sky is an extraordinary blue this morning, with a stiff breeze from the north and frost on the ground. I expect our flock of sheep will arrive from their summer pastures soon. We are ready! Root crops are in the cellars, grapes have been pressed, hay and forage for the animals are put up, although Cwenhild still thinks there may be one last cutting of hay. Our herbs are dried and stored. I do wish we had more rose hips and dried berries but, barring unforeseen catastrophes, we will make do.

A letter arrived from Carlisle telling of a visit from the bishop to Lanercost in two weeks. Of course, he and his retinue will also visit Lambley. Thank goodness they will be housed at Lanercost. I will discourage their presence at Lambley any more than is absolutely necessary to avoid any unwanted attention from some of his retinue to my young novices and oblates. The primary purpose of his visit is to attend the initial profession of vows from three of our novices, Bernia, Kendra, and Avice, as well as the perpetual renewal of vows for all the sisters. The second reason for his visit is to evaluate our stores and ascertain our tithe to the diocese. I pray that his stay is a short one!

OCTOBER

4 October 1455

The Harvest

The weather has been most cooperative for the final cutting and harvesting of hay. Though scything and gathering the hay is wearying, the harvest is an assurance that the animals will have enough for the winter. Eawynn and I walk slowly to watch the hay being unloaded from the wagons into the haylofts this morning. She asks to walk to the river beyond Lanercost Abbey. Her steps are sure and strong, but she is tired by the time we return to her room. Thankfully, it has grown cooler, and the forests are ablaze in golden leaves! The nights are almost cold enough to start fires in the fireplaces, but the wood that is stacked and stored for the winter months needs to be conserved. It worries me that we have not had rain in over a month. It seems there is a dry spell every fall.

Bishop William Percy will arrive with his entourage in a week. I think we are prepared for his visit. When Nicholas Close was bishop there were never any issues with the behavior of his entourage. The post of bishop is political. Bishops and archbishops are replaced at the whim of the king. One only needs to remember Thomas Becket and his fate. He was Lord Chancellor to Henry II. He was not even a priest when he was appointed to the post of Archbishop of Canterbury. The present bishop is very lax about the behavior of some of his retinue and tends to look the other way when they take advantage of our hospitality. We already learned hard lessons on a previous visit in October of 1453 when one of his priests made some very unwelcome overtures to a few of our younger novices. We had to have him bodily removed from the novices' sleeping quarters. The bishop blamed the girls for leading him on. I requested that the priest in question stay at Lanercost in the future. Gratefully, this priest was absent last year.

Since many of our stores are kept in separate cellars, which have been made quite inaccessible for purposes of accounting the quantity of goods, the tithe to the bishop will be reasonable. The younger children, boys as well as girls, and novices will be kept very busy for the duration of the visit.

11 October 1455
The Bishop

William Percy, the Bishop of Carlisle, arrived this afternoon at Lanercost. He immediately sent one of his priests, who introduced himself as Father Andrew, to inform us that he and a few others will visit Lambley mid-morning tomorrow. They plan to audit our holdings of root crops, fruits, hay, and grains to ascertain a fair tithe. We will meet with the bishop at the church of the Blessed Mary Magdalene after our midday meal for the service of profession. Kendra, Bernia, Avice, and the widow, Martha Beaufort, will be making their initial profession of vows, while the remainder of us will renew our vows. I expect the service will be short.

There will also be a service immediately following ours for the brothers or other religious of Lanercost to be initiated as monks or into the priesthood. Father Andrew told us that their group would be leaving for York immediately after the services and would not be able to stay for any celebration.

He did not disclose why they were traveling to York, but I can only think it involves the archbishop and possibly the political situation.

At our celebration in the evening, I would be lying if I said I missed them. Sister Margarethe has a wonderful evening meal of roast goose prepared, with a glass of our special mead as a treat, and small cakes made with dried fruit and honey for dessert. I notice that Sister Avice helps a great deal with the serving. I ask Margarethe afterwards about Avice. Apparently, Avice likes cooking. I do not know why I thought she would prefer working with the children under Sister Mathilde.

Although Eawynn takes her meals in her room most of the time, mostly to avoid awkward conversations, she joins us for the celebratory meal. Both Margarethe and I tend to monitor how much Eawynn eats. She has little appetite but makes herself eat for the sake of the child. This is not the Eawynn of old, who had a very hearty appetite. I pray daily to Our Lady that Eawynn stays strong enough to deliver a healthy baby. After that, I fear the worst. For a time, I worried that Eawynn would not be able to care for a baby born from such circumstances. The topic of the baby, and her feelings toward it, came up only once, and I will see that it is never mentioned again. It was Brigitta who inquired of Eawynn, quite innocently, if it would be possible to love the child of a rapist. I thought Eawynn was going to slap her. Eawynn angrily hissed that the baby was hers, only hers, and completely hers.

13 October 1455
Eawynn

Eawynn seems to have gained some strength back, although this changes from day to day. Too much exertion one day results in exhaustion the next. Much to her chagrin, I have restricted the activities that she may undertake to sewing and mending, activities that she previously avoided as much as possible. Even research and writing in the library with Yvonne is too strenuous, as she must stand for extended periods of time. Today, we walked out to the barn to view the flocks that are returning from the summer pastures. The shepherds were in the process of moving the flocks into the abbey's enclosures. As much as she enjoyed the walk, I fear it tired her.

15 October 1455

A Cold Wind

We are all breathing easier now that the bishop and his retinue departed without incident. Every fall I fear that our hidden stores of root crops and preserves will be found. There is a frigid north wind this morning. Thankfully, the shepherds and their flocks are fully returned. They are grazing in our nearby pastures and can be brought into the holding pens if the weather turns brutal. I should not be surprised by how much the two puppies have grown, but I am. They left as playful puppies and returned as trained guardians of the flocks. They are ever watchful and never leave their charges. They regard me with complete disinterest. I pray Our Lady will look over us in the coming months. Winter may be a time for reflection, for reading and mending and weaving, but it can also be very difficult.

Although there has been very little improvement in Eawynn's condition, she seems in good spirits. She often tries to participate in activities, but her energy drains quickly, and she needs to rest. I have contrived to have a large bed, and she sleeps with me at night, but her sleep is restless. I fear she is in pain, but she denies it.

18 October 1455

Winter

Today, the weather has been cold and bleak. The wind was relentless all afternoon, and it is sleeting this evening, which makes being outside miserable. When she came in for the midday meal and a quick visit with Eawynn, Cwenhild said the poor sheep were huddled together for warmth. Thank goodness for their warm winter coats.

We are blessed that we are ready for this season. Although it is still autumn, it already feels like winter, and I fear that winter will be longer than usual this year. Regardless, we all need this time of rest. Winter is the time for the earth to sleep and heal. This time of rest and renewal is also important for the forests and meadows that God has granted to our care. We can care for these precious places and nourish them, or we can use them up. While I understand the need, it saddens me to know that so many of our great forests had previously been cleared for pastureland, firewood, and lumber, but I am strengthened in the knowledge that many are now growing back. Reoccurring outbreaks of the Black Death since the 1300s have decimated the human population in England. Many former homes and hearths have been abandoned. The forests are growing back in England and, from what I have heard, all over Europe as well.

20 October 1455

Eawynn

Eawynn is ailing again, very weak and pale. I have asked Gisela to stay with us for a few days and tend to her. Gisela agrees only on the condition we provide transportation every morning and evening, as she has much to tend to at her own cottage. Donal has agreed to provide Gisela as well as the novices with transportation. They will come every morning and return early in the afternoon, before it grows dark. He has provided them with horses, so the journey takes only a quarter of an hour each way. Ellie and Maud are accustomed to walking, but they tend to dawdle. Margarethe will need to find something for the girls to do while they are here.

I sit with Eawynn this evening, holding her hand. I reminisce aloud about days gone by, about the adventures of our youth. She nods her head as I continue and smiles, then squeezes my hand. There is one memory that is etched in my brain as if it were yesterday. Fifteen years ago, Eawynn and I were traveling with a group of four brothers from Lanercost to Carlilse. It was early spring, and the sheep were in the process of being shorn. Eawynn and I were the only women asked to go by the abbess so we could negotiate the sale of our wool for Lambley separately from the brothers of Lanercost. We were only carrying a small sample of our finest wool. Our negotiations had been quite successful, and we were in the process of returning from Carlisle. The group had made camp in a copse of trees on a hillside of the moor. We were already asleep when raiders struck our camp. They tied the brothers up and separated them from us, while they ransacked the camp looking for anything of value. They left us in our tent, guarded by a formidable looking scoundrel with red hair and a red beard. A giant of a man. The raiders acted like they were angry when they found we had nothing of any great value. We did not even have much food, as we were only a day's ride from the abbey. They released the brothers in the morning, with instructions to travel to the abbey and give a note to the abbess that Eawynn and I were being held for ransom. They also described a place to retrieve us that was two days ride over the Scottish border.

How can I describe our captors? They were not outlaws. It seemed that this raid had been conducted more for their enjoyment than for any hope of gaining wealth or resources. They did not handle us roughly but did insist that we remove our wimples and veils. I could not understand the purpose of this, until I noticed that one of our captors, a tall young man with dark hair and eyes, surprisingly clean shaven, had a more than passing interest in Eawynn. She also realized that she was becoming the recipient of unwanted attention. At that point we refused to be separated for any reason. We ate, slept, and took care of our bodily needs together. Any friendly advances, and there were quite a few, were ignored. No harm came to us, and we were treated with civility. The realization came that these were not common ruffians, but some young Scottish nobility, out for some fun.

We traveled for two days with them, reached the appointed area, and waited. Much to our surprise, help arrived within a day. We were approached the following morning by a troop of about ten soldiers, accompanied by three of the brothers from Lanercost. Our captors quickly disappeared into the brush, vanishing like mist on a summer's morning. Apparently, only one brother went on to inform the abbess of our situation. The other three had ridden back to Carlisle to enlist the aid of the bishop. He was responsible for quickly gathering a guard of soldiers to rescue us. As I finish my tale, Eawynn nods and smiles, her eyes closed. I proceed to make myself ready for bed.

22 October 1455

Our Lady, Let Me Not Lose Hope

My spirit is a desert, dying of thirst. Every day is time standing still, waiting. The world seems devoid of color, just gray horizons in the distance. What is my purpose? What is God's purpose for me? Why do I have these bouts of hopelessness? Eawynn is slowly slipping away from me, and I cannot bear it, but I must show a brave face.

Gisela feels that the baby may come early. Eawynn calculates that the baby is due the second week of December. Gisela is insisting on complete bed rest for the remainder of the pregnancy. Eawynn is allowed to get up to use the privy, or to walk with assistance to the dining area, which is not far, but that is all. It is common for physicians to prescribe that women be confined throughout their pregnancy, but Gisela believes that practice to be unhealthy. She feels that some activity, especially outdoors, is best to ensure the mother is healthy after the birth, but only if the woman is healthy to begin with. It is not the pregnancy that is making her ill. I fear it is the wasting sickness, for which there is no cure.

NOVEMBER

6 November 1455

A Prayer to the Blessed Mother

Today, more than ever, I must rely on the gracious kindness and wisdom of our eternal mother for guidance. She has never failed me, even when I have failed myself. I pray earnestly and daily for Eawynn's health to be restored.

> "When we, unhappy mortals,
> shamed from generation to generation
> are waylaid on our pilgrim path,
> you call to us with a prophetic voice
> and lift us up from our hard fall.
> Praise to you, O Mary!"

A prayer of Hildegarde of Bingen.

14 November 1455

Distracted

I have had difficulty settling myself down to do anything. I finally decide that I need to begin writing again, even if I only write of the day-to-day events. It has been cold, raining on and off for three days. A flux has passed through the entire community rendering everyone helpless for at least a day. Thankfully, due to her seclusion, Eawynn was not affected. The brothers at Lanercost have also been spared. We have ceased all contact with them for the duration. As the disease seems to spread throughout the community, there are always a few who are well enough to tend to our animals. The illness seems to be fading now, and I am grateful no one was seriously ill. I am curious as to the cause. If it was something we ate, would not all of us have become sick at the same time? How does it spread? Is it spread from one person to another? If we knew, we could take measures against this happening again.

I force myself to practice my lute and my harp again. It has been several months since I touched them with any dedication. I enjoy making up new tunes, but I have had few new ideas all summer. Every time I try, nothing comes.

25 November 1455

A Cold Awakening

We are shivering at Prime this morning as the fire has gone out in our small chapel fireplace. Did anyone check it after Compline, or during the night? I cannot remember. I usually go through Compline half asleep. The singing at Prime is pitiful at best. I can hear teeth chattering from the cold. Even Judith and Brigitta cannot keep the melodies going. Prime is perhaps my favorite of our times of prayer, just not today! It takes everyone a while to thaw out enough to see to our needlework and knitting this morning. Confinement seems to keep Eawynn's condition stable. She is not better, but at least she is not worse. Since she began sleeping with me at night so I can monitor her, I have noticed that the baby seems more active at night. Last night, the constant kicking woke both of us several times.

Outside is a beautiful scene, as it snowed all day yesterday and last night. The snow is up to our knees. Everything looks so pure and clean, although I am sure the workers did not appreciate digging their way to the stables this morning. The storm has passed and the sunlight on the surface of the snow is dazzling. Once, this glorious sight would have filled me with joy. Now, the future fills me with dread.

26 November 1455

The Novices Return

This morning, Ellie and Maud return for the winter from Gisela's cottage in the woods, bringing with them several stocks of herbs that she uses for healing, as well as copious notes they have taken about finding these herbs, and the methods of drying and preparation. They have even illustrated a small leaflet with beautiful drawings of these plants. A thorough inventory of what is stored in the way of herbs and tinctures must be undertaken to assure that there is enough to last until next summer. We help the local population as needed, but we need to ensure there is enough to keep us healthy as well. There are plenty of dried berries and rose hips.

I will need to familiarize myself with the information the girls have learned. They have requested to visit Gisela occasionally, and I have no objection. I suspect that Gisela is not a follower of Christ, but I trust her to keep her opinions to herself so as not to unduly influence the girls. When I first met with Gisela, before the girls were apprenticed, she expressed grave reservations about behavior she had witnessed several times from Christians that she could not agree with, although she stated that she had no problem with the actual teachings of Christ. I agree with her that there are hypocrites among us who use the mantle of Christianity to further their own interests. They persecute those who do not agree with them, even other Christians.

30 November 1455

A Serpent in Our Midst

Like all communities, our two communities are not all kindness and civility, although I certainly wish it were so. As the abbess at Lambley, it often comes to me to settle the little disputes, the unkind words, and sometimes the downright meanness. Although I really dislike the role of arbitrator, peacemaker, and sometimes judge, I must remind myself that these incidents can also be a time for growth. I usually call all those involved, even the spectators, and let them discuss the problem and look for solutions. This does not always work.

Most members of our community are kind and caring towards each other. We generally discourage unkind actions or words, but occasionally, we have someone who is cunning and deliberately mean. Such is the case this week with an older, wealthy widow, Martha Beaufort. She joined our community about six months ago, claiming a vocation for the Lord. It started with small situations that were hard to prove. This woman is very devious and clever. She has even tried to involve the abbot at Lanercost. Both Sisters Margarethe and Yvonne have spoken to me, relating that they have heard her question my decisions. Sister Beaufort dislikes Cwenhild and her rudeness to Cwenhild is apparent to all of us, although Cwenhild shrugs it off and ignores her. Sister Beaufort also objects to Brigitta's attendance at the liturgical hours because Brigitta is not a novice. Although I have confronted Sister Beaufort with facts, she is now claiming to be a victim. I will need to make a hard decision, as she has divided the community with her actions. The problem is how to treat her with compassion, when I feel so much apprehension about the damage she has already done.

I should not have titled this journal page with the word serpent. I find most of the snakes in our barn are excellent at keeping the rodent population down. I have always wondered why Satan was disguised as a serpent in the Garden of Eden. I cannot even think of an animal so despicable as to be used for that purpose. Maybe a wolverine. Then again, maybe not. Being intentionally despicable seems to be part of the human design. I just need to digest that for a moment, the fact that humans are made in the image and likeness God.

DECEMBER

2 December 1455

Slander

The widow, who is now Sister Martha Beaufort, has accused me of showing favoritism to several nuns, but especially to Eawynn, and has even hinted that our relationship is more than mere friendship. As if anyone would believe this at our age and with Eawynn's precarious health! Certainly, this would make a scandalous story. We have never felt a need for discretion, and we have no need now. Many in the convent know that we have slept together for years. We have always declared ourselves to be close friends and true sisters. We have never shown any untoward signs of affection publicly. At one time, we slept together for the company of comfort. We do so now so that I can watch over Eawynn, whose time grows near.

I publicly denounced the older widowed nun as being slanderous and preposterous!

I do not believe God cares who we love.

3 December 1455
Patience and a Plan

I have asked Our Lady for the patience to calm the dissension in our community in such a way that no one is isolated or injured. I meet with several older, long-serving members of our community, which includes not only the sisters who are in charge of various areas, but also lay women who have served us for some time, many of whom have come to me with concerns. We agree to work with patience to teach others, both by quiet admonition and by example, to immediately quell any talk of gossip or slander that we hear by simply refusing to engage in any discussion that involves such.

Hopefully, this will eventually take root as a preferred form of reaction, and the entire mess will settle down. If not, I will need to take a more active role and address the entire community to take no part in any slanderous gossip, but to do so passively, by simply not engaging.

4 December 1455

The Story of Job

We never know just how strong we are until we have been tested beyond endurance and yet still prevail. I do believe that life tests us, not to break us, but so that we can truly know our strength. Unfortunately for some, the trials of life are too much to bear, and for some, the circumstances of their lives leave them bitter. I often wonder why humans have such different life stories, talents, and experiences. It seems unfair that some have so much, and others are born with so little.

After carefully reading the story of Job again, I became aware that God did not cause Job's afflictions directly, as I had previously thought. God told Satan that Job was a pure man who would never renounce Him, no matter what. Satan disagreed. God then allowed Satan to test Job beyond endurance. As if our Creator would ever feel the need to prove a human's love for him.

Job suffered horribly and needlessly to prove a point on a bet between God and Satan. It was not enough that he lost his home, his herds, and suffered with boils; he also lost his children. Because of Job's faith, God promised Job that he would restore everything many times over. How does one restore a child? With another child? Losing a child is a grief that does not heal. This must be the projection of human jealousy upon the divine nature of God. I cannot believe our Creator could be so petty as to allow so much suffering to prove a point. If it is so, then I want no part of this God.

Last night, the baby moved around much less than usual. This morning was the same. Eawynn is very worried that something is wrong. Gisela has stopped visiting as often due to the weather, but I will make her aware of this new development.

7 December 1455

Damp Wool and Disrespect

I cy rain is making a pattering sound on the dead leaves this afternoon. What a cold, windy, dreary day! Everything feels damp. The smell of damp, woolen outer clothes drying near the fireplaces fills the air, along with the smoke. We are seated close to the fire with our handiwork. One side of me is very warm, almost too warm, but the other side is so cold that I must keep turning around. Even with my woolen socks, my feet are cold. I think my porridge grew cold coming from the stoves to the dining table this morning!

In the midst of this we have received a letter from the Archbishop of York, another summons. I cannot imagine traveling in this weather. Hopefully, it will clear up soon. I will not leave with Eawynn so near her time. I will send word to the archbishop that one of our number is very ill, and that I will leave as soon as the situation resolves itself, one way or the other. I did not include specifics.

I had Cwenhild send someone to bring Gisela to the abbey, as the nasty weather persists. When Gisela examines Eawynn, she says the babe has dropped into position. She also reassures Eawynn that the lack of movement right before birth is normal. She returns to her cottage after, saying said she will return tomorrow and stay until after the birth.

At least the discord amongst the community has died down, and we are treating each other with more compassion and respect. Our troublemaker, Sister Beaufort, seems to have gotten the message, but I fear this is not over. She did approach me last week to complain that others are avoiding her, that some are not even responding when she speaks to them. Of course, she blames me.

8 December 1455

Time

It is morning. Eawynn wakes earlier than usual, complaining of a backache and contractions. The contractions seemed to go on for some time, then stop, and then return. I am hopeful that Gisela will arrive soon.

It is evening. The contractions have become very regular. Gisela arrives and has checked Eawynn twice and has confirmed that this is not a false labor. We alternate between rubbing her shoulders and her legs, as she complains of cramping. Gisela has shown her how to breathe through each contraction by panting. Eawynn has not been allowed food since midday but has had broth to drink for strength. I did not realize that solid food during labor could cause problems. Eawynn falls asleep between contractions, even though there is very little time between them. Gisela reassured me that sleeping between contractions is normal and helps to preserve strength. Having Gisela here gives me courage.

I walk outside for a moment, at Cwenhild's coaxing, to see the night sky. The colors come often in the winter months, but not like this. The sky is ablaze with every color, swirling and dancing across the entire sky, as if the sky is breathing. I can only remember an experience like this once before, when I was young, just after I had first come to Lambley. Even so, it was not as brilliant as this. I return to Eawynn's side, wishing that she could see the lights, but her attention is totally inward. It is as if she is listening to music the rest of us cannot hear.

9 December 1455

Birth

Just before midnight, Gisela allows Eawynn to push. She says the baby is crowning and ready. With all the strength she has, Eawynn pushes, never crying out, barely making a whimper. I know she is exhausted. The baby is partially out with the cord around its neck when Gisela shouts at Eawynn to stop pushing. I hear Gisela flip the cord off the baby's neck with a snapping sound. Eawynn is told she can push again, and she does with tremendous effort. The child is born. Its lips are blue. Gisela breathes into its tiny mouth just as it lets out a loud wail. The baby is a girl, with reddish fuzz covering her head and a lusty cry. Eawynn reaches out to hold her tiny daughter immediately, desperately trying to stay awake. As she starts to doze, Gisela takes the baby and cleans her. The baby is rooting around, trying to suck. With Gisela's help, the little one latches onto Eawynn's breast easily, but is frustrated when nothing is produced. We have a wet nurse with a baby of her own already in residence, in case Eawynn is unable to nurse. I hate to wake the wet nurse, but it is necessary to feed the baby. We put her with the wet nurse in the same room for now. She is a kindly woman in her late twenties, with ample milk for her own child as well as Eawynn's baby.

After waking, Eawynn asks to hold her daughter again. She announces that she will name the child Isolde. She is adamant that the child be kept in the same room with her, even when nursing from the wet nurse. It is obvious that she loves the child fiercely. Throughout the afternoon, several visitors come by quietly to congratulate Eawynn and to see Isolde. Margarethe and Mathilde sneak in long enough to plant a kiss on Eawynn's forehead. Cwenhild stays longer, standing by the cradle that Timothy made and watching the child sleep with a tender expression that I had never seen on her face before, not even after delivering a baby lamb.

Brigitta tiptoes in while both mother and child are asleep, grins and tiptoes out. Now that Isolde is cleaned up and swaddled, I can see the tiny, pouting rosebud of a mouth. As I place my finger near her tiny hand, she grips it tightly. I never really thought of a newborn as having much of a personality, but I was wrong. Isolde is very demanding when she is hungry.

Tonight, the fiery dance of lights in the sky continues. I insist that Eawynn be carried outside in a chair to see this fantastic display. She agrees to go out, but only if she can hold Isolde. We watch the shimmering show in silent wonder. In my mind, I can hear the celestial music that should accompany it. Would that I were talented enough to reproduce such music, but I think doing so would be impossible. As we gradually grow colder, we take Eawynn and the babe back inside to their beds.

12 December 1455

A Visit to York

We leave for York this morning. It is difficult to leave Eawynn, but I am under orders from the archbishop. I know Eawynn and her tiny daughter will be well cared for, but I will worry about Eawynn's health every moment that I am away. The sun is up and reflecting brilliantly on the trees and grass that are covered with ice. It is almost blinding in its beauty. The sky is a deep blue, and the weather looks to remain clear. It will take us almost five days to get to York. As Eawynn cannot travel, I have asked Sister Avice, who took her initial vows last October, to scribe for me. She is a competent horseman and should complete the journey without slowing us down.

From the archbishop's correspondence, I gather the meeting is about something important, although I have no idea what. My mind jumps to the worst conclusions. Can someone have informed him about the burial of Adelheid and her child in consecrated ground? It has been one of my worst fears, although I feel completely justified in my decision and my actions. God does not punish someone for circumstances beyond their control. God does not punish the actions of those born into poverty and misery for trying to survive. I believe in a God who understands the hearts of all people and loves them no matter what. It is the hypocrites who wield their power over the lives of so many that need to answer for their actions.

16 December 1455

Yorkminster

As we ride into York, I feel a familiar thrill upon viewing the great Yorkminster Cathedral, which is nearing completion. I have only seen it a few times. My heart is always divided when I view such a work of wonder dedicated to God, because I am then reminded of the toil and suffering that went into its construction.

22 December 1455

Martha Beaufort

We returned home this morning after meeting with the archbishop. The archbishop, William Booth, kept us waiting for over three hours in a very cold, unheated alcove. I miss the previous Archbishop, John Kemp, who supported my work and believed in me. Booth is not a man I can trust to have the best interests of our convents at heart. He told me that he had heard of disturbing events at our convent. He questioned my ability to act effectively as abbess, and mentioned that he was thinking of replacing me, that he would have already replaced me except that he feared it might provoke an uproar. Evidently, he must have thought

I would be supported by my sisters, as well as the abbot and brothers at Landercost. His suggestion for my replacement was none other than our wealthy troublemaker, Sister Martha Beaufort. Imagine my surprise!

I believe I finally convinced him that she would make a wonderful abbess elsewhere. Such a ruckus over nothing. Although Avice was extremely helpful, especially in helping me manage with my twisted left leg, I missed Eawynn. She has better insight and instinct about situations than I do. Her counsel has often kept me from doing something foolish. Avice has grown tremendously since she professed her initial vows, and I am proud of her progress, but I cannot confide in her the same way. My leg hurts from riding for five days each way. I must remind myself that those in power in the Church are not necessarily men of God, they are political appointees. They are often the sons of wealthy or noble families who do not stand to inherit, and so are granted, for purchase, high ranking positions in the Church. In fact, real men of God in these positions are somewhat of an anomaly. I consider myself blessed to have met a few. The present archbishop of York is the creature of his master, Henry VI of Lancaster.

23 December 1455
Home

Visiting Eawynn is my priority upon our arrival back at the abbey. Immediately upon returning from a journey, I normally make sure my mare is well-cared for, but this time I simply hand her reins over to a stable boy and leave. I walk straight to our room without even removing my cloak. Eawynn is asleep. I can see the faint bruising under her eyes and the bluish tint on her mouth. Baby Isolde is also fast asleep in her cradle, while the wet nurse, Anna, is in my adjoining room tending to her own child, a month-old baby boy named Bran. She smiles as I enter.

Happily, Isolde is thriving, but Anna tells me that she is very worried about Eawynn. She mentions that Gisela comes by every few days to check on them both. Anna tells me how much she misses her family and wants very much to return home to them. For the present she is needed here. The abbey pays her well enough to ensure she will stay. I offer to have her other child brought to stay with her and suggest that her husband would be welcome to visit as well. I suggest that we arrange a bedroom of her own for her, with cots for her children, that is close enough to Eawynn's room to be convenient.

I am sitting by Eawynn's bedside having a quiet conversation with Cwenhild and Mathilde when Eawynn awakens. She smiles wearily as I reach out and hold her hand. Her hand feels cold to the touch, so I order more blankets for her, even though the small fireplace has been well banked, and the room is quite warm. Since the wet nurse and her child have been sleeping in my room, I order a cot to be placed in Eawynn's room that I can use for now, until other arrangements can be made.

26 December 1455

A Time to Rest

It is the day after the birthday of Our Lord. What a special time to reflect on his message and his sacrifice. Outside we have a fresh blanket of snow. It is so quiet. It does seem so much quieter on a winter's morning with snow on the ground. Is there a reason for this?

The earth is sleeping, resting and recuperating from the enormous energy expended to make everything grow in the summer months. This is also a time for us to rest. We take care of the daily tasks that must be done and spend a great deal of time in quiet contemplation as we go about the tasks of knitting and sewing. Rosamund's young apprentice, Alfred, is creating the most intricate and gorgeous needlework I have ever seen. It is a tapestry of the church of the Blessed Mary Magdalene! I believe his skills have completely surpassed the rest of us.

Eawynn seems better. She can sit up and spends most of her time simply holding Isolde. I marvel at the way she coos at the baby and even insists on cuddling her when she is asleep. She surrenders Isolde to Anna only when the child must be fed. She is devastated that someone else must breastfeed her and change her clouts. Eawynn and I have been close friends for a long time, and I have never seen her so attached to anyone as she is to this child. Her appetite seems to have improved, and I am hopeful that she will heal.

29 December 1455
Martha Beaufort

Since our return from York, Sister Martha Beaufort has become truly insufferable. She questions every decision I make, sometimes publicly, even implying that she should be given the position of mistress of novices because I am too lax about their development. This attitude is absurd, coming from someone who spent four months as a novice and knows nothing about the administration of a monastery.

Today, my deliverance has come! A letter from the archbishop arrived this afternoon, requesting that Martha Beaufort be escorted to York where she will be placed as prioress of St Clement, an Augustinian Priory that answers directly to the archbishop. Evidently, Sister Martha is someone he needs to placate because she is a Beaufort. She is to leave as soon as possible. I will personally help her pack her belongings. I will allow her to take her remaining inheritance with her. I will offer prayers for the good sisters of St Clement. They will need them.

I am considering the possibility of sending both Sister Riona and Sister Helena as well, as they both seem to get on well with Sister Beaufort. I will inquire into this matter as soon as Martha Beaufort has been securely placed at St Clement.

31 December 1455

The Seasons

As the light begins to return in this cycle of the seasons, we spend some necessary time in quiet contemplation, not the simple vows that are part of our normal waking and working hours, but the solitary contemplation that comes without distractions. For me, this is more than the silence we observe going about our daily work, it is a time of deep, solitary quiet. I request that all nuns spend an hour every day, except the Sabbath, in complete solitude. Those nuns who are in charge of the various activities of the convent will need to arrange this, as we cannot all attend to this at the same time. I make no demands about how the hour is spent. It can be on a walk, sitting in the gardens, or in the chapel. It can be spent anywhere, so long as the hour is spent in solitude and contemplation. We will continue this practice until Easter.

How reasonable that the cycle of days should be divided into separate portions. The time of sleep and renewal is followed by a time of intense planting and preparation, that fully manifests in growth and production. Following this, the harvest and a different kind of preparation for the winter sleep begins again. How fortunate that our lives follow the same pattern.

My thoughts have often considered the many trappings and traditions of the Church that rule the day-to-day moments of our lives. I imagine most religions have these. I question their relevance and purpose except to control the lives of the participants in some way. More and more I feel the need to ignore all the little "do" and "do nots," preached with the fiery threats of some hellish afterlife if we do not comply. Only the important basics remain, to treat all of creation with respect, compassion, and above all, to love. God is love. God loves all. We should love all as well.

LINDA MARIE BROWN

THE YEAR OF OUR LORD

1456

333

JANUARY

3 January 1456

A Blizzard

How quickly the silence of winter becomes a threat to survival! The snow is falling so thickly through the afternoon sky that the tree line beyond the garden is not visible. It has been snowing since the beginning of the new year. Unfreezing water for livestock and keeping the paths to the barns and the holding pens cleared so that fodder can be distributed have become the top priorities for both abbeys. Cwenhild has put together a rotating list of those who must carry water and break up the ice in the watering troughs. I am with Bernia and Kendra, a group of three, two young nuns and me with my twisted leg. Even though I am not as strong or capable as some of the younger sisters, I find that working with the others instead of ordering them about helps keep morale up. Naturally, Sisters Riona and Helena are

334

exempt. They claim that performing this type of labor is not in their agreement. They quickly make themselves scarce by retiring to the sewing room. I let them go. It is more trouble to fight them than to just ignore them. I will write to the archbishop soon to see if they can be rehoused with Prioress Martha Beaufort in York.

When Alyce, Eugenia, and old Sister Joan began to complain about the hardship of what is undeniably a difficult and exhausting job, I draw everyone together for a speech, a talk about priorities. A bad attitude does not help a bad situation. This blizzard threatens our very survival, and we will do what we must to survive. As each group finishes their task, they come in by the fire and thaw out, until it is time to go back outside again. Hopefully, the blizzard will stop soon. There has been little time to rest as we must maintain vigilance for the younger stock. At least the chickens and ducks seem content and secure in their coops. We have yet to establish contact with Lanercost. The bright side of this new year is that Sister Martha Beaufort is now a Prioress in York.

Eawynn is up and about, taking short walks around her room with Isolde. While I visit, she helps set up a table and chair for a desk and requests that Yvonne bring her some work to do while Isolde sleeps. When I suggest needlework, she scoffs and says she would rather clean out pigsties. Gisela recommends that the wet nurse Anna stay at least six months. At that time, some soft foods and goat's milk can be introduced into Isolde's diet. Anna's other child, a darling little boy of two years, has also come to stay with us. He spends much time with Henri in the orphans' wing of the abbey, looked after by Mathilde and her novices. Apparently, he is a favorite. Anna's young husband has also visited a few times, but only in the evening as his work during the day keeps him very busy. He is a blacksmith in a small hamlet between here and Brampton.

9 January 1456

Compassion

An incident occurred yesterday that greatly disturbed me, so much so that I spent the better part of a sleepless night considering the events in our lives that shape us into the complex creatures that we are. A young boy of fourteen in Brampton was beaten very badly by his father. His mother and brothers feared for his life. I do not understand why they brought the boy here instead of to

Gisela, as the distance to the convent is twice the distance to the healer's cottage.

As the mother and one of her other sons dropped the boy off, she spoke with me, trying to explain and excuse her husband's behavior. She told me that this boy is very different from her other sons. He does not like boyish activities. He acts in a very feminine way. It seems the father had been drinking before he came home. The very sight of his son sent the father into a rage, claiming he would kill the boy. I have seen boys like this before. They often endure terrible abuse from the community in which they live. I helped Mathilde bind his wounds and sent Maud to fetch Gisela. Gisela came quickly, as quickly as one can come in this freezing weather. At least it is not snowing. Gisela set three broken bones and reported that his skull had also been fractured. He will need bed rest, and we will tend to him here. His name is Cuilen. If he survives, perhaps we can find a place for him here or at Lanercost. I will speak to the abbot.

What kept me awake last night was trying to understand, to make sense of what it is that causes these tragedies; the lack of kindness and consideration between family members, the child whose mother neither loves nor protects her child as she should, the child abandoned by the father, the physical and verbal abuse that is allowed. Often, what saves those who experience abuse is the grace of kindness from someone outside the immediate family, a stranger or a tutor. It is our experiences that shape us and cause our growth and resilience, but also affect our ability to love. We can become compassionate towards those who suffer, or we can become bitter and hate filled. As often as I have tried to forgive, I find there remains a small part of my heart that is hardened against those who have intentionally injured me. I have asked our all-compassionate Creator to help me to forgive completely, yet I find I am still attached to my injuries after all these years.

I pray to Our Lady that I behave deliberately and with compassion toward all, aware that I do not know their hidden suffering, and aware of how my actions and words have the power to injure or to heal.

13 January 1456

Cuilen

Cuilen's health increases daily. I sit with him for a while every morning. I make sure he is never left alone. He complains very little, only to say that his head hurts. When Gisela hears that his head is hurting, she advises keeping his room dark, as light apparently makes the pain worse. We do not allow him to leave his bed, as a head injury can be made much worse if he moves around. His other wounds seem to be healing. Our novice, Judith Devereaux, has taken it upon herself to watch over him. I heard her singing to him this evening, very softly, as if to sing him to sleep. Eawynn also spends some time sitting with him, sometimes with Isolde in her arms. She thinks he is a tender and sensitive soul. He does not talk about his family at all. Eawynn believes he has suffered a great deal, both physically and emotionally. His mother came to visit once, and he barely responded to her. She is grateful that we are caring for him, but she does not want him to return home. It is finally time to speak with Abbot Alexander Walton about Cuilen's future.

17 January 1456

Sickness Returns

As I venture into the barnyard this morning, I meet Cwenhild, who has more contact with the laborers than I have. She informs me that several people have become sick in the surrounding area, a sickness that affects breathing and is accompanied by a severe cough and fever. Margarethe informs me that she has already been handing out our berry tinctures and herbal mixtures to those who have come to the kitchen door requesting help. I have been so preoccupied with Eawynn and Cuilen that I was unaware of these developments. Two of the elderly in the nearby village have died, and one child is gravely ill. I fear the little one will not survive, as he was sickly to begin with. So far, those who live at the abbey are unaffected, but I feel it is only a matter of time. I am requiring the village folk who work here to stay home, if they, or any of their family members, start experiencing symptoms.

19 January 1456

More Sickness

The number of those who are sick is steadily increasing. Gisela has contacted me, requesting some of our herbs, dried berries, and rose hips, as she has also been inundated with villagers requesting assistance, and I sent Maud to her with supplies. Gisela has been such an immense help this past year by agreeing to teach our two novices her herbal knowledge, and I am grateful. We pray daily for the health and recovery of those affected.

Spending time with Eawynn has become my favorite time of the day. Isolde is very active, lying on her back in her cradle while she examines her fingers. We have brought her some of Henri's toys that he has outgrown. They catch the light as they hang and move above her crib. Her eyes follow the movement. She seems to recognize faces, as her eyes follow Eawynn around the room. I believe I saw a hint of a smile yesterday. Due to the outbreak of sickness, access to have to Eawynn and any of the children in our care has been greatly restricted.

20 January 1456

Cuilen

I walk through the path that has been cleared to Lanercost this morning to speak with the abbot about Cuilen. I take Judith with me to help me along the way. It is very cold, and the sunlight reflecting off the snow is dazzling, almost blinding. Although dirt has been thrown on parts of the path, some spots are still quite slippery. I must step carefully. Sometimes I think I am not the right person to explain this situation to the abbot, but who would be? I leave Judith in a waiting room while Abbot Alexander Walton greets me and immediately offers me a seat by the fire, then orders hot tea. I begin by telling him the details of Cuilen's arrival, describing his condition, his healing, and his apparent disposition. The abbot expresses concern for him but is not certain that Lanercost would be a good place for him. He feels that there might be brothers who would despise him because of his femininity. I did not say so, but I suspect there are many monks and priests who are like Cuilen. So, the abbot is not sure if he can help, and it might be up to me to find a place for this young man. At least the abbot agrees to meet with Cuilen once he is completely healed. Truthfully, I do not know whether Cuilen likes girls or boys. How do I even bring up this subject with him? Do I really want to know? This is not a situation I have ever dealt with before. Perhaps Eawynn can help, as she still spends a little time with him every day, and they seem to enjoy each other's company.

21 January 1456
Retribution

The illness sweeping through our community and the surrounding area is very serious. It does not discriminate between God-fearing and heathen but does seem to affect the very old and the very young much worse than the rest. The symptoms are similar to an illness that occurred several years ago, although this time many more in the surrounding community have died. The simple cough with a few days of fever either subsides within a short time or increases with symptoms of bloody flux. It is terrible to stand by helplessly, especially with the children. Our stores of herbals are almost gone. Inexplicably, many of our religious community who were very ill during the last episode have only experienced mild symptoms this time. Cwenhild, Kendra, and Bernia became ill before anyone else. They are still weak but are well on their way to recovery. Yvonne and I have not been affected by this illness. Those who are not sick work themselves to the bone helping others. I am beside myself trying to make sense of this.

The bishop sent two Doctors of Medicine from Carlisle to assist us. They attempted to help us at Lambley, but they were worse than useless, and I sent them away. They were filthy creatures who proposed the most ridiculous remedies, such as sheep's urine. The unfortunate people in the surrounding area that they treated grew worse and died. I have more faith in Gisela's remedies.

Unfortunately, I have heard rumors from Cwenhild that things are becoming ugly in the village. She listens to the talk of the shepherds and barn laborers and brings the news to me. I would like to know the origin of this gossip. Someone is spreading the belief that this plague is God's retribution for our sinfulness, the sin being that there are those who are not Christians who are allowed to live among us, a small community of Jews as well as those who follow the older beliefs. Sometimes, those who are stricken with grief over the loss of a loved one will willingly blame anyone who is different. I find this reasoning, or lack of reasoning, to be very frustrating, but it is impossible to try changing their minds without becoming a target as well. I pray this passes quickly before the situation becomes dangerous.

22 January 1456

Tragedy

We received word this afternoon from Alaric's son, Timothy, that a group of villagers turned Gisela out into the snow and burned her cottage. I quickly send Sisters Alyce Marie and Eugenia, who are both fully recovered from the illness and often walk to the village for supplies for the kitchen, to the home of Gisela's adult son to see if she has sheltered there. The sisters return to inform me that his home is being watched. They spoke with Gisela's son, who informed them that he has not seen her. To turn an older woman out in the deep of winter! What cruelty! I have a few of the shepherds seeking her in the countryside. It will be brutally cold tonight. We at the convent are better protected against the wrath of the villagers than Gisela's family, although they are professed Christians. If we can find her, we can secretly provide shelter until we find a solution. Although I would be devastated at losing her, it is unthinkable that we would also lose her vast knowledge of healing.

Prayer to Our Lady

O most gracious Mother of divine wisdom.
Who did not abandon your Son at the cross.
We plead with you.
Do not abandon your children.
We know you watch over all God's children.
All the children of the earth are yours.
We most humbly implore you.
Protect those who are persecuted from the wrath
of angry mobs.
Aid us in our time of great need!

25 January 1456

Our Healer is Found

Gisela has been found! God be praised! Donal thought to check the summer pastures and found her in one of our shepherd huts. He left her with firewood and what little food he had brought with him. I sent him back with more supplies, enough to keep her for a few days. Even if the villagers find her there, I doubt they would burn one of our buildings, but I have no idea how she might be treated. Only people that I trust know her whereabouts.

27 January 1456

Good News

The news from Gisela is good. She is managing well, and the abbey will keep her supplied. After her assistance in our time of need, I feel strongly that she deserves our support. Eawynn suggests that we have her brought secretly to the convent for the remainder of the winter. It is a good idea. I need to figure out how to go about doing this.

This morning, after persuading Eawynn to take a short walk outside, we sit bundled up, side-by-side in the courtyard, watching the birds that are eating the grain and dried breadcrumbs tossed out on the snow from the kitchen, and pecking at the suet hanging from a tree limb. What a multitude of shapes, colors and sizes! They are fierce in their rivalries in this cold weather. Some flit about, while others scold and bully. The jays and magpies are the worst. I love to watch the little titmice and chickadees. Their feathers are all puffed out. I think this must help them stay warm somehow.

Eawynn nudges me in the side to watch as one of the kitchen cats, a multicolored cat of orange, black and white, silently stalks the birds from behind a bush. The cat moves slowly and stealthily, advancing forward step by step, low to the ground. Suddenly it rushes at the birds in a veritable flurry of feathers, but they all escape! The cat finally leaves, and the entire sequence of avian squabbling begins again. The variety of birds is simply astounding! The entire drama is entertaining, but I feel Eawynn growing weary. She is not as animated as she would normally be at such a display. Eawynn tries to hide her exhaustion, but I can see how easily she tires. We walk arm-in-arm back to the convent and to her room, where I leave her, sitting with Isolde in a rocking chair that we borrowed from the children's wing.

29 January 1456
The Plague has Ended

Yesterday, at our midday meal, Cwenhild told us that another chicken had gone missing from the henhouse a few weeks ago, and as her body had not been found, it was assumed that a predator had carried her away. She said no chickens have disappeared since then, which she found to be odd, as she has never solved the mystery of how two chickens previously disappeared. Her news today is that the chicken has been found, with a brood of nine chicks! Evidently this chicken has a secret hiding place in the hen house that no one knows about. Marvelous and mysterious are the ways of chickens! It is a little early in the year for baby chicks to hatch, but Cwenhild thinks they will survive, snuggled beneath their mama's ample wings.

The illness that has plagued us seems to have subsided. Only one of our number died, a young girl who worked in the kitchens. We are fortunate. We received better care than most of the families in the surrounding area.

Gisela is surviving in the shepherd's hut. It is a crude structure but must serve for now. Someone that I trust, Timothy or Donal, checks on her and brings supplies every three or four days. I have no idea how this will work out. I can hope and trust in God, but it is our efforts to assist her that have saved her for now.

FEBRUARY

1 February 1456

Cuilen

What is to be done with Cuilen? This is a question that has been plaguing me for days. He is feeling much better, sitting up in a chair and taking short walks around the room. I have tasked Eawynn with gaining his confidence and, if possible, persuading him to confide in her as she stops by to see him for a bit each day. She has even brought Isolde with her, in hopes of making Cuilen feel at ease enough to tell her about himself. He has been mostly unresponsive to her questions, although he admitted that he likes small helpless creatures, especially babies. He also likes to sing. I have heard him singing with Judith. He has a lovely tenor voice.

I also asked Judith, since she seems quite fond of him. She has had much better luck in gaining his confidence. I think she must have confided some of her own thoughts and feelings. Unlike most of our novices, Judith does not seem to have any physical attractions, either to men or to women. Her only desire is to serve God. She has been teased about her complete devotion to God by some of the other novices, mostly by Ellie. When Sister Agatha and I speak to the other novices and insist that the teasing stop, they tell me a great deal more than I really want to know about their own feelings. I admit, they embarrass me, and I think they actually enjoy embarrassing me. They do not dislike Judith, but think she is odd. Most of them freely admit that they are attracted to some of the young men who work on the grounds or deliver goods from the village. Some are even attracted to a few of the brothers at Lanercost. On the other hand, Cwenhild has made no secret of the fact that she prefers women, even though she has taken a vow of celibacy that she claims she will never break. But I digress.

Cuilen confided in Judith that he likes everyone, but also that he likes to dress in women's clothing. He finds women's type of dress more pleasing, and he likes jewelry. In all honesty, I have no idea what to do with all this information.

I do not think I can let him wander around the convent dressed as a woman. I cannot even imagine the uproar that would cause.

3 February 1456
My Meager Efforts

The weather has been dreary the last few days: overcast, very windy, and cold. This afternoon, at least, the sun is shining. I am dragging myself through the hours of the day. We have an hour allotted for silent contemplation during Lent. Today I drift off in Eawynn's room by the fire, until Sister Agatha wakes me. She shakes me gently on the shoulder, and I wake up with a start, not knowing where I am or what time of day it is. She gives me a moment to compose myself, then speaks in a voice that is very near tears. She wants, no, needs my assistance with some novices, who are feeling restless from being cooped up. They are having difficulty being quiet and are trying her patience. Agatha is very young to oversee the novices, but there is no alternative except to learn as she goes. In a moment of inspiration or insanity, I suggest that she gather up everyone who is restless, have them bundle up and go outside. Eawynn, who is sitting near me, suggests they have a snowball fight. Whoever heard of such a thing? I have never even seen or been in a snowball fight. Apparently, Eawynn has. We watch from a window in the learning room as Bernia and Kendra join the novices in the meadow where the children play. They make balls of snow in their hands and throw them at each other. A few snowballs even hit their mark, resulting in loud squeals of protest. After a short time, they grow weary of flinging the snowballs and turn their creative talents to building snow figures. At this point, Agatha comes back inside, thanks Eawynn for the suggestion, and collapses in a chair, out of breath, but smiling. I am a little concerned as one of the snow figures begins to bear a striking resemblance to an attractive young brother at Lanercost. Several of the girls spend a great deal of time perfecting this snow figure. Eawynn remarks that she is impressed with their attention to detail.

Finally, tired of being outside, they troop back inside, leaving their coats and boots in the mud room that Timothy had completed. I have hot tea brought to the sewing room, and we make our way there, where they crowd around the fireplace to thaw out. The rest of our time is spent quietly, spinning and weaving cloth, sewing, repairing, and knitting garments. My swollen fingers protest at these duties. The cold of winter affects my joints much worse than the blessed warmth of summer. I let this time of industry pass for the hour of solitude that is required of all religious until Easter. I allow myself and all religious members of our community an hour every day to pursue whatever our hearts need or desire. Today, what was needed by the novices was to play in the snow. This should happen more often. I think young adults need this as much as our children do.

Unlike the novices, I like to spend this free time practicing the harp or lute. When I feel inspired, I also attempt to write melodies. When I was younger, I liked to take walks or rides with Eawynn if the weather was nice. Lately, I like to nap. Just before retiring for the night, I walk outside for a few moments. The moon is out, and the sky is ablaze with stars, a few even appear to move. The snow and ice covering the tree limbs sparkle like crystals in the moonlight. My heart nearly stops in awe at the unspeakable beauty of it all.

7 February 1455

Community Service

Tomorrow, the abbeys will resume the schedule of visitation to the surrounding community to see how all are coping, especially after the illness that decimated our part of England this past winter. Some of the brothers from Lanercost have once again offered to help us, and I will ensure that no women from Lambley will travel without male companionship. It may take several days to cover all the outlying areas. I will no longer take part, as I am reluctant to participate after my ill-fated journey with Eawynn last March. Those who were sick have recovered fairly quickly at both abbeys. I am certain there must be families and individuals, especially the elderly, who may have been overlooked or forgotten. All will be visited. I feel strongly that this is our mission.

The Church should serve its community, not the other way around. Lambley Abbey does not ask people in the area for alms, as the local people have so little to begin with. Both abbeys are mostly self-sustaining, although visiting pilgrims and some of the wealthy families in the vicinity often offer donations.

All too often, to maintain the facade of power, wealth, and beauty, churches require more than they give back. There are so many in authority who are drunk on the power and wealth they can wield. They have completely forgotten the mission of our Lord. As Christ said to Peter in the Gospel of John, chapter 2, verse 17, "Feed my sheep."

9 February 1456

The Hands of God

It is still cold, but the bad weather has held off. Although overcast, there has been no additional snow. The schedule of community visitation began yesterday as groups of nuns, accompanied by brothers from Lanercost, spent the morning in Brampton village going door to door to find out if or how they might assist, noting who needed food and/or medical assistance. Brother Edward traveled with Bernia and Kendra, returning by late morning to the abbey. Edward later related to me that the two young nuns handled the various situations well. Fortunately, except for a few cases, the people of the village have been actively assisting each other.

Upon their return, Kendra told me of an elderly man without family who lived alone and was unable to adequately care for himself but was also very stubborn and difficult to deal with. The other case that greatly concerned them was a widow with five children and no male family members to assist her. The children were doing poorly, having been ill. This family had little food to sustain them or firewood to keep them warm. Today, Bernia and Kendra took supplies to both homes, and Edward, along with Timothy, offered to help the old man, as he requires someone strong to aid him. These two cases will be checked periodically.

Tomorrow the groups will begin journeying into the surrounding countryside. We pray daily at Prime that God will alleviate the terrible suffering brought on by the illness and this harsh winter. We also pray to Our Lady for guidance in all our actions. In these dire situations, our hands are the hands of God.

14 February 1456

Animals in Need

Cwenhild, aided by Brigitta, Avice, and a few brothers from Lanercost have spent two days traveling through the area outside the village. I have waited for their reports each evening as they return, tired and in distress about what they have encountered. They made their way through the countryside as best they could, carrying supplies on pack horses so that they could give aid immediately. A few of the hovels with elderly required medical attention and food. Surprisingly, there were several dwellings that were empty except for starving animals that had been abandoned, some still closed inside. In one cottage they found three deceased bodies, a woman with two children, that had been dead for quite some time. The bodies were frozen. There is little anyone can do now as the ground is too hard to bury them. This will need to be dealt with at a later time.

I am troubled about the animals. The dwellings with animals inside, mostly dogs, were left open so the animals could at least get out and fend for themselves. We can spare little food for them at this point. The abandoned livestock were given enough food and water to last until they can be retrieved. I have asked the shepherds to bring these animals to the abbeys as soon as possible. They will find homes for the livestock. I am sure not everyone was visited, but better weather is needed before anyone ventures farther away from the abbeys. It is an arduous business, and it is beginning to snow again. The women I sent are exhausted and need time to recover. God grant us the courage and stamina to continue His work.

15 February 1456

Gisela

I walk to the stables to speak with Alaric's grandson, Timothy, this morning. He has been bringing supplies to Gisela. I ask him to bring her to Lambley to stay for the remaining cold months. There is a small room at the end of the corridor near my study that is not in use where she can reside for now. One of the stable laborers must have been listening to my conversation with Timothy, as he angrily confronts me for assisting a heathen, making it clear that he thinks we should turn her out. I remind him that God is the judge, that we should not stand in judgment of someone who has spent her life serving her community. I also caution him to hold his tongue and threaten to remove him from our abbey if he spreads the tale that we have sheltered the healer. How can I judge someone whose beliefs differ from my own without at least attempting to understand her? This will be an opportunity for mutual learning. I can only hope I hear no more of this.

Christ gave us the commandments that supersede all others. Love God and love each other. It is really that simple. These are not all the laws, actions, and consequences found in Leviticus. These are not all the rules and regulations put forth by Paul. Love God. Love each other. Christ did not say love only Christians. He did not say we can pick and choose whom to love. He did not say persecute Jews, Muslims and heathens. Christ said love. God is love. So simple. So, so simple. Just love. Why do we have to make it complicated?

16 February 1456
Eawynn

While others in our community are assisting the surrounding community, Eawynn spends most of her time either napping or holding Isolde, who is now gurgling and smiling at everyone. Eawynn is also working a bit each day in the library with Yvonne. She is excited about some old, musty manuscripts from the twelfth century, recently received from a university in Cambridge, that require translating from Latin to the vernacular. Evidently, they are not sacred, but secular. Even so, I will be very glad to have Gisela with us for Eawynn's sake. She seems to have stabilized but has shown no real improvement. Exhausted, she retires early every night. Last night, she requested that I sit with her for a while. Doing so, she took my hand and asked me to swear by God and Holy Mary that I would raise

Isolde if anything happened to her. I kissed her on the forehead and told her that her fears were foolish, although, in my heart, I know they are not.

17 February 1456

Lambing Season

Lambing season has begun! Every year it is the same. Our first lamb arrived this morning. I do not look forward to the racket that will ensue, but I pray for healthy lambs and ewes because it is still quite cold. The shepherds are on duty all hours of the day now to monitor and assist with the deliveries.

Timothy arrived with Gisela this afternoon from the shepherd's hut where she has been hiding. I have not had time to speak with her in depth about her situation yet, except to learn that she is estranged from her grown children and their families. She told me that they have accepted the Christian faith. Because she has not, they will have nothing to do with her. The room furnished for her at Lambley has a small hearth, a bed, and a simple desk and chair. It is quite secluded, but cozy. The two girls who stayed with her, Ellie and Maud, have volunteered to supply her with whatever she needs. I prefer to keep her separated from the rest of the community. There is no point in inviting trouble. I hope she will be comfortable.

18 February 1456

Gisela

It is late afternoon now. I am spending some time becoming better acquainted with Gisela. Eawynn joins us for a short while before she leaves to visit the children's wing. I ask Gisela about herself. She does not know exactly how old she is. From her appearance, I would estimate that she is about my age, perhaps a few years younger. She is an attractive, older woman with a motherly build, long, thick hair that has started to become gray, and startling blue eyes. She relates that she has never learned to read or write, but has developed her own system for recording things, such as her herbal remedies. Her recorded knowledge was lost when her home was burned. What knowledge she has now is what she can remember, or what was written down by Ellie and Maud, who spent time with her. It is enough. It has to be enough.

At first, she is reluctant to talk about her beliefs, but relents when I press the issue, trying to make her understand that my intent is not to judge, but to understand. It is evident that she is much more comfortable discussing medical matters and herbal remedies. To help put her at ease, I tell her about myself, that I have studied many religions, including the religions of the Ancient Greeks and Romans, as well as the Norse gods, and I find all religions to be of great interest.

Slowly, she confides in me that her beliefs have come primarily from her father's mother, who also taught her herbal lore. Believing that everything has a spirit, even rocks and mountains, connects her to the natural world. She feels that everything is connected, part of the whole of creation, and deserves respect. I have not come across this kind of belief in my research. The concept of worship is foreign to her, although she cares deeply for all living things. Over the years she has expanded the herbal knowledge that had been passed on to her, both by trial and error, and by observation of cause and effect. Until recently, she was respected as a healer in the community. Somehow, very recently, that began to change. She does not know or understand the source of this distrust from the community, but suspects it has to do with what she calls the "new religion." I do not know for certain, but I suspect the distrust was intentionally started by the two medical doctors sent from Carlisle and encouraged even more by the local physician. Essentially, they have poisoned the well.

22 February 1456

Gisela

Today, Sister Yvonne and I spend several additional hours in conversation with Gisela, with Eawynn in and out of attendance. I am surprised at Yvonne's interest. She must have discovered that we were sheltering Gisela from Eawynn, who has worked closely with Yvonne in the library for years. Yvonne is quiet, but evidently, very observant. When I ask why she wants to be included in our discussion, she replies that her interest is purely historical. She thinks that Gisela is from an age of beliefs that is passing by and will soon disappear. She wants to record those beliefs as accurately as possible.

Trading information about methods of healing has been the main topic of our discussions. Yvonne knows a great deal about the history and art of healing in ancient times, much of which is as ridiculous as what our modern physicians do. She is a true historian, being much more interested in the research aspect of healing than Eawynn. Every attempt is made to honor Gisela's beliefs and wisdom. I make no attempt to covert Gisela to Christianity. I think that would betray the trust we have built with her. She expresses a desire to return to the shepherd's hut when the weather warms up, as it is on abbey grounds, and she feels safe there. The shepherds may need to build another shelter for themselves, or for her, however it works out. In a way, she is now a member of our community.

Just as I am fascinated by Gisela's vision of life and death, so she is curious about ours, although she already seems to know a great deal about Christianity, no doubt from her adult children who are Christians. Having been to Carlisle, she has seen the church and priory there. She cannot reconcile the teachings of a poor Jewish carpenter with the obvious wealth of Christian bishops and priests. Christ, she said, was a homeless man who depended on others for food and lodging. Her limited acquaintance with priests has caused her to view them as predators who use the guise of religion to fund their own excesses. Her one exception to this is Father Kenric, the priest at Lanercost, whom she believes to be a sincere and humble man.

Her most important objection to Christianity is the belief that Christ died so that our sins would be forgiven. She feels this encourages those who sin to continue sinning, as they are repeatedly forgiven, but never suffer any real consequences for their actions. While I know that our Savior wants us to be like Him and to make amends for our transgressions, I cannot argue with the point that many in the Church seem to take advantage of this practice. Gisela is one of the most outspoken and honest women that I have ever known. Sometimes she even causes me to doubt my own faith. We will just have to accept each other as we are.

25 February 1456

Marriage

The weather has been very warm the last few days, almost springlike, but it started to snow again this evening and is growing colder. Winter has returned, just when many lambs are being born. There are newly built areas inside for the ewes and their lambs, and the shepherds will monitor those pregnant ewes who are left outside at all times. It is hard work, especially when there is trouble with the birth. I have watched the shepherds turn a lamb or kid around inside its mother when it could not come out properly. Sadly, sometimes both the mother and its lamb are lost.

In our discussion today, Gisela asks me why the priests and nuns do not marry. What an excellent question. I am totally at a loss. To my surprise, Eawynn speaks up. She says that priests and brothers are married to the Church, while nuns take vows as Brides of Christ, and also because our Lord did not marry. Yvonne is present and shows no surprise at all that Eawynn speaks aloud, but just smiles at me and nods. Then she whispers to me that she has known for a very long time that Eawynn is not really mute and gives a little laugh. Gisela just watches us. I am not sure she understands the implications. So Eawynn's secret is out, a little at least. I wonder who else knows or suspects.

As to why priests and nuns do not marry, in truth, I do not know the answer. I am not sure it is a healthy thing to live without a close companion. I have been fortunate that I have had Eawynn all these years as the companion of my heart. Gisela laughs heartily at Eawynn's explanation and says it is a foolish reason, that must have been designed by men. Not one of us disagrees.

MARCH

1 March 1456
Noise and a Puzzle

The noise from the barns continues, all day and sometimes during the night! Babies, babies everywhere; lambs, kids, a few calves and a colt off one of the work mares. I thank God for such abundance and good fortune as we have not lost many during the birthing, and as much as I enjoy walking out to see them all, I wish they would hush! Our shepherds sleep standing up these days. Hopefully, we will have enough hay and fodder for all the animals to last until the grass begins to grow.

Everyone becomes very quiet as we break our fast this morning when I announce that a bag of grain for flour has gone missing in the kitchen pantry, along with a basket of eggs. Although breakfast is not a time where conversations are encouraged, I tend to look the other way as long as they happen quietly. The very silence of the sisters, novices, and those serving us is deafening. Our good cook, Sister Margarethe, informed me earlier this morning that she thought things seemed to go missing, but she had not been completely sure until she started keeping a daily inventory. Evidently this has been going on for some time. The abbey has already handed out all that can be spared to the needy and still have enough left to provide for us through the remainder of the winter. It is a puzzle that needs to be solved.

3 March 1456

A Loss and a Gain

Guda went to God late last night. Since retiring as head of the kitchen, her health has been steadily declining. Her passing will be celebrated this weekend. I have personally seen that her body has been washed and wrapped in linens. Her body will rest in our little mausoleum until spring, when the ground thaws.

I was present at Guda's bedside, holding her hand when she died. She went peacefully, unafraid. It was quite late when we finished getting her body ready for burial. I immediately went to sleep, only to be awakened later that night by tiny mewing noises. My black, fluffy cat had delivered three kittens in the corner of my room on an old blanket that she must have pulled off my chair. I had forgotten that she was in the family way. The kittens are so tiny and helpless, yet so perfect.

Lately, I have been too busy and preoccupied. This is a message from Our Lady that I need to slow down. Through everything, the cycle of life and death continues, and we must accept our place in it all. God will provide, and Our Gracious Lady has always given me the strength to continue. As I sit on the side of my bed watching the mother cat nurse her babies, I can just see the pale beginning of dawn in the eastern sky.

Feeling that I need to personally tell Guda's family, I travel with Avice to Guda's brother's cottage just beyond the local village this morning. We go on horseback accompanied by Timothy. Guda never married and has only one living sibling, who is also getting on in years. He has a daughter, whose family resides with him. They are grateful for our news, having expected it for some time. They are quite happy for her to be buried on abbey grounds. Guda has been at the abbey longer than I have. It feels strange for her to be gone from us, but I know she is with God.

7 March 1456

The Mystery is Solved

The mystery of the missing items has finally been solved by a very observant Sister Margarethe. One of our young novices, Mildred, or Maud as she is more frequently called, has been handing items off to a young man in the village. She was confronted this morning while holding some eggs and cheese from the pantry as she waited for him in a copse of trees behind the convent. A couple of men from the barns were at the ready and detained him. Evidently, Margarethe had all plans well in hand and ready to set in motion.

So, what are the consequences to be? It is a complicated situation. I have often witnessed the romantic yearnings of our young girls, many of whom did not choose to be here, but were sent by their families. Maud was a strong willed and rebellious child when she came here as an oblate two years ago. Although she was difficult at first, I thought she had finally accepted her place at Lambley. Being wonderfully gifted at drawing pictures, it was Maud who drew all the pictures of the herbs while she was staying with Gisela. I am having difficulty understanding why she would go to such great lengths, stealing from the pantry for a young man's attention. Maud is from a large, landed family, with several girls to find husbands for. The young man is the son of the local butcher. His family has no great need for the stolen items. What could be the purpose behind all this? A decision will not be made until I figure that out. Meanwhile, if I report the thefts, the consequences for both will be dire, and I have no wish for that. I have asked Margarethe and all others who were involved in the apprehension of the young man to keep silent about this incident until I have made my decision. We have let the young man leave and placed Maud in seclusion. Gracious Lady, grant me wisdom.

14 March 1456

Dawn

It is almost dawn. The sky is beginning to lighten, and I hear the beginning of birdsong. It has been a long winter, but the promise of spring is in the air. Even so, I have never felt so weary, weary and cold to the very marrow of my bones. My strength in handling the day-to-day affairs of the abbey is diminished. Perhaps it is just the consequence of growing older. So many decisions to make, and so many who depend on my wisdom to make correct choices. Gracious

Lady, grant me the strength to continue. I feel the need for your presence by my side.

It is afternoon and I have just received a message from the Bishop of Carlisle. This year the bishop will be sending one of his priests, a Monsignor Matthew, from Carlisle to assist us. There is no need for this priest, except that perhaps this priest is being sent by the bishop to spy on us. Father Kenric, the priest from Lanercost Abbey, who usually says our Sunday Masses at the church of the Blessed Mary Magdalene, would have sufficed very well for the Easter. The bishop has also requested that the Easter Mass be restricted to the religious of Lambley and Lanercost Abbeys. We have always invited the community near the abbeys as well as the lay persons who work at the abbeys to attend the Mass. To avoid a catastrophe, I walk to speak with Abbot Walton.

20 March 1456

The Kingdom of God

Eawynn wakes me early this morning and we walk slowly through the abbey grounds, the sunlight slanting through the trees and onto the patches of frost on the ground. It is chilly, but not freezing. Spring is all around us, the promise of rebirth. Tiny flowers have appeared through the frost-covered grass, crocuses, and snowdrops. At the barns, the workers attend to feeding and milking. There is activity everywhere. I love seeing all the babies. Even in these dark times, they are God's reminder that change continues, nothing lasts forever. Empires and tyrants rise and fall, both politically and in the Church, which is as much a political institution as a religious one. Has it always been this way? I often wonder what the original disciples of Christ would think.

As I greet the men about their labors, and later, the women in the kitchen, I try to remember that the spirit of the Creator dwells in everyone, in fact, in everything, from the young man who coerced our young novice to steal, to the healer now residing in our convent. The kingdom of God is not some far-off place. It is here. It is now. "Neither shall they say, Lo here! or, lo there! for, behold, the kingdom of God is within you." Luke (17:21)

23 March 1456

The Kitchen

The head of our kitchen, Sister Margarethe, has been away for the past three days visiting her family. This morning, the porridge is cold and lumpy, again. The store of honey is low, rendering the congealed mass of cooked grains barely edible. I only force it down because I am hungry. I notice that several others do not finish their bowls, although no one complains out loud. Last evening's repast was not much better. It is interesting to note how adversely this affects everyone's mood, including my own. May Margarethe's journey be short and her return to us safe, and soon!

25 March 1456

Holy Week

Holy Week begins with the first day of Our Lord's passion, when he was arrested in the Garden of Gethsemane and handed over to the Romans. What a coincidence that, despite our grumbling since Margarethe's absence, we once again begin the day with cold, congealed porridge. I ponder whether I should feel grateful for all our blessings, that we have food, despite its taste and texture. Then I decide that being grateful is not really the issue and set out to investigate who exactly is responsible for the inedible servings that continue to arrive at the table during mealtimes. At this point, the quality, or lack of, seems deliberate. Margarethe arrives late in the afternoon, just in time for crispy, burned fish from the river, served with undercooked greens. She has some blistering words for the kitchen laborers. I have no need to investigate further or address the issue after Margarethe's acid rebuke of the woman that was left in charge. Faith has been restored that tomorrow's meals will be greatly improved, although it is still a time of fasting, so I might be greatly disappointed. Something is needed to improve our spirits.

26 March 1456

Avice

A vice and I spent yesterday outside with two novices, helping Margarethe prepare the herb and vegetable beds for planting, carting our small wagons filled with seasoned animal dung and mixing it into the soil. By nightfall I was bone tired. All that bending over affected my back, but at least I slept well. During our work, Margarethe was uncharacteristically quiet. When we had finished, out of hearing of the others, I inquired about her family. She responded that everyone was well, but that she had other concerns that she wished to discuss with me whenever it would be convenient.

This morning, after breaking our fast with hot porridge and goat milk, Margarethe meets with me in my study. She requests that she be allowed to dismiss the woman who was left in charge of the kitchen while she was absent. The woman has been employed for many years and is very knowledgeable about the work but has been very difficult to work with since Guda gave up the position. The woman seems to bear a grudge against Margarethe and questions her decisions constantly, making the situation in the kitchen stressful for everyone. Surprised about how anxious she has become since taking over Guda's position, I inquire if she has taken time to speak with the woman, one-on-one. Margarethe responds that she only tried once and was made to feel like a fool. The woman resents Margarethe because she feels the job should have been hers. She is doing everything in her power to sabotage the situation, including attempting to turn the others against Margarethe. Having had no idea of the strain this has placed on Margarethe, I ask how I can help. She replies that many of the kitchen helpers have also become difficult to work with, and she does not feel she has the authority to reprimand them. I will get this situation sorted out so Margarethe can get the kitchen running smoothly again. I suggest that Sister Avice become a permanent help in the kitchen. I know that Avice liked working there as a novice.

Sunday is Easter, the time when we celebrate the risen Lord. I will speak to the kitchen staff this afternoon, after I have dismissed the troublemaker. Then I will need to further consider how I must approach this situation. Also, there seem to be kittens everywhere!! Very amusing but sometimes dangerous when they are underfoot! I must be careful where I step, especially at night.

26 March 1456
Evening

The troublemaker has been dismissed, although I have conditionally allowed both her daughter and daughter-in-law to continue as kitchen laborers. The woman was angry and extremely rude, even to me. I had Timothy and Donal nearby, as I expected trouble. She was given her pay for her labor and escorted off the abbey grounds. I requested a meeting with the rest of the kitchen staff after the evening meal, which was well-cooked and as what might be appropriate for Holy Saturday. My speech was simple. Margarethe was in charge and her orders were to be followed. I would back up any decision she made with regards to who was hired and who was dismissed. I added that I expected the Easter celebration to be excellent, as it has always been in the past, that I would not accept less than their best efforts.

Monsignor Matthew has arrived at Lanercost Abbey. When I spoke with the abbot, who had also received a message from the bishop, he suggested that we allow this to run its course. We will follow Monsignor's instructions, whatever they are.

27 March 1456

Monsignor Matthew

It is the most holy time of the year when we celebrate the passion of our Lord. This year I have been made most aware of the complex nature of humanity. As we make the preparations for the sorrow of His crucifixion, and the joy of His resurrection and triumph over death, the division between those who truly follow in his footsteps, who serve others as Christ served us, and those who use this celebration as an occasion for their own self-aggrandizement, becomes ever more apparent.

Monsignor Matthew is an example of those who use a celebration as a showcase for his own importance, strutting around like a turkey cock and ordering changes in the most minute of details. He objects to the music we have chosen for the Easter celebration and dictates the songs that we must sing. Abbot Walton and the brothers from Lanercost are very obliging, but I can tell that they are uneasy about all the changes. To make matters more difficult, a few of my fellow nuns, Sisters Riona and Helena, are worshiping at this priest's feet and reacting to his every utterance as if it comes from God himself! Nothing satisfies Monsignor Matthew.

He is also spending time at both abbeys snooping around and asking questions that are none of his business. He is especially interested in seeing the records of our flocks of sheep, sales of wool, stored provisions and so forth from last fall. Eawynn oversees the records. As abbess, it is my job to introduce him to Eawynn and ask that he be given the information he requests. I warn Eawynn of his request in advance and ask her to meet us in the library. I lead him to the library and introduce him to Eawynn, using signing to communicate with Eawynn. My inability to keep a smile off my face as I watched her act deaf as well as dumb almost gives her away. I must stand back and focus on something outside through one of the windows to keep from laughing. She does not make communication easy for him, repeatedly motioning for him to write down his questions. Then, she forces him to wait as she takes her time rummaging through piles of books looking for the records he wants. To my surprise, she finally produces the information and points out the details to him while watching him make notes of it all. I am worried that we might have to come up with additional revenue until he turns and walks away, when Eawynn informs me that she always keeps two sets of records. The records she showed Monsignor Matthew reflect exactly what the bishop had recorded on his visit last fall, as well as the details of what goods were sent. Unfortunately for Lanercost, she does not keep two sets of books for them. I sincerely hope their records match. For the remainder of

Monsignor Matthew's visit, I try to make myself scarce, simply to preserve my sanity.

Fortunately, there is a monk in the company of Monsignor Matthew, Brother Walter, who is a learned and humble man, and we spend some time in conversation away from the whirl of activity surrounding the preparations. He is as ignorant as we are of the bishop's intentions. The amount of time and resources spent on the actual liturgies of Holy Week this year would have been better spent helping the poor of our community, most of whom have been excluded from our celebrations. In the past, I have always extended invitations to all in the surrounding area. I would much prefer simplicity to this gaudy display of wealth. I will be relieved when this priest from Carlisle is gone.

28 March 1456

Easter Celebrations

Our celebrations for Easter Sunday have officially concluded with a Mass this morning presided over by the Monsignor. I breathe a sigh of relief when Monsignor Matthew and his retinue leave after the noonday meal to return to Carlisle. I spoke with Abbot Walton after

test

Monsignor Matthew arrived, and he agreed when it became evident that the community would not be invited to the Easter Mass, that another Easter mass will be celebrated for the community at the church of the Blessed Mary Magdalene in the evening with Father Kenric acting as celebrant. Cwenhild previously asked all the barn laborers to spread the news to the local community. Judith and Brigitta were overjoyed at the news, as was Cuilen. We will hold our own Easter celebration, this evening and every Sunday until the time of Our Lord's ascension. Thrilled that we can enact and sing what we have practiced for so long, we will raise our hearts and songs to God, in our own way, in our own voices, in our own time!

29 March 1456

Awareness and Amends

I must ask Timothy to make me a new walking stick, as the one I am using now is becoming difficult to grip. I am preoccupied as I take an early morning walk around the grounds this morning with Eawynn. It is good to get her outside, but our walks are brief. We sit for a spell on one of the benches in the flower garden. I should be more aware of my surroundings because I enjoy listening to the birds, but I barely notice them. Eawynn already knows of my conversation with Margarethe and the events that transpired with the rest of the kitchen staff. The Easter meal had been acceptable, although different than usual, and probably not up to Guda's standards. Change is usually uncomfortable. We will adjust.

My discussion with Eawynn concerns my role in all of this. Having never considered that placing someone in such a position of authority and responsibility in the kitchen could cause such anxiety as to be debilitating, I feel remiss in my duty as abbess. Being aware of the fears and feelings of the nuns that are in positions of authority under me is my responsibility, and I feel I have failed in this regard. I need to reconsider my role as abbess, particularly the boundaries and limits of my authority.

Eawynn considers for a moment before responding. To the best of her knowledge, my interference with Sister Rosamund or Sister Yvonne was never needed, because both were committed and competent. Neither Yvonne nor Rosamund has ever had any need for my input with regards to the areas which were their respective domain. Eawynn advises that I do likewise with the others, by allowing all those in positions of authority more freedom, by trusting Margarethe to be able to choose or remove her own help. Eawynn did agree that Avice might do well working with Margarethe, but that I should let Margarethe make that decision. I listen to her but letting go of the reins is difficult for me. Perhaps the issue with Sister Margarethe is that Margarethe does not feel she has my support. I must make amends. It is the grave responsibility of those whose every decision affects the lives of others to consider how those in their care will be impacted. We must all support each other as the Blessed Mother supports us.

Eawynn has always been my confidant as well as my advisor, and I value her opinions. Ever since she professed as a nun, she has been the person I depend on when I really need a different perspective. Lately, she tries to show interest, but it is obvious to me that her spirit is tired.

APRIL

2 April 1456

Maud

Any judgement of Maud's actions has been delayed until I have fully understood the events that led up to her thievery. This morning, I send for her to come to my study. When I ask her to describe the whole ordeal from start to finish, she discloses to me that she met the butcher's son when she was working with Ellie at Gisela's cottage. Gisela would send Maud into the nearby village for supplies. She contacted the young man there. Evidently, she was very attracted to him, although he is at least seven or eight years older than she is. I believe he enjoyed the power that he seemed to have over her, although that is speculation on my part. Young girls are often susceptible to this kind of manipulation.

Maud says the man was very kind to her at first. She refuses to go into any great detail but does say that he made demands of her. The demands were in the form of taking things from the convent for him, to prove that she cared for him. He is an attractive young man, and I believe this was a game for him. The outcome is that she became a thief to receive his attention. Just how far that attention progressed she will not reveal.

How can I fault a lonely, impressionable girl for being used in this manner? I tell her that she must make amends with Sister Margarethe for the cost of her pilfering from the pantry. I will leave the details of that up to Margarethe. I need to speak with the abbot about how to approach the young man and his family, and this will take some time. It is a delicate situation, especially when considering the reputation of the girl, but there must be consequences for the young man. He is old enough that he must take responsibility for his actions. Theft is a serious offense.

5 April 1456

Cuilen

I meet Cuilen in the hall outside the children's quarters and ask to speak with him. He follows me to my study where I bid him to sit. Nervous, he remains standing. I sit because I have been walking, and my legs are tired. I have been so busy that the problem of having an adolescent boy in a convent of nuns has been overlooked. Cuilen appears to be fully recovered from the beating he received. He shifts his feet nervously side to side and stares at the floor. I insist that he sit, telling him that I do not bite, that I just want to discuss his situation with him. He fidgets and remains standing. I ask him how he spends his days. He replies that he works with Brigitta and Cwenhild in the barns in the mornings. After the midday meal, he spends time with Judith, who is teaching him how to read music. He looks up and says, almost defensively, "I am becoming quite good at reading music, and I am learning to play the wooden flute. Sister Yvonne has helped me to better my reading and writing skills. When I have free time, I help Sister Mathilde with the children."

I express surprise that he is keeping so busy. I also notice that he is dressed as a young man, with no jewelry what-so-ever. Changing this subject, I tell him that we will visit the abbot soon, as I think there might be a place for him there. He responds, "But I do not wish to become a monk or priest. I want to be a musician and a teacher!"

As kindly as I am able, I say, "Cuilen, you cannot stay here indefinitely. You were here to be healed, nothing more. The abbot at Lanercost will not require you to become a monk or priest. The brothers can further your education, and I do not mind if you continue your studies with Judith. We will visit the abbot the day after tomorrow in the morning. I will make the appointment today."

I stand to dismiss him. He looks at me with questioning eyes, and I continue, "Cuilen, you will make a fine teacher and musician, and you may certainly visit us often, you are simply too old to live in a convent." With that, he nods and turns to leave. At the door, he turns back and whispers, "Thank you."

6 April 1456

Martha

It is always a little upsetting to see some of our community working so hard, while others take every opportunity to relax, taking long walks or sitting in the gardens for hours. Their excuse is often that they need the time for spiritual contemplation. Sister Joan, who works in the library with Sister Yvonne, spends a great deal of time in spiritual contemplation, as do Sisters Helena and Riona. When I ask Yvonne, who is always busy, why Joan has so much free time, Yvonne replies that trying to make Joan actually do anything that she does not want to do is simply not worth the waste of energy. Yvonne volunteers that Joan enjoys copying music and is excellent as to the details, but she somehow manages to avoid copying text. When I raise the issue with Joan, she responds indignantly that her time spent listening to the Lord is much more important than her labor in the library, her reason being that she is like Mary, from the story of the sisters in the Gospel of Luke.

The story of Mary and Martha in the Gospel of Luke has always annoyed me. When Our Lord visited their house, Martha worked very hard to welcome him, but Mary simply sat at his feet and listened to him. When Martha complained, Jesus admonished her for criticizing her sister.

I have sympathy for Martha. I am a Martha, always working and worrying. Today, I heard the voice of Our Lady telling me that I must learn to listen and be still, that when I worry it means that I do not have faith. I must put my complete trust in God's care every minute of the day. This will be very difficult for me. Even so, I still think there are those in our community that use the excuse of spiritual contemplation as a means to avoid labor. There must be a balance. Without the Marthas of this world, nothing would get done.

7 April 1456

Decisions

Cuilen shows up at the door to my study shortly after the morning meal. I assume he eats with the children as I have never seen him in the dining hall when the nuns eat. I pick up my cane and we begin our walk together toward Lanercost Abbey. As he strides beside me, I realize that he has grown taller in the few months that he has been with us. I tell him that I need answers to a few questions before we speak with Abbot Walton, such as why he is dressing as a boy and not affecting to act feminine like he did when he was brought by his mother. He says his feelings have not changed, but he likes being here at the abbey, and he does not want to give anyone an excuse to send him away. He adds, with a slight smile, that this is the first time he has ever had friends. Confident that I can talk the abbot into taking this boy, we continue toward the abbey.

Abbot Walton greets me when we arrive and introduces himself to Cuilen. He asks Cuilen to sit in a waiting room while he speaks with me. I walk with the abbot to his study, we sit, and he asks all the questions that I have been expecting. I explain how Cuilen acts, what he does with his days, and what his ambitions are. Then I request of the abbot that he give the boy a chance, explaining that I cannot have an adolescent boy walking freely around the convent, and I need to find a solution to this situation. Abandoning the boy is not an option. The abbot asks why Cuilen cannot be a laborer in the barns, with the other young men who work for us. Not answering his question, I ask him to please, just speak with the boy. If his answer is no, then I will consider other options.

Cuilen is sent for, and I am asked to sit in the waiting room. Their conversation lasts long enough for me to sit a while, pace around the room, and gaze out the window at the gardens where several brothers are working. "That is what I should be doing," I think, "instead of cooling my heels while the abbot questions the boy." The door opens and I am invited back in. Cuilen is to fetch his few belongings. He will be accepted on a trial basis.

We walk back to Lambley, silently for the most part, both deep in thought. As we approach the convent door, I turn and ask, "Do you think you can get along with the other boys who are your age? It might be difficult."

He shrugs and smiles timidly. "I think I can survive just about anything, as long as it is not physical. I do not care what others might think. I have friends here now that I can talk to, Judith and Brigitta, even Cwenhild. I will be all right." With that I pat his shoulder, and we part ways.

10 April 1456

Bunnies

There is a pile of brush that has been accumulating throughout the winter. It has grown quite large, as the men are cleaning up all the windfall from around the abbey. It is located in one of the meadows, far away from any structures that might be set on fire. As it rained three days ago, one of the abbey's workmen thought that it would be a good time to burn it soon, early in the morning when dew is on the grass and the wind is down. He stopped by my study to ask my permission to burn it tomorrow morning. I was surprised, because I had thought that Cwenhild would have been in charge of this. When I asked why he had not spoken with Cwenhild, he replied that he had, but she had referred him to me. His asking is usually just a formality, because I rarely object to their ideas, but I stopped to look at it on my walk today. I almost missed the tiny nest of newborn bunnies nestled just inside the edge of the pile. Such a precious sight! Another reminder that in spite of all the conflict between humankind, the miracles of our Creator never cease. Grateful that I had been made aware, I informed him that he would have to wait to burn the brush piles until the birthing season of tiny woodland babies is over.

My only regret is that Eawynn did not accompany me. She would have loved to have seen the bunny nest. I described it in detail, and while she seemed interested, it is as if a light has gone out in her. She tries so hard to put a good face on it, but I can see how weak she has become. Her only joy seems to be spending time with her daughter, who is sitting up and rolling over. With her reddish gold curls, Isolde looks more like her mother every day.

11 April 1456

Brigitta and Cwenhild

I have heard disturbing rumors about Cwenhild and Brigitta from several sources. Imagine what a hypocrite I would be if I considered that one of my favorite people is taking advantage of an adolescent girl. Not only that, but Brigitta has already been married, although we still do not know the circumstances, or even her true name.

I walk through the barn this morning to speak with Cwenhild, but also to lay this ugliness to rest. She is busy with Brigitta milking two goats. I stand and watch until they notice me, then I give a little wave. Cwenhild stands up and beckons me closer. She has not been her merry self since Adelheid's death, and the ordeal of Eawynn's rape has also weighed heavily on her young shoulders. How old is she now? Twenty-three? Twenty-four? I mention that there have been rumors, but what I am most concerned about is how they are being affected by the rumors. Cwenhild smiles and Brigitta laughs out loud. "I heard the rumors two weeks ago from Timothy, that I had seduced Brigitta, that we are lovers," Cwenhild says, and continues, "When Brigitta heard them, she insisted on holding my hand or walking around with her arm around my waist." I try to picture this, as the top of Brigitta's head barely comes up to Cwenhild's shoulder. "I have taken a vow of celibacy, and I have not broken it," she continues. I reply that I really do not care if she has or not, as long as it is consensual, as I consider Brigitta an adult.

I am astounded when Brigitta interrupts, "Cwenhild is my best friend. We are not lovers, and I have been thinking about becoming a novice." I reply they will need to come to my study soon, and we will need to talk. I know nothing about Brigitta's background. She has always refused to tell us who she really is or where she is from. I am certain that questions will come up when she is ready to profess, if not before. If the abbot or the bishop learn that she is a runaway, they might try to send her back. I am not sure if she understands this.

19 April 1456

The Call for Communal Action

An important reading has given me much to think about, from the Acts of the Apostles (2:42-45), "They devoted themselves to the teaching of the apostles and to the communal life, to the breaking of bread and to prayers. All who believed were together and had all things in common; they would sell their property and divide among them all according to each one's need."

As a community, we at Lambley Abbey do whatever we can to assist those in our surrounding area: the old, the infirm, the poor. There are landowners and artisans in the surrounding area who have so much more than they need, and not because they have labored more or are more deserving. When the harvests are poor, I have watched as people, especially children and the elderly, starve and die from lack of care. How can we, as followers of Christ, justify this inequality? The Catholic Church's display of its wealth, with its cathedrals and palaces that I have seen during my travels, is marvelous and extraordinary to behold. However, the awesome beauty of a cathedral is nothing compared to the beauty of our woodlands. What a waste, so heedless of our Lord's teachings to truly live and take care of each other! How can we promote a system of living where all are fed, all are clothed and taken care of? I have no answers to these big problems. We can only do what is possible in our own small way.

26 April 1456
Music

As usual, Sisters Avice, Agatha, and the novices have been working daily in the gardens under the supervision of Margarethe, weeding and planting. I join them for a short time, but must stop to rest, and sit on a nearby bench. Stooping over for any length of time is hard on this back and these knees. While resting, the sound of one of our young kitchen girls singing drifts on the morning air. The song is not one of mine, nor sacred, but a sweet lilting song of love and loss. I do not hear as well as I once did, but still it moved me. Sound. One of our connections with this world, this amazing creation from the energy that is God. An energy that is found in everything. I thank the Creator always for the gifts that enable us to experience God in such a profound way.

The lovely sadness of the song took me back to a time when Eawynn and I thought we might be parted for the rest of our lives, when she was sent away to Lacock Abbey to escape an arranged marriage. We sneaked out and walked the hills for hours the night before she left. The moon was out with enough light for us to find our way. The woodlands looked enchanted, and I could almost believe the stories of woodland sprites and elves! We held hands as we walked and vowed that we would be forever together in spirit. We were so young. Our future was so uncertain, and yet she came back to me.

MAY

1 May 1456
May Day

I was not involved with setting up the maypoles yesterday, although I heard that Brigitta repeated her feat from last year of tying the ribbons to the top of the tall maypole. Instead, I have been busy helping Cuilen to gather his things and say his goodbyes. He is acting like he will never see anyone again, although he will only be a short walk away. I am certain the abbot will allow him to visit us. I have also not been available to practice the singing for the dances and the crowning of the statue of Our Lady. This is the first year since I came to Lambley that I have missed this.

As I walk to the area where the poles are set up, to watch the children dance the maypole dance this morning, realization manifests that I have been remiss about visiting the older children for several months, as I have been preoccupied with Eawynn and Isolde. Eawynn is in the playground area, sitting in a chair that someone has been thoughtful enough to bring out. She is holding Isolde, who is taking everything in with wide eyes. She claps delightedly as instrumental music begins, and the children line up. They begin to weave the ribbons around the short pole as soon as the singing starts, led by Judith and Brigitta, who is wearing a dress. I cannot remember ever seeing Brigitta in a dress. I spy Lynet and Odelyn among those who are in the dance and realize that there are children here that I do not recognize. Both girls appear to be excited and happy. The dance and singing go on until the ribbons are tied at the bottom of the pole, and a crowd soon gathers around the table where sweet cakes and sweet tea are served. I nod my approval to Mathilde with her young charges and make my way to Eawynn's side. I take Isolde from her as Cwenhild helps her from the chair and assists her to walk back to her room. I follow with Isolde, who is determined to pull my veil off.

Surprise fills me in the afternoon as our beautiful novices gather around to dance the maypole dance, dressed in their white dresses, their hair bedecked with flowers. The music is strange to me. I hear instruments. A harp, a lute, and a wooden flute play a lilting melody that I do not recognize, then the song begins. The group of singers is made up of a few young men from Lanercost and some of the younger sisters, led by Judith and Cuilen. The song is lovely, surpassing every song to Mary that I have ever heard, with interweaving melodies that somehow also harmonize. When the dance is finished, a more solemn song begins as the novices walk in procession, two by two, toward the grotto where the statue of Mary is crowned with a wreath of flowers woven together. I turn as I feel a hand on my shoulder. It is Eawynn, supported this time by Sister Yvonne, her eyes are filled with tears. The realization hits me that this is the last Maypole celebration she will see. She will not see Isolde grow up to dance in the children's dance. I turn to hug her gently and walk with her back to her room.

3 May 1456

The Here and Now

This morning the flocks of sheep from both abbeys left for summer pastures. I think it is still a little too cold, but the herders reassure me that there is already enough grass for grazing. Gisela travels with them. Having spent the last week in preparation for leaving, she is anxious to go. She will stay in the little shepherd's hut until the flocks return in the fall. The herdsmen will keep watch over her, and she will likely help them as well. The shepherds also take supplies to build another shelter. I will miss Gisela. She has given me much to think about. All my life I have been taught to focus on the life after death, in paradise with Christ, and that worldly things are temptations that pull us away from God. Gisela is focused on life here and now. For her, God is present in everything. Because of her, there is part of me that also seeks for God here, that seeks to live fully now. Is that wrong? It seems that we are missing something if our focus is always on some distant future. We are missing the only thing that ever really exists, the present.

13 May 1456

The Divine Feminine

As we move through the Easter season, I have given some thought to the third member of the blessed Trinity. The Bible tells us the Holy Spirit was sent to the disciples by God after the ascension of our Lord, to be present as a comforter for mankind. The Holy Spirit is the embodiment of the love between God and his son, our Lord. When Christ promised that he would not abandon his flock, that he would not leave them as orphans, he promised a comforter, the Holy Spirit. In the Eastern tradition the comforter is seen as feminine, the divine feminine of our Creator. What a treasure to be able to call on our Mother God in times of need.

22 May 1456

Rebellion

There has been unrest here in the north of England, which is growing worse as time passes. There is much dissension against the king who is acting irrationally once again, but also against the Yorkist factions. Yorkist rebels appear daily in the area, although to date they have left our monasteries alone. As a result of the friction between the Lancasters and the Yorks over the throne, the Scots have taken this opportunity to make more raids south of the border just to stir the pot. It gives me pause to question those who claim to rule by divine right. They are almost always the most ungodly of men. The bishops who are appointed by the king are certainly not chosen because they are God-fearing. These are political appointments, put in place to support the ruler against the Yorkist usurper. Religion has become nothing but a political tool. Such is our world today! What has happened to the Sermon on the Mount? When did we lose sight of His true teachings? Those in authority give lip service to Christianity only to further their own interests.

Even here in the convent, I question the vocation of many of our sisters who did not become brides of Christ by choice. Many have accepted their fate, and some have even grown to love it, but not all. I worry a great deal about the two new girls that have come to us, accepted because of generous donations from their family. They are sisters. Edith Massey is thirteen and Amelia Massey is eleven. Their father does not intend for them to take religious vows. If he finds suitable marriages for them, they will return home. They have not reconciled themselves with this choice. Edith is sowing seeds of rebellion among the novices. Managing the novices' schedules has become increasingly difficult for Sister Agatha, as some are outright refusing to learn the various skills needed to become a nun. Preferably, Agatha can get them under control by herself. If not, I will need to intervene.

I am an older woman. My time left here on earth is growing shorter, and I am tired. I will put off how to deal with these new troublemakers until I have discussed the situation with Eawynn and Sister Agatha. Perhaps Sister Margarethe, who was the previous mistress of novices, can offer some suggestions. There are mountains of freshly shorn wool to clean and card. These are tasks I will suggest the troublemakers could easily learn. There are other means of bringing them under control that I would prefer not to use but will if I must. Thinking about it is giving me a headache. Just for today, I will praise God and thank Our Gracious Lady for all that I have been given.

13 May 1456

Discipline

Margarethe has taken the situation in hand. Edith and Amelia Massey have been separated from the rest of the novices and oblates. They are spending time in solitude until Margarethe decides what to do. She has threatened to send them to separate convents in the south of England. Eawynn has had little strength to even join the conversation. I fear she is slipping away from us, and I am helpless to stop it.

24 May 1456

God

I step into the chapel of Saint Mary Magdalene this morning to spend some solitary time in prayer for Eawynn's health, in front of the small tabernacle that contains the body of Our Lord. It is cool and quiet. Some workmen are repairing the steps to the sacristy in the back. I ignore them and they ignore me. I often look for peace and solace in this place but find none today.

As I leave, I stride back toward the convent on a path beside a stone wall where two cows are pastured with their growing calves, lying in the shade of an oak tree. I stop and stand still. Birds sing, and bees and butterflies flit from flower to flower. A woodpecker knocks on a tree behind me, and some ravens scold.

We are busy building great cathedrals to God all over Europe where the living God is kept, contained in an ornate golden box. Eawynn has seen the great cathedral at Salisbury, and I have been to the one in York. God cannot be contained. No matter the peace I feel or do not feel in the chapel, God is in the vibrant life that surrounds us. The essence of God is pervasive. We do not need to seek God. God is here, everywhere.

27 May 1456

Wisdom and Patience

Blessed Mother, grant me wisdom and patience. Sister Agatha has come to inform me that Maud, who was pilfering from the kitchen pantry, is pregnant. What a surprise! Many questions arise in my mind. Should her family be informed, and if so, will they take her back? What about informing the family of the butcher's son? Should Maud be released from her profession? She is still a novice. She has not taken the initial vows to become a nun. Should she be allowed to continue, in which case the baby would be put up for adoption? Would her family want the child if it is a boy? She cannot keep the child and remain a novice. If she chooses to keep the child, but has nowhere else to go, what course should be taken then? So much depends on the decisions of the families.

Eawynn has stopped all pretense of working in the library. I bring a comfortable chair in from my room, for her to sit in during the day, bundled up, even though it is quite warm. Anna, the wet nurse, brings Isolde in to see her several times during the day. The child is sitting up and attempting to move around the floor. I can see how much Eawynn adores this little girl, even so, she soon tires and begins to nod off. Eawynn can no longer be left alone with Isolde. She is too weak. Every spare moment that I have during the day, I come to check on Eawynn. This is not like the illnesses we experience that pass from one to another. There is a sickness inside her. She is so thin and pale. I know the worst will come soon, too soon.

JUNE

2 June 1456

Decisions

Both Maud's family and the young man's family have been contacted and apprised of Maud's situation. Her family is refusing to help, which is not surprising, as they have several children to care for. They are blaming the convent for lack of supervision. Perhaps they have a point.

The young man flatly denies that he is responsible. He states that Maud had other liaisons with young men who work at the convent in the barns and fields, but he refuses to point a finger at anyone. Claiming that the girl seduced him, he hinted that she brought him gifts of her own volition, so that he would have sexual relations with her. It is his word against hers, although none of the other young men who work in town or on the abbey grounds have come forward to support his claim. Furthermore, his family is backing him. His father, the butcher, told me that Maud often visited the butcher's shop to speak with his son, that she actively sought him out. There will not be any consequences for this young man.

Maud has been made aware that she will not receive help from either family. Holding fast to her story that it was only the butcher's son, and only a few times, she breaks down and cries in despair. Perhaps I am naive, but I believe her. I believe her because I must, because I cannot see any other opportunities for this situation to have occurred. Her choices are limited. That she will have the baby is certain. By placing it up for adoption or in an orphanage, although not ours, she can retain her position as a novice. If she decides to keep the child, we will provide her with a place to stay and work here at the abbey. Although she has shown a talent for copying texts and for drawing, work has not proven to be one of her strengths in the past. I hope this will change if she chooses this path.

Maud and her situation have been a distraction from Eawynn's sickness. Her illness has no visible symptoms, such as cough or fever. Her condition is characterized by lack of appetite, fatigue, and apathy. Sleeping sporadically throughout the day, even as she rests in a chair, she has little to no interest in the events taking place around her. A light comes to her eyes and her face brightens only when Isolde visits. I pray daily to Our Lady for Eawynn's recovery. This evening in a moment of lucidity, she draws me close and whispers, "Let me go."

5 June 1456

Betwixt and Between

Maud has decided to keep her child and stay with us here at Lambley as a lay person. While she enjoys working with Sister Yvonne in the library, she has also expressed a wish to continue learning herbal lore to become a healer and perhaps even a midwife. Eventually, she may even find a good husband. Changing her mind is also a choice at this point, as she still has a few months to go before the birth.

Eawynn did not get up this morning. As I was late for Prime, I did not check on her until after the service was over.

Arriving at her room, I had trouble waking her, and even when she appeared to be awake, she was not coherent. It was as if she did not know where she was. The feeling of helplessness that overcomes me when I am with her has rendered me unable to perform the daily duties of an abbess. I am sick with worry.

6 June 1456

Eawynn

Eawynn has taken to her bed and cannot get up. I can barely get her to drink herbal teas. The color has faded from her cheeks and her lips are pale. I send for Gisela. I know in my heart that it is the wasting sickness.

This evening, Eawynn looks up at me and asks to be carried outside to see the sun set and watch the moon rise. She no longer bothers to sign but uses her voice. We are still sitting here on a bench, wrapped in blankets, long after darkness has fallen. I hold her close to keep her warm. She touches my cheek softly and, whispering, asks me to promise to care for Isolde. Tears stream down her face as she worries that Isolde will be alone. Hugging her to me and cradling her head on my shoulder, I vow that I will love Isolde as my own, until my final breath. Then I beg Eawynn not to leave me. I finally have her carried back inside, and I sleep by her in a chair for the remainder of the night.

7 June 1456
My Heart

Gisela arrives at noon from the shepherds' pasture. Eawynn remains asleep most of the time. Gisela gives her a draught of some liquid to take the pain away, but it makes her sleep. I believe it is the same tincture that Gisela made up for Thomas, using the milk of the poppy. I am useless as abbess now. I cannot leave her side. People ask me questions and I cannot even respond. I have no thoughts but of Eawynn. I sit by her side, holding her hand in case she wakes.

Suddenly, as if appearing out of thin air, Yvonne is on the other side of Eawynn's bed, drawing up another chair and taking her other hand. She peers at me, tears streaming silently down her face and dripping onto the guimpe of her habit. Quietly she reaches across to touch my face. "You know I loved her too, Isentrude, "she whispers. "We worked together for twenty years. She was as close to me as anyone, even Edward. He blames himself, you know, for not being with you both that day. I have told him this sickness is unrelated, but he does not believe me." We spend the evening with her, but she does not wake. Margarethe has taken charge of the abbey. She has placed Sister Avice, as young as she is, in charge of the kitchen.

8 June 1456

Grace

This morning, Eawynn wakes and refuses to swallow the pain medicine. She whispers for me to bring Isolde to her. Unable to hold Isolde by herself, I hold the baby close to Eawynn where she slowly extends her hand to stroke the baby's face. Gisela responds to a knock on the door and opens it to reveal Father Kenric, who is garbed as if for Mass. He enters quietly and makes his way to the other side of Eawynn's bed. "I am here to receive your confession so that you may go to God without hindrance for your sins," he says softly, as he pulls up a chair and sits, producing small vials of holy water and oil from within his cassock.

"I have already confessed my sins to God," Eawynn whispers. "I have no need of a priest."

Father Kenric's face darkens, then he replies, "True confession only comes through a priest."

I whispered to Eawynn, "What harm can it do, Eawynn? It will not hurt you to confess." With that I stand with Isolde, who is starting to fidget, and hand her to Gisela, who begins to pace around the room with her.

"Very well," Eawynn replies, her breath becoming increasingly labored, "I confess that there are people that I love more than I will ever love God. And I will not repent."

Father Kenric gives a small sigh of resignation. "Very well, God does not punish someone for loving others. I will also baptize the baby while I am here." With that he stands up, makes the sign of the cross and anoints first Eawynn, then Isolde, baptizing her in the name of the Holy Trinity. He smiles at Isolde, who is making cooing noises at him and stretching out her hands and departs. Eawynn has already lapsed back into sleep. I take Isolde back as Gisela tries unsuccessfully to wake Eawynn to take the pain tincture. I return the baby to Gisela who takes her back to Mathilde, and I sit down again by Eawynn's side, holding her hand.

9 June 1456

Despair

How can I go on? Eawynn passed on during the night. I held her hand when I sat by her during the night. I must have dozed off and slept for quite some time. When I awoke, her hand was cold. I do not think I can exist without her. Others have taken over the plans for the funeral Mass, the burial. I want to be buried with her. I move by putting one foot in front of the other. Someone brings me food, but it tastes like ashes. The world is gray. The light of my life is gone.

SEPTEMBER

23 September 1456

After

D ays, weeks have passed, and I have no recollection of them. I did not write. I could not write. Today, I picked up pen and paper again.

A strange but fleeting sensation passes over me as I walk in the graveyard this morning, with Kendra carrying Isolde beside me, as I do every morning to lay fresh flowers on Eawynn's grave. She would laugh at me if she knew. How ridiculous, trying to find fresh flowers in autumn. I will not think of winter yet, although it is already winter in my heart. Eawynn is buried in a cold grave, never to see a sunrise again, never to see her beautiful child grow into a woman.

Sister Margarethe has taken over as itinerant abbess. Gisela has returned to the summer pastures. She will be back here soon, when the flocks return.

A pair of magpies is perched on the top of a stone fence. Isolde points at them, delighted at their chatter. For a moment I feel as though I am a part of the birds, seeing and feeling what they feel. It is a fleeting moment of utter peace and acceptance, then it is gone. It causes me to consider how God must sense life. Eawynn is gone, but a part of her will always be in Isolde, and a part of her will always be in me. I sense her presence and hear her laughter at the oddest moments.

I have always thought God to be someone apart, the Creator who watches over his creation, but now I wonder if I might be completely incorrect. Suppose the Creator is truly present and part of all creation, aware of everything, and experiencing everything that happens from the smallest particle to the largest tree? To think of God this way connects everything. Even the smallest particles are part of the creation we call God.

26 September 1456

Repetition

Knowing that I should spend more time in quiet meditation, I find that most days now I must stay busy, or I will lose myself completely. Quiet contemplation is difficult, as my mind wanders aimlessly. I do not want to meditate. I do not want to think or to listen. I must keep moving. We harvest vegetables and clean out the storage cellars for the root crops. The cellars contain a myriad of small spiders, rodents, insects, and occasionally snakes, that must be dealt with. I tend to shoo away snakes, but only temporarily.

It began raining last night and continues this morning. Rain is needed. The weather has been hot and much drier than normal for this time of year. The hours and days pass by in a haze, a blur of sound and sight, until I can barely distinguish one from the next. It is the same cycle of birth and death that flows through all of creation. While I am not insensitive to pain and death, I am numb, sleepwalking through the hours of the day. The only time I am truly present is the time I spend each day with Isolde. I will keep her mother alive in her memory as she grows older. I have promised to care for her. This beautiful child is my only reason for waking up each morning.

The wheel of time continues. Day passes into night, summer into fall, fall to winter and so on. I am old and tired. I see the same joys and sadnesses, the same selfishness, the same mistakes replayed over and over. Every day I spend time sitting by Eawynn's grave speaking to her. Today, Yvonne joins me, moving up behind me silently to place a hand on my shoulder. We continue like that for a long time.

EPILOGUE

Isentrude's journal was discovered under some other books in her room by Sister Rosamund, as she and I were cleaning Sister Isentrude's room shortly after her death. Handing the journal to me, Sister Rosamund remarked that books and historical accounts are my domain. Of course, I read the journal. Valuing Sister Cwenhild's opinion, which is often very different from mine, I also asked her to read it. Although other journals are mentioned in this one, they have not been located. Sister Cwenhild and I have agreed that Sister Isentrude's thoughts on religion and God might be best suited for another time, one that is more advanced in the understanding of creation. Sister Cwenhild suggested that the journal be stored in the very back of a closet located in the bell tower of the Blessed Mary Magdalene's chapel, behind several old missals and psalm books.

422

The last entry of the journal was written a few months after Sister Isentrude retired as abbess of Lambley Abbey. She died on the twentieth of June 1466, a little over ten years after Sister Eawynn's death. She kept her promise to care for Eawynn's daughter, Isolde, who is growing into the image of her beautiful mother. I was blessed to have spent so many years working side by side with two such remarkable women. They were ever true to their vision of God.

It is my belief that in the years following Eawynn's death, Sister Isentrude has kept her dearest Eawynn up to date on all the important events. She would have given Eawynn daily detailed reports on Isolde's progress and achievements. She would have surprised Eawynn with the news that Brigitta became a novice shortly after Eawynn's death and is now a fully professed sister, who still works closely with Sister Cwenhild. She would have reported that Maud delivered a baby girl, Arwen, and that Maud and Arwen reside with Gisela, who now has a small cottage on the abbey grounds. Maud has become a fine healer and midwife and has not married.

Mother Margarethe, who has been the abbess since Sister Isentrude retired, thought it fitting that Sister Isentrude be laid to rest next to her beloved Eawynn. The last years of Sister Isentrude's life were spent caring for Isolde and working in the library with me, taking Eawynn's place in both tasks. While Sister Isentrude remained steadfast, her health slowly deteriorated. When she was not in the library or the children's wing, and the weather was agreeable, she would walk to the graveyard and sit in a chair that Timothy had made and placed near Eawynn's grave. When asked why she spent so much time there, she would always say that she and Eawynn had much to discuss.

10 August 1466

Sister Yvonne Dacre

ACKNOWLEDGEMENTS

There are many who helped me on this journey that began during the year of Covid, 2020, the endeavor of writing a novel that incorporates parts of my own story. As a woman, teacher, and musician who has worked in religious settings for many years, the writing reflects my own questions and opinions.

My daughter, Dr. Stephanie Harper, and one of my dearest friends, Darlene Smith, encouraged, cajoled and repeatedly told me to "unpack this" and asked for "more details here" as they edited my initial manuscript and final copy. Many friends read the manuscript in the initial stages as well as the final. They critiqued and encouraged. I am grateful for their input. They are, in no specific order: Mare Martin, Fern Martin, Peaches Gulino, Anne Castille, Geri Rizzo, and Denise Comeaux. My grateful thanks.

Cover illustration by Pluto, my very talented granddaughter.

MUSINGS OF A MEDIEVAL ABBESS